# a Mad turn

*anti-methods of Mad studies*

edited by Phil Smith

AUTON
OMOUS
PRESS

Weird Books for Weird People

Autonomous Press is an independent publisher focusing on works about neurodivergence, queerness, and the various ways they can intersect with each other and with other aspects of identity and lived experience. We are a partnership including writers, poets, artists, musicians, community scholars, and professors. Each partner takes on a share of the work of managing the press and production, and all of our workers are co-owners.

Paperback: 978-1-945955-50-1

Ebook: 978-1-945955-51-8

Edited by phil smith

Cover art by Casandra Johns

# acknowledgements

books don't write themselves. either do editors. or authors, for that matter. writing doesn't exist until it is read by an audience. you, dear reader, made this book come into being.

the people i work with at Autonomous Press do important work, for the right reasons. they've helped me be a better editor and writer. they've given me opportunities to do stuff i've wanted to do for a long while.

the writing and visual art of Jacquie Pruder St. Antoine has spurred me on to do more, and more better. i don't think Jacquie knows how important they've been to my own learning and growth.

the work of the authors in this book made the project a reality. they didn't just write the chapters. they created a reason for me to edit it, to call it into existence.

# Contents

# a Mad turn

## an introduction

*phil smith*

what is Madness?1

is Madness a Badness?

is Madness a Sadness?

who benefits from it?

what is it made from?

where does it arise?

who decides what it is?

this is a book.

this is a book about Madness.

this is a book about studying     Madness.

this is a book about studying     Madness

---

1    a brief note about why i write the way i write: "My work has been increasingly opposed to the representation of knowledge and exploration that is academified (L. Johnk, personal communication, May 21, 2016). My writing has become increasingly performative, both in the writing of it, and in the for-the-page and oral presentation of it. At conferences, I've performed, with others, scripted, poly-vocal, intentionally-en-jumbled, crosstalking, choral, mad, glossolalic verbal-magic, soundfield explosions of almost-sense. Versions for the page are increasingly enjambed, twisted, disorderly, concretist, entangled, anti-linear, cripped, echolalic, rhizomatic wonders of liminal written prestidigitation" (Smith, 2018, p. 30).

and is   made
by a group of people.
the group of people
who made this studying Madness book
are Mad.
it is important that Mad people
made this studying Mad book
because too often Mad people
don't have a say,
     like,

| in what | Madness |
|---------|---------|
| and studying | Madness |
| looks | like |
| smells | like |
| sounds | like |
| feels | like |
| tastes | like. |

the movement
to take back
and own
the meaning and making and studying
of Madness
by Mad people is a
     growing new thing
and this book
is part of that
     growing new thing.
this Mad made book

opposes the colonialist
[Jefferson]
[star ship]

ENTERPRISE

that constitutes
the    psy
        spy

            sly
            crucify
            buy
            awry
            codify
            decry
            botfly
            lie
            com                  plex
            crime(agaiNst hoomanity)    plex.

Madness ain't no Badness.
Madness ain't no Sadness.
Madness is Made©
outta whole cloth
by the people who brought you racism
                          colonialism
                          classism
                          sexism
                          heterosexism
                          xenophobia

cishetnormativity.

| | |
|---|---|
| this book about | Madness |
| and studying | Madness |
| explores what | Madness |
| is and what studying | Madness |
| is and how Mad people study | Madness. |
| the Mad people studying | Madness |

come at it from a variety of perspectives.

they    come at it from    education

anthropology

english

community health

women, gender, and

sexuality studies

poetry

disability studies

backgrounds.

| | |
|---|---|
| some identify as | Trans. |
| some identify as | Neuroqueer. |
| some identify as | Disabled. |
| some identify as | Autistic. |
| all identify as | Mad. |

•

the first bit in this book, "[de][re][dough ray] fining Madness," looks at what Madness iz and iz not, coming from a Mad perspective. here, Madness is understood as ambiguous multiple mysterious emancipatory revolutionary knowledge contingent constructed political and risky.

the next chapter, "{k}not defining mad studies," seeks to understand what Mad Studies is and isn't, was and wasn't, will be and won't be, again from a Mad perspective. it understands Mad Studies as undisciplined nonsensical radical subversive political anticolonial recalcitrant antireified critical unsettling cross|inter|transdisciplinary polyphonic resistant counterhegemonic and illogical. it is a defining undefining, knowing that Madness and Mad Studies resist knowing.

The next chapters are examples of what Mad Studies work might look like. Jersey Cosantino's "Epiphanic haunting: An autoethnographic origin story of Madness and gender nonconformity haunting," explores the idea of epiphanic haunting by revisiting and reliving the author's origin story of Madness and gender identity. Made through an analysis of Denzin's (2014) interpretation of performance autoethnography, Durham's (2014) definition of epiphanic moments, and Gordon's (2008) commentary on sociological haunting, they look at traces of memory that defy the boundaries of past, present, and future, challenging sanist notions of making knowledge. Looking at the formative and embodied memory of a childhood viewing of Stanley Kubrick's (1980) horror film *The Shining* within the realm of epiphanic haunting, Cosantino begins to see their memory and its remnants as inextricably linked to overt and covert forces of systemic privilege and oppression.

Adam Davies, in their chapter "Maddening moments: Or how I came to trust myself," looks at how madness is intricately connected to societal fears of violence, excessive affect, and dangerousness. Seeing things only through rationality conceptualizes madness through pathology, fear, and illness. But there are also important learnings that can come from being disoriented. Davies looks at what they term *maddening moments* have played into their research and teaching. By paying attention to embodied feelings, sensations, and moments of madness, they remain curious and able to rethink their relationship with madness. Like other Mad people who are constantly questioned about their/our understandings and interpretations of the world, paying attention to self-knowledge and embodied sensations was difficult, especially when dominant constructions of mental illness only consider our feelings and sensations as pathology. Madness can be unsettling for many who are invested in bio-medical approaches to mental illness and who might be uneasy when Mad people honour their/our own experiences. It was not always easy for Davies to listen to their gut feelings and embodied responses. They learned to ignore when their body was communicating that a situation was not right or even when they felt a reasonable amount of anxiety.

In Rebecca-Eli M. Long's piece, "Knitting Like Mad," they knit to keep themself safe, treating yarn as a lifeline, refusing to set it down even when their wrists and shoulders ache from repetitive motions. When they brought it to an ethnographic field site at the local senior center, it became a helpful way of connecting to people, supporting their neurodivergent communication style. They started to wonder what knitting might be able to communicate as a broader way of storying research interactions. It provides a methodological intervention that supports their Mad, neurodivergent bodymind, through reshaping the social space involved in conducting research. They connect this approach with histories of craftivism (activism through crafting) as well as the challenges to self-narration and expression they experienced as a researcher.

In their chapter "Paranoia and reliably unreliable narrators," Samuel Shelton describes ideas and concepts they arrived at based on their experiences of Madness informed and negotiated through their simultaneous experiences of queerness and transness. They focus on the process of becoming a Mad scholar and how that process has been both one of confusion and frustration as well as one of restoration. The chapter offers an intimate account of the transformative powers of Madness, especially in relation to Shelton's queer gender and sexuality. Along the way, they also address the yet-unwelcome, undervalued position of Madness within dominant intellectual spaces as demonstrated by their experiences of unmet needs in academia. Shelton's purpose is to advance conversations about academic sanism and its intersections with other sources of inequity and injustice.

Monica K. Shields' chapter, "What came after the jungle," through their story about living for 40 years in the jungle of Puerto Rico and what came after, talks about what the doing that is neuroqueer, the being of all the posts, and how they connect (or don't) to the bodyminds of Mad people. Oh, and cockroaches. I should mention the cockroaches, how they crunch when you chew 'em.

slp and Aubry Threlkeld, in their chapter "Reinscribing Madness through poetry: Irrationality and interdependence in the wor(l)d," understand Mad subjectivity as being shaped by cultural traumas (Alexander, 2012)—not only biomedical trauma as inflicted experience, but mad subjectivities as arising within social processes, institutions, mores, values, etc., where "good mental health" is an oppressive norm. They question, alter, explore, and add to Mad Studies through a particular process-based approach to writing—one Mad way to explore Mad experience. They argue that when Mad people write about traumatic and saneist experiences, writing can also promote identity formation, easing, and sometimes healing. Poetry can be a location for processing experience, in and out of therapeutic confines—reinscription, in our experience, a conscious *re*writing of and over previous text, is still further a method for understanding mad experience. They take previous writings of personal experience and reinscribe them—in this case, gchat erasure poems. Repetition here is myriad, offering comfort and new outcomes, at the most literal level. They return, together, to discussions that are profound, playful, and banal—a literal retelling which is a reliving, reaffirming, and re-enlivening their relationship, creating new texts, new sometimes transformative experiences, through selective destruction of text. Reinscription, in some ways, is the same thing done over and over again, yielding different results—a way of understanding madness and the world.

In j. logan smilges' "The Trans depressive," they look at which comes first: being trans or being depressed? Typically, people think the former: trans people become depressed, especially early on in their transitions when many struggle to secure the social recognition they want. Less often do people think the latter: depressed people might turn out trans. And when this latter possibility is considered, it is usually done rather cynically—the depressed person comes to realize that they were trans all along, thus implicitly recentering trans as the source of their depression. But what, asks Smilges, if we take seriously the generative potentialities of depression, its ways of producing both new orientations to the world and new variations of the gendered self? They offer an alternative angle from which to understand the interanimation of trans and Madness not only as intersecting lines of experience but as mutually reinforcing categories. The trans depressive reveals the contingence of gender nonconformance and mental disability. Able-mindedness is bound up with cisnormativity, thereby assembling trans and madness as residual yet hinged modes of existence. The depressed person, they argue, is necessarily trans. The gender dysphoria diagnosis adheres depression to gender variance, manufacturing the trans depressive while simultaneously working toward its eradication. Smilges attempts a recovery: exposing the generativity of depression, the affectivity of trans, and situates the trans depressive as a crucial tool in the project of a Mad liberation.

In their chapter, "The Blackbird's Sonnet," Jacquie Pruder St. Antoine takes a new look at what a Mad turn might mean. They ask, how do you imagine that which you cannot conceive? They admit they don't know what new ways of being/

knowing/doing will look like, not a clue. St. Antoine is a tree/ soil/flesh/animal/star/person. One of the Mad ones. Madness, they say, is an individual experience, but one that illuminates the saneist/ableist/sexist/racist/classist forces that build the -ism forces. These forces are entangled with their experiences and can be only examined through their own cloudy lens. To examine Madness ethnographically would be to continue the Othering that has plagued not only their life, but the lives of their fellow Mad wanderers. It would be a continuation of the powers that have sought to eliminate them, or at least the parts of that are viewed as undesirable. We've done enough of that. But it can't just be their story, ya know? It has to be color and scent, paint and yarn and buttons, shrieking laughter in the night and deep grieving wails, lines and slashes, new words (or worlds) that are real, imagined, or something wholly out of this strata. Nah, words aren't right for describing what it is like to be Other. It is needles in kitchens and glowing green digits on your stove clock. Other is the *whomp, whomp, whomp* in your ears and swimming in the pond among frogs. Other is broken and whole, spilled paint and broken glass. These are the moments and the glitter of the Others and how we *do* and *be* the Mad turn.

The final chapter, a poetic offering entitled "the possibilities of a post-psy Mad Studies: another damn man[maid] ifesto," takes un-tools and anti-methods offered by Deleuze and Guattari, as well as Lather and St. Pierre. It steps beyond and away from quantitative methods (on which the psy-complex is predominantly based) and even more recent qualitative methods, that have long dominated empirical understandings of the world, to imagine post-method, even post-science Mad doing-being-knowing, ways that this current book steps towards, and into new possibilities for exploring what it means to be Mad in the whirled world.

this book

iz    a step toward

a turn toward

the Mad Studies yet-to-come

a Mad Studies

that Mad people will build

twisting and turning and singing and dancing

a new thinking-being-doing-knowing.

let's go.

## Roofer essences

Smith, P. (2018). *Writhing writing: Moving towards a mad poetics*. Autonomous Press.

# [de][re][dough ray] fining Madness

*phil smith*

> "But what then in the end, you, the madman?"
> (Artaud, 1948, p.9)

> "Everyone sees madness through their own lens.
> Mad people see it through a lens that burns the ground
> they stand on."
> (O'Hagan, 2014, p.46)

what is Madness?
defining it is    hard
        not    soft

                2 dew –
a slippery slope of    this-ness
and            not-ness
that voids and avoids meaning.    (Kafai, 2013).
it "should retain its aura of mystery,
and it should always leave room
for different views and stories,
where some 'mad' people or 'survivors'
want a place

in the exploration of the unknown,
where there is still room to laugh
about one's madness,
and where some 'patients'
want to offer different stories,
different perspectives,
different views on 'madness',
sometimes mysterious,
but sometimes very mundane"        Netchitailova,
                                   2019, p.1510).

Madness is "deliberately ambiguous;"
wise Mad people want to "avoid essentializing and determin-
ing madness"                       (Rodéhn, 2022).

●

still, things can be said of       it
and about                          it.
Richard Ingram
who thunk up the idea of Mad Studies, sez
"As we are always dealing
with multiplicities,
trying to pin down madness
as one thing is,
I think,
to miss the point:
It is a million things"            (Ingram, 2016, p.
                                   15).

so, yeah.
still, I'll give it
(them?)
a go.
madness iz, first of all,
a claim
a REclaim                                           (Dwornik, 2021;
                                                    Rodéhn, 2022)
to identity:
"...the use of the terms 'mad' and 'madness'
signifies the reappropriation of language
  where 'the Mad' - or C/S/X -
speak out to reclaim and define their experiences
in relation to psychiatry..."            (Baylosis, 2019,
                                         p. 1)

though some reject the term
Mad
deeming it unreclaimable                 (Beresford,
                                         2020).

it is a
"reprisal that rejects
the pathological and degrading labels"
                                         (Breslow, 2019,
                                         p. 60)

assigned to Mad people
by the   psy-complex
         spy-complex

    lie-complex

    deny-complex

    buy-complex

    die-complex.

Mad also

"refers to the emancipatory and self-affirmative stances of
Mad pride and Mad activism"          (Koivisto, 2019,

                                        p. 24).

Mad is noun and verb both

at the same rhyme time                (Thorneycroft,

                                        2020).

itsa weigh

to say

who i yam

who we are,

across multiple communities

and groops                                  (Brewer, 2018)

(c=consumer)

(s=survivor)

(x=ex-patient).

Mad is not a term accepted

by alla deez folx beecaws

"there is no consensus about language

in this field.

Whatever terms we use

and however we use them,

we are inevitably likely to offend.

We apologize for this
and hope we cause
the least possible offense."                    (Daly, Costa, &
                                                Beresford, 2019,
                                                p. 9)


                              •


Madness iz
a "permanent revolution in the life of a person"
                                   (Cooper, 1978, p.
                                   36).
not that a person        revolve(r)s
                         turns (and turns about)
                         spins
                         wheels (cart).
rather, it takes   hold uv a person
                   hauled uv a person
                   wholed uv a person
like a junkyard dog
grabs on
and shakes
and shakes
and shakes
                   (it all about, do the hokey-pokey).
never
ever
ever

letting go.
it izza "way of knowing" (Cooper, 1978, p. 155).

that is, Madness is a set
of knowledges (Rose, 2022).
nod jest won
bud    many
       meany
       money

                    uv     and
                    4      and
                    above  and
                    threw  and
                    about
the whirled and how it  works.
                           twerks.
                           quirks.

it is a way of    seeing
                  exploring
                  experiencing
                  understanding
                  being
                  doing
the       wired
          weird
          word
          whored
          hurled

whorled
whirled,

      the people     in

                    on

                    threw id,

our relationships to the whirled world
and each udder
spinning spinning spinning.
it iz

      "contingent,
      permeable,
      leaky,
and     revisable"                (Thorneycroft,
                                      2020, p. 93).

2 often, Madness
as wee in the (wild wild) West
have come to
know it as cr(e)aterfied
by duh (dis)enlighten(dark)ment      (Porter, 2002)
is miss|under|overstood to be
abbynormal, and binary –
that is, it always       stands
                not    sits
in opposition to the normative     (Kafai, 2013).
but really: "Madness and sanity
are not two different garments;
they are the warp and weft
of the same fabric"              (O'Hagan, 2014,
                                        p. 16).

sanity/insanity

are not separate;

are not differnmints;

are not apart(meant);

they are the same thingyringydingy.

Madness is socially

and culturally

{re}{de} constructed                       (Breslow, 2019;

Davies, Brewer,

& Shay, 2022;

Dwornick, 2021;

Macdonald,

Charnock, &

Scutt, 2018)

and completely

"enmeshed

with other socially and discursively produced

articulations of difference

including but not limited to      race,

gender, and

sexuality"

(Snyder, Pitt,

Shaouda,

Voronka, Reid, &

Landry,

2019, p. 488).

it is      in nately

in tersectional.

Mad people increasingly see themselves
as part of the neurodiversity movement

Graby, 2015).

## bud: hoo de[re]fines it

for much too long
Madness has been  understood
and      created
and      codified
and      portrayed
by those who are (said to be)
not Mad:
"Madness has been described
again
and again
by people who have never experienced it"

(O'Hagan, 2014,

p. 46).

the un-Mad.

the Normies.  ("the tyrannies of normalcy")

(Voronka, 2017,

p. 336)

the not-weerd.

psychiatrists and academic researchers

(Brosnan, 2018;

Macdonald,

Charnock,&

Scutt, 2018).

bluntly,

> "...scholarship on psychiatric disability
> continues to be controlled by researchers
> whose expertise is defined in large part
> by virtue of their neutral and objective
> *second-hand* observational knowledge
> and explicitly clinical expertise..."
>
> (Jones & Brown,
> 2013).

the meaning and understanding and
creation
of Madness
came to the un-Mad
in its AC/DC current (misin)form
through a "psychological turn"
post-1750, in Locke-step
with cartesian linear binary empirical philosopheyes

(Porter, 2002, p.

127)

undt taken up for reelz after 1800 anno domino
with the advent
(impending birth of jeezus?)
uv psychiatry

(Porter, 2002, p.

153).

in itz present form
it is reinforced and held in plaize
by neoliberalism, which:

"...places responsibility for unhappiness, disruptive behavior, and emotional suffering on the individual, as though the individual's well-being arises solely from his or her chemical and genetic makeup, and not from unjust social environments."

(Whitaker, 2019,

p. xiii)

by neoliberalism, i mean
"...a concept often used to
refer to government policies
that sustain inequalities of
wealth, privatization of
public goods and services,
and the privileging of
business interests by
government."

(van Veen,

Teghtsoonian,

& Morrow, 2019,

p. 67)

Mad people ask, essentially,
"What and whose knowledge counts?"   (Brosnan, 2018).
what count(er)s is dis:
Madness "is always immediately political"

(Cooper, 1978, p.

18).

| political, yet how | iron | ick |
| --- | --- | --- |
| | [copper enforced] | ick |
| that Mad people | are not allowed to be | |
| part of the polis | | |

are not allowed to be

city zens.

Madddddniz iz

a      RE     volt

          electric energy

          arcing

across and against the   hegemony

          he(d)gemon(e)y

          a fence keeping sum out

          a fence keeping capital safe for sum

of the Western shootemup

status   quo

        dough

        peso

        blow

        dinero

        roll

the insidious violence

of late capitalism.

as such,

"All madmen are political dissidents.

Each of our madnesses

is our political dissidence."        (Cooper, 1978, p.

        134).

so it is

that Mad people      rebel

        (not the Confederacy)

against all

again stall.

the psy-complex, too,

is      political

      poly toke all

and seeks to     force

      fierce

      farce

the Mad

to become    disordered

     dismembered

     disenfranchised.

the      psy-complex

does this through

     psychiatrization:

     "...the processes and mechanisms

     through which certain persons,

     adult or child, come into psychiatry

     as a political realm... when their body,

     their psychology, and/or particular

     expressions of emotional and

     psychological distress are

     constructed as 'mental illness' or 'disorder.'"

          (Liegghio, 2016,

          p. 111)

psychiatrization iz alzo abowed

"the dissemination and infiltration of psychiatric knowledge, theories, and ideas about the (human) mind beyond the immediate domain of psychiatry and throughout the wider culture and society"                                      (Koivisto, 2019,

p. 26)

psychiatrization          intersects with

intersex with

criminalization

and     institutionalization          (Ben-Moshe,

2011).

and so rebelling against all

as the Mad will – must – do

involves some considerable risk:

"...mere disagreement

with a psychiatric label

and/or the legitimacy

of a past or current hospitalization

is often recast

as a neuropsychiatric deficit

or further sign

of underlying psychopathology"          (Jones & Brown,

2013).

because Mad people

ya know

are unreliable knowers

by definition.

as a result of the vio lense

perpetrated on their      bodyminds

                      bawdy-mineds

                      soulhearts

                      sole-harts

by the psy spy calm plex panopticon,

Mad people "carry the violent effects

of pathologizing rhetoric

in our bodyminds

as         flashbacks,

             memories,

             shivers,

             nightmares,

             stories"                      (Johnk & Kahn,

                                        2019, p.34).

some Mad bodymind soulhearts

understand what the

             psy-complex

             psy-clops

po(o)rtrays as disordered

but iz really instead

"responses to socio-politico-economic conditions of conflict,

entrenched social inequality, and chronic poverty"

                               (Mills &

                               Fernando, 2014,

                               p. 189).

                               (Mills, 2015, p. 23).

Mad people see it as

             "a form of colonization"

Mad people     fight

spight

might

night     (take) back against these

poor    trayals

be     trayals

by acts of     re     sistance

per     sistance

in     sistance

sister dance:

resist    ance that is

resist    dance that is

resist    ants that is

secret,

sly,

covered up.

Resistance that is     "cryptic,

opaque

and    veiled."

(Mills, 2015, 22)

## sanism iz

sanism is

"discrimination against those

who have been given a psychiatric diagnosis

and/or who are perceived to be 'mentally ill,'"

(Wolframe,

2013)

a term first used by Rebecca Birnbaum

(Wolframe,

2013).

it iz an "over-arching belief

that those who identify

as or who are labeled

"Mad" are dangerous

and/or incompetent"    Davies, Brewer,

& Shay, 2022,

p.21).

sanism "includes different manifestations

of stigma and microaggressions which...

may include having low expectations..."

resulting in the belief that Mad people

"are not capable of doing things independently;

are in need of constant supervision;

are unpredictable;

are violent;

and/or irrational"                    (Breslow, 2019,

Sanism "is invested            61).

in shoring up

the sane body and mind,

and in that shoring

the loathing

of mad bodies manifests"

(Thorneycroft,

2020, p. 96).

sanism

iz an    ism schism

a      psy

      spy made by    empirical

               of the empire    scientists

                                 scion twists.

## Mad Made peeple want to define what Madness iz

"Mad people's definition of it has seldom made it into the dictionary or into conversation, media stories, literature or mental health discourse. Our definition of madness can even elude us. We lack a validating language to make meaning from it. Our madness stands outside in the dark, knocking on the door to meaning, struggling to get in."

                            (O'Hagan, 2014,

                            p. 46).

Mad peeple

peeple Made Mad©

make meaning

by claiming Madness

as theirs

and not that uv da    psy

                     spy

                          complex

                  cy      clops.

it's hours.

u canned half id.

## Reefer Ants

Artaud, A. (1948/2020). *Artaud, the Mômo* [trans. C. Eshleman]. Diaphanes.

Baylosis, C. (2019). Mad studies and an ethics of listening. *Journal of Ethics in Mental Health,* 10, 1-18.

Ben-Moshe, L. (2011). Disabling incarceration: Connecting disability to divergent confinements

in the USA. *Critical Sociology* 37(7), 385-403. doi: 10.1177/0896920511430864

Beresford, P. (2020). 'Mad', Mad studies and advancing inclusive resistance. *Disability & Society, 35*(8), 1337-1342. doi: 10.1080/09687599.2019.1692168

Birnbaum, R. (2010). "My father's advocacy for a right to treatment." *Journal of the American Academy of Psychiatry and the Law, 38*(1), 115-23.

Breslow, K. (2019). Perspectives in AE – What troubled persons industry professionals can learn  from Mad Studies. *New Horizons in Adult Education and Human Development, 31*(1), 59-64.

Brewer, E. (2018). Coming out Mad, coming out Disabled. In E. Donaldson (Ed.) *Literatures of Madness: Disability Studies and mental health* (pp. 11-30). Palgrave Macmillan. doi:  10.1007/978-3-319-92666-7_2

Brosnan, L. (2018). Who's talking about us without us? A survivor research interjection into an  academic psychiatry debate on compulsory community treatment orders in Ireland. *Laws, 7*(33). doi:10.3390/laws7040033

Cooper, D. (1978). *The language of madness.* Penguin Books.

Daley, A., Costa, L. & Beresford, P. (2019). Introduction. In
A. Daley, L. Costa, & P. Beresford (eds.) *Madness, violence,
and power: A critical collection* (pp. 3-18). University of
Toronto Press.

Davies, A. Brewer, K., & Shay, B. (2022). Sanism in early
childhood education and care: Cultivating space for
Madness and Mad educators in ECEC. *eceLINK, 6*(1),
18-30.

Dwornik, A. (2021). The interface of Mad Studies and indigenous ways of knowing: Innovation, co-creation, and
decolonization. *Critical Social Work 22*(2), 25-39.

Graby, S. (2015). Neurodiversity: Bridging the gap between
the disabled people's movement and the mental health
system survivor's movement. In H. Spandler, J. Anderson,
and B. Sapey (Eds.) *Madness, distress and the politics of dis-
ablement* (231-242). Policy Press. doi: 10.2307/j.ctt1t898sg

Ingram, R. (2016). Doing Mad Studies: Making (non)sense
together. *Intersectionalities: A
Global Journal of 2016 Social Work Analysis, Research, Policy,
and Practice, 5*(3), 11- 17.

Johnk, L. and Kahn, S. (2019). "Cripping the fuck out:" A
Queer Crip Mad manifesta against the Medical Industrial Complex. *feral feminisms, 9*, 26-38.

Jones, N. & Brown, R. (2013). The Absence of psychiatric
c/s/x perspectives in academic discourse: Consequences
and implications. *Disability Studies Quarterly, 33*(1). doi:
10.18061/dsq.v33i1.3433

Kafai, S. (2013). The mad border body: A political in-betweenness. *Disability Studies Quarterly, 33*(1). doi:
10.18061/dsq.v33i1.3438

Koivisto, M. (2019). *The art of egress: Madness, horror, and
the art of depsychiatrization.* Aalto ARTS Books.

Liegghio, M. (2016). Too young to Be mad: Disabling encounters with 'normal' from the perspectives of psychiatrized
youth. *Intersectionalities: A Global Journal of 2016 Social
Work Analysis, Research, Polity, and Practice, 5*(3), 110-129.

Macdonald, S. J., Charnock, A. & Scutt, J. (2018). "Mad
Studies and social work: Conceptualising the subjectivities of service user/survivors that experience significant
mental health problems." *Social Work and Social Sciences
Review,19*(3), 98-118.

Mills, C. (2015). Symptom, seduction, subversion: Reading resistance to psychiatry through a post-colonial
lens. *CUSP: critical cultures and cultural critiques in psychology, 1,* 22-46.

Mills, C. and Fernando, S. (2014). Globalising mental health
or pathologising the global south? Mapping the ethics,
theory and practice of global mental health. *Disability
and the Global South, 1*(2), 188-202.

Netchitailova, E. (2019) The mystery of madness through
art and Mad Studies. *Disability & Society, 34*(9-10), 1509-
1515, doi: 10.1080/09687599.2019.1619236

O'Hagan, M. (2014). *Madness made me.* Open Box.

Porter, R. (2002). *Madness: A brief history.* Oxford University
Press.

Rodéhn, C. (2022). Introducing Mad Studies and mad reading to game studies. *The International Journal of Computer Game Research*, 22(1).

Rose, D. (2022). *Mad knowledges and user-led research*. Palgrave Macmillan.

Snyder, S., Pitt, K-A., Shanouda, F., Voronka, J., Reid, J., and Landry, D. (2019). Unlearning through Mad Studies: Disruptive pedagogical praxis. *Curriculum Inquiry, 49*(4), 485-502. doi: 10.1080/03626784.2019.1664254

Thorneycroft, R. (2020). Crip theory and Mad Studies: Intersections and points of departure. *Canadian Journal of Disability Studies, 9*(1), 91-121.

van, Veen, C., Teghtsoonian, K., and Morrow, M. (2019). Enacting violence and care:

Neoliberalism, knowledge claims, and resistance. In A. Daley, L. Costa, & P. Beresford (eds.) *Madness, violence, and power: A critical collection* (pp. 63-79). University of Toronto Press.

Voronka, J. (2017). Turning mad knowledge into affective labor: The case of the peer support worker. *American Quarterly, 69*(2), 333-338. doi:10.1353/aq.2017.0029

Whitaker, R. (2019). Foreward. In A. Daley, L. Costa, & P. Beresford (eds.) *Madness, violence, and power: A critical collection* (pp. xi-xiii). University of Toronto Press.

Wolframe, P. (2013). The madwoman in the academy, or, revealing the invisible straightjacket: Theorizing and teaching sanism and sane privilege. *Disability Studies Quarterly, 33*(1). doi:10.18061/dsq.v33i1.3425

# {k}not defining Mad studies

*phil smith*

Mad Studies started to become
a thing
created out of the imagination
of crazy people.
people who began
to envision
what it might be like
to explore what          doing

being

thinking

living

Mad Mad Mad Mad Mad
means
inna whirled
that denies its very reality.
one of these people
Richard Ingram
described it as an
"in/discipline... both a discipline
and an indiscipline"                    (Ingram, 2016, p. 13),
noting that "we are always

caught in these doubles,
and there is no way around this"             (Ingram, 2016, p. 13).
as a cultural geography
outside of whatever reason might be,
Ingram sees Mad Studies
as a landscape encompassing
"...making sense at times
and not making sense at other times...
continually bringing up
questions of nonsense
and introducing nonsense."                   (Ingram, 2016, p.
                                             15).

Mad Studies
"has the potential to interrupt
hegemonic ways of          knowing,
                           being, and
                           learning"
                                             (Snyder, Pitt,
                                             Shaouda,
                                             Voronka, Reid, &
it works across the                          Landry, 2019, p. 485).
barbed-wire      fine fences
that      con    fine and
          con              strain
discip           lines
in ways that

"reconfigure boundaries" (Snyder, Pitt,
Shaouda,
Voronka, Reid, &
Landry, 2019, p.
488).

Mad Studies is an uncanon (Johnk & Kahn, 2019),
eclectic (Kunzel, 2017)
radical (Dworkin, 2021;
Landry
& Church, 2016)

a "shift of perspective" (Rodéhn, 2022)
an umbrella term (Breslow, 2019;
Thorneycroft,
2020)

"unruly" and "subversive" (LeFrançois &
Voronka,
2022, p. 106)

"a politicized space...
a collective project" (LeFrançois,
Beresford,
& Russo, 2016, p. 1)

"recalcitrant,... uncontainable,
disorderly, unstable, ungovernable
and resistant to rule-based definition,
whilst obstinately defying and eschewing
dominant neoliberal, colonialist
and positivistic/racist understandings
of knowledge production

about madness"                    (LeFrançois &
                                  Voronka,

                                  2022, p. 109).

Mad Studies is
"led by us and our experiential knowledge as survivors;
engages committed allies; and
is demedicalised and based on a social approach"

                                  (Beresford, 2016; p.

                                  352).

it is an anti-reified
oppositionally defiant
set of "collective interventions
into ways of knowing
that come from outside
the academic industrial complex,
or that challenge its boundaries
and authority"                    (Gorman &
                                  LeFrançois,

                                  2018, p. 111).

Mad Studies "...provides a systemic critique of
                psy-violence,
                epistemic injustice...
                and sanism..."    (Gorman &
                                  LeFrançois,

                                  2018, p. 108).

it continuously
"questions and unsettles
biomedical understandings

of mental illness,

and frames psychiatric experiences

as diverse forms of human emotional or spiritual expression"

(Dworkin, 2021, p.

25).

it "seeks to develop an alternative praxis and epistemology
to the medical model of psychiatry" and

"interrogates psychiatry and exposes its hidden inequalities
and systemic practices of epistemic violence"

Mad Studies works to create          (Johnston, 2019).

"counter-hegemonic interpretations"

within a

"radical, interdisciplinary" sphere          (Landry & Church,

2016,

p. 173).

it "takes inspiration from          subjectivities,

embodiments,

narrative,

experiences,

and     aspirations

of those who have been a part of institutional psychiatric
systems"          (Milaney, Rankin, &

Zaretsky, 2022).

it can be described as the

"cooperative study, on an international scale, of the experiential knowledges of mental health service users and survivors"

(Newman, Boxall,

Jury,

& Dickinson, 2019).

it      slips

and    slides

and    swoops

and    elides

"across a multitude of disciplines

including but not limited to    cultural studies,

history,

sociology,

gender studies,

and    philosophy"

(Dworkin, 2021,

p. 31).

to which I'd add    Queer

studies

Black studies

Indigenous studies

Educational studies

literature

cinema studies

art criticism

and and and and.

Mad Studies is  cross

inter

trans    disciplinary.

it "creates a platform for deconstructing and decolonizing

contemporary psychiatric practices... Mad Studies celebrates madness as an expression of human emotional experience, and calls for the recognition of a mad identity that is free of discrimination and definition." (Dworkin, 2021, p. 35).

Mad Studies pays in tention

a tention

in tension to

"psychiatric survivor analyses...

mad readings of the wider world...

documenting and teaching mad people's history...

exposing and providing a systemic critique of psy violence"

(LeFrançois,

Beresford,

& Russo, 2016, p. 2)

Mad Studies is not, however, monolithic:

"not all service users or consumers

are anti-psychiatry,

and some individuals who endorse Mad Studies

choose to take medication to resolve

what is causing them distress" (Breslow, 2019, p. 61).

at the heart of Mad Studies

is Mad Pride,

"a transnational movement

that validates and celebrates

the lives, identities, and communities

of Mad and neurodivergent people,

including people
who identify as crazy,

> psychocrip,
>
> neuroqueer,
>
> Autistic,
>
> Borderline,
>
> Bipolar,
>
> ADHD,

and     mentally ill"     (Johnk & Kahn,
p.35).

Mad Studies arises out of both
scholarship and activism           (Brewer, 2018).
in doing so, it is essential that Mad
Studies explore
intersections between sanism and racism
in order to understand
"the over criminalization and dehumanization of racialized
people and indigenous peoples who experience distress and
suffering"
as well as to "to resist the effects of appropriation and colonization"                              (Joseph, 2019, p. 4).
it must work diligently
to avoid the hegemony of Eurocentrism
and to build bridges
between the global South and North     (Beresford, 2020).
Mad Studies
goes out of its way to "resist and challenge categories"
                                  (Rodéhn, 2022).

mebbe it's easier to say
what Mad Studies i snot:
"...colluding with Big Pharma,
piss-poor fabricated research on the 'mentally ill,'
vapid neo-liberal imperatives,
and the morally bankrupt psy-enterprise"

(Castrodale, 2017,

p. 52).

critically, Mad Studies

takes

breaks

snakes

"a radical departure

from the urge

to make mad subjects

both knowable and governable,

or to make sense

of that which cannot

and should not be reduced

to the rationalist's desire

for       uniformity,

consistency,

universality

and      conformity

to the dominant logics

of the sanestream"      LeFrançois &

Voronka,

2022, p. 108).

it avoids logic
knowing that this is a path
that leads down a Made Mad© Hare
rabbit hole leading to

    sanism

    racism

    neoliberalism -

the arkhos of the psy-complex -
in (dis)order to
"open spaces for that which is unspeakable within western"

        (LeFrançois &
        Voronka,
        2022, p. 109)

onto-epistemes.
it is essential    too

       2

       to

understand that
Mad studies is not done
figuring itself out,
and that no person
or body
or group
or school of thought
gets to decide
what it is
or where it is

or where it's going

(Costa, 2014;
Gorman &
LeFrançois, 2018).

Mad Studies iz  about

and by

Mad people

(Castrodale, 2017;
Costa, 2014;
Macdonald,
Charnock, & Scutt,
2018; McWade,
2015).

Mad people
are the only real and true
"authorities on their own state of being"

(Johnston & Steckle,
2018, p. 236).

still, some caution about making
the boundaries of Mad Studies
too hard and fast
encouraging those who engage
in studying Madness
not to get bogged down
in excluding people, ideas, and approaches
but to explore them
as useful and interesting tensions

(Spandler and
Poursanidou, 2019).

Mad Studies, in critiquing the  psy

        spy

             die

             lie

                    compl(iance)ex

it looks at ways that

      "...biomedical systems
have acted with some mechanisms
that contribute to hiding
the social and political determinants
of health,
while focusing their attention
on the biological causation...
The biomedical system
operates 'reification' processes
that reframe socioeconomic factors,
human relationships, people,
and their experiences
as      things,
          objects,
and     true facts of nature.
This contributes
to the construction
of a social reality
that aims to preserve
a particular political order,
reintegrating suffering people
in a shared order of meanings

and thus cancelling out

the     social,

          economic,

and    political

dimensions ...

If we believe

that our diabetes or depression

is mainly related

to a biological alteration

of our cells...

from which we can be healed

only by taking a drug,

we will not question

inequality of our society...

and the way in which

medicine frames the world..."

(Aillon, & Cardito,

2020, p. 12)

Mad Stud       tease is

illogical

unreasonable

anti-hierarchic

counter-institutional

oppositionally defiant

complex

intersectional

antidisciplinary

counterhegemonic

incoherent

irrational

alinear

nonsensical

illucid.

## Roar fer senses

Aillon, J.-L. & Cardito, M. (2020). Health and degrowth in times of pandemic. *Visions for Sustainability, 14*, 3-23. doi: 10.13135/2384-8677/5419

Beresford, P (2016). From psycho-politics to mad studies: Learning from the legacy of Peter Sedgwick. *Critical and Radical Social Work, 4*(3), 343-355. doi: 10.1332/204986016 X14651166264237

Beresford, P. (2020). 'Mad', Mad studies and advancing inclusive resistance. *Disability & Society, 35* (8), 1337-1342. doi: 10.1080/09687599.2019.1692168

Breslow, K. (2019). Perspectives in AE – What troubled persons industry professionals can learn from Mad Studies. *New Horizons in Adult Education and Human Development, 31*(1), 59-64.

Brewer, E. (2018). Coming out Mad, coming out Disabled. In E. Donaldson (Ed.) *Literatures of Madness: Disability Studies and mental health* (pp. 11-30). Palgrave Macmillan. doi: 10.1007/978-3-319-92666-7_2

Castrodale, M. (2017). Critical disability studies and mad studies: Enabling new pedagogies in practice. *The Canadian Journal for the Study of Adult Education, 29*(1) 49–66.

Costa, L. (2014). Mad studies: What is it and why you should care. *The Bulletin, 518,* 4–5 (Online publication, http://www.csinfo.ca/bulletin.php). Toronto, ON: The Consumer/Survivor  Resource Centre.

Dwornik, A. (2021). The interface of Mad Studies and in-digenous ways of knowing: Innovation, co-creation, and decolonization. *Critical Social Work* 22(2), 25-39.

Gorman, R. & LeFrançois, B.A. (2018). Mad studies. In B.M.Z. Cohen (Ed.). *Routledge International Handbook of Critical Mental Health (pp. 107-114).* London: Routledge.

Ingram, R. (2016). Doing Mad Studies: Making (non)sense together. *Intersectionalities: A Global Journal of 2016 Social Work Analysis, Research, Polity, and Practice, 5*(3), 11-17.

Johnk, L. and Kahn, S. (2019). "Cripping the fuck out:" A Queer Crip Mad manifesta against the Medical Industri-al Complex. *feral feminisms, 9,* 26-38.

Johnston, M. (2020). "He sees patients as lesser people": Exploring mental health service users' critiques and appraisals of psychiatrists in Canada. *Disability & Society,* 35(2). 258-279. doi: 10.1080/09687599.2019.1634524

Johnston, M., and Steckle, R. (2018). Psychiatric post-anar-chism: A new direction for insurrection in     the mental health system. *The Annual Review of Interdisciplinary Justice Research, 7,* 232-257.

Joseph, A. (2019). Constituting "lived experience" discourses in mental health: The ethics of racialized identification/ representation and the erasure of intergeneration colonial violence. *The Journal of Ethics in Mental Health, 10.*

Kunzel, R. (2017). Queer history, mad history, and the politics of health. *American Quarterly, 69*(2), 315-319. doi: 10.1353/aq.2017.0026

Landry, D., & Church, K. (2016). Teaching (like) crazy in a mad positive school: Exploring the charms of recursion. In J. Russo & A. Sweeney (Eds), *Searching for a rose garden: Challenging psychiatry, fostering Mad Studies* (pp. 172-182). PCCS Books.

LeFrançois, B., Beresford, P., & Russo, J. (2016). Editorial: Destination Mad Studies. *Intersectionalities: A Global Journal of Social Work Analysis, Research, Polity, and Practice, 5*(3), 1-10.

LeFrançois, B. A., & Voronka, J. (2022). Mad epistemologies and maddening the ethics of knowledge production. In T. Macias (Ed.) *Un/ethical un/knowing: Ethical reflections on methodology and politics in social science research* (pp.105-130). Canadian Scholars Press Inc.

Macdonald, S. J., Charnock, A. & Scutt, J. (2018). "Mad Studies and social work: Conceptualising the subjectivities of service user/survivors that experience significant mental health problems." *Social Work and Social Sciences Review, 19*(3), 98-118 .

McWade, B. (2015). *Mad Studies: Making space for Mad knowledge and activism in the academy.* Keynote Lecture. Changing Worlds: Engaging Science and Technology in Art, Academia and Activism. University of Vienna.

Milaney, K. Rankin, J., & Zaretsky, L. (2022). The modern day asylum: A Mad Studies informed approach to understanding de-institutionalization, madness and chronic homelessness. *Canadian Journal of Disability Studies*, 11(1).

Newman, J., Boxall, K., Jury, R., & Dickinson, J. (2019). Professional education and Mad Studies:Learning and teaching about service users' understandings of mental and emotional distress. *Disability & Society*, 34 (9-10),1523-1547. doi: 10.1080/09687599.2019.1594697

Rodéhn, C. (2022). Introducing Mad Studies and mad reading to game studies. *The International Journal of Computer Game Research*, 22(1).

Snyder, S., Pitt, K-A., Shanouda, F., Voronka, J., Reid, J., and Landry, D. (2019). Unlearning through Mad Studies: Disruptive pedagogical praxis. *Curriculum Inquiry*, 49(4), 485-502. doi: 10.1080/03626784.2019.1664254

Spandler, H. and Poursanidou, D. (2019). Who is included in the Mad Studies project? *The Journal of Ethics in Mental Health*, 10.

Thorneycroft, R. (2020). Crip theory and Mad Studies: Intersections and points of departure. *Canadian Journal of Disability Studies*, 9(1), 91-121.

# Epiphanic Haunting

## An Autoethnographic Origin Story of Madness and Gender Nonconformity

*Jersey Cosantino*

## Haunting
### *The Origin of Fear*

> *What we 'look for' is un/fortunately what we shall find.*
> -Trinh T. Minh-ha, *Woman, Native, Other*, 1989, p. 141

When I was young, *too young*, my father showed me scary movies, exposing me to the world of horror and gore at such a pivotal moment in my self-development that these films ended up leaving a deep and lasting imprint on my psyche. I know my father made sure my mother did not know that I watched these films. If she had known, my mother would have, undoubtedly, protested; *and* I know that these movies were only one small part of a chain of what I would later consider disturbing episodes that challenged my threshold for enduring fear.

For example, when I was no more than 5 or 6 years old, I excitedly went to the train station with my father to watch the trains. We stayed there for quite some time, watching the trains slowly pull into the station, passengers getting on and off. Then there was a loud noise and faint lights in the distance, and my father walked me closer to the edge of the platform. Unsure of what was about to happen, both eager to know and anxious about what was to come, with the noise getting louder and closer, I tried to back up but found myself unable to move through the wall that was my muscular, brutish father standing firmly behind me.

As the noise increased unbearably and fear and panic overwhelmed me, I could feel my father's strong hands pressing down hard on my shoulders, freezing me in place. The high-speed train whizzed by me in a blur as I stood only a foot or two from the platform's edge. I could feel the platform and me shake to the core. Terrified, I screamed and cried, but the train's noise ensured my small shrieks could not be heard. My dad did not ease his grip until the train was well out of view. In what would become a pattern for similar incidents for years to come, I met my father's sickeningly joyful face with my terror, snot, and tears. It took me time to realize that my father took some weird, sadistic joy in scaring me as a young child, the same joy he did a terrible job of trying to hide when he would intentionally let our rather vicious dog too close to strangers who would, without even trying to pet the dog, get bitten. After the paperboy left with a finger covered in blood, his parents tried to sue us, but I don't remember what ever came of it.

My dog, like me, was angry - *very, very* angry. We both grew up in a household of alcoholism (mom), domestic violence (dad), unaddressed mental health conditions (very much mom, but *also* dad), and emotional and psychological abuse (mom *and* dad). These memories of the high-speed train and watching countless horror movies tapped into a well of panic and fear that had been brewing inside of me since the moment I became aware I existed. I was not only terrified of the monsters that I saw on the screen but *also* of the garage door opening each evening, announcing the arrival of my enraged father, home from work, and the sound of twist-off cap wine and Disaronno bottles, announcing nights of my mother's hateful shouting, spiteful comments, curses, blackouts, and night terrors.

I was primed to engage with cinematic horror in such a way that the gruesome violence that I saw on screen never seemed fully *un*real. Each morning, fixing the pillows on the living room couch where my mother slept (and still sleeps) each night, or opening the curtains covering the window in the bathroom, I would often find spots of blood, blaming myself for not protecting her, something that I always tried to do. Using my imagination, I would attempt to put together the pieces of what must have occurred between closing my eyes to fall asleep and discovering in the morning the aftermath of my father's violence.

The way my mother would turn so quickly, transitioning from an overly excitable, often kind, and generous mother to a vicious, out of control monster - *a change so fast that I would try night after night to identify the turn, the time it took, the number of clicks of screw-off bottles it would take, the indicators that it was about to happen* - to the way that my father would be laughing one minute and then throwing something or punching someone the next - *so fast that I swear you could feel the energy of the room change, going cold, my mind frantically sputtering, searching for what I said or did that set him off* - it is no wonder that my young mind blurred the boundaries between the television screen and my own, lived reality.

Film, TV, music videos – these all became modes of escape, opportunities to leave a world that I always desperately wanted to flee, seeing in film a version of "truth" that either elicited profound fear or deep longing, depending on the version of self and context of self portrayed on screen. Sometimes this fear and this longing would coincide, coming together in a similar way to what I felt on the train platform. My body tingled with the excitement of knowing what was behind that steadily growing noise and shuddered in panic at the encroaching fear of the unknown. The sheer power of the "cinematic world" (Denzin, 2003, p. 58) and media in general includes the ability to reflect possibilities of ourselves to ourselves (Denzin, 2003, p. 58). These cultural representations of who we are and who we might become infuse our everyday lived experiences, merging our evolving sense of self with the identity categories crafted for us by our "cinematic society" (Denzin, 2003, p. 58). Given these options, what worlds do we choose to inhabit? What possibilities of self are made accessible, and which remain just out of reach?

Seeing as cinema and media can offer us tools to navigate the complexities and uncertainties of life (Denzin, 2003, p. 61), the meanings that my young, impressionable, not-fully-developed brain happened to create were ones that were dictated by and embraced within a fully lifelike, theatrical version of reality (Denzin, 2003, p. 60 and 69). It is in this "reality" in which various performers on screen and within the confines of the horrors of my own home mirrored one another (Denzin, 2003, p. 69), ebbed and flowed through one another, breaking the fourth wall (the invisible or implied barrier between actors on a stage or screen and the viewing audience) so often that I was frequently confused as to whether I should flee *or* if I should follow. Among these moments, few hold such profound significance as my memories of watching Stanley Kubrick's 1980 cinematic adaptation of Stephen King's terrifying novel, *The Shining*, a film whose lasting reverberations I can still feel to this day.

## *The Shining (as Memory)*

> [F]*rom 1900-1930, cinema became* [*a crucial*] *part of the American society...The cinematic, surveillance society soon became...filled with subjects (voyeurs) who obsessively looked and gazed at one another, as they became, at the same time, obsessive listeners, eavesdroppers...new versions of the spoken and seen self. A new social type was created: the voyeur, or Peeping Tom, who would...*[*raise*] *the concepts of looking and listening to new levels.*
> -Norman K. Denzin, *Performance Ethnography: Critical Pedagogy and the Politics of Culture*, 2003, p. 61

For as long as I can remember, I have been haunted by this incredibly vivid memory of a scene in *The Shining* where the main character, Jack Torrance, played by Jack Nicholson, walks down the hallway of the empty Overlook Hotel where he and his family are staying and caretaking. Jack, peeking into a series of partially open hotel rooms, brings the viewer into his frame of sight, revealing the devious deeds of the hotel's ghostly guests. I remember so clearly the images of women in fancy suits with hand-drawn mustaches kissing feminine-presenting lovers and variously gender nonconforming and nonbinary characters engaging in, or about to engage in, nonnormative sexual acts, clad in leather with whips, chains, masks, and toys all at their disposal, ready to elicit - *pleasure?* or *pain?* - I was entirely unsure but I had a nervous sense that it might be a little of *both*.

Seeing as this memory was acquired as a child, I did not yet have names for what I saw - queer, orgy, BDSM, fetish, kink, drag, transgender, gender fluidity. Furthermore, as I alluded to earlier, I was often exposed to films and TV shows that were intended for an older viewing audience, leaving me with questions upon questions and no one available or, often, willing to answer them for me. Thus, this memory, this epiphany - or shall I say *epiphanic moment* - took residence in my bodymind (to speak to the ways in which the body and mind are forever intertwined) as a complicated, swirling pool of longing, aversion, and curiosity. As quickly as I remember this scene being - a mere blip in the two and a half hour-long film - my young, malleable mind desired nothing more than to rewind those moments over and over again until I made sense of all that I was seeing.

If only I could watch that scene on loop and discover why this small glimpse into a world of perversion was pulling me in so strongly. If only I could go back and catch the eye of the woman in a suit with a penciled-on mustache who looks coyly over her shoulder at Jack, but also *through* Jack, straight into my eyes breaking not only the fourth wall but everything I knew, or *thought* I knew, about gender, sexuality, expression, and identity. Oh, *if only*.

## An Epiphanic Haunting

Durham (2014) defines "epiphanic moments" as moments where a significant realization or awareness occurs that helps us know more deeply how we are positioned in the world and in relationship to each other (p. 13). Epiphanic moments often occur when our understanding of our identity and/or how we are represented by others and larger society is radically disrupted – shaken to its core (Durham, 2014, p. 13). I would describe this memory of *The Shining* as nothing less than a sincere crisis of identity (Durham, 2014, p. 13) that, over the course of my lifetime, has had significant implications on the ways that I performed my gender identity and expression and the aspects and clues of true self that I proudly acknowledged or desperately sought to ignore and hide.

Furthermore, this brief theatrical representation of gender nonconformity and queer sexuality becomes particularly complicated by its placement within the context of a horror film that blurs the real and unreal and includes audio and visual delusions and interactions with the supernatural.

Building on Durham's (2013) definition of epiphanic moments, I would characterize this gender identity and Madness origin story as an *epiphanic haunting*2 in which my own embodied interaction with these ghostly hotel guests left such deeply seated traces within my psyche that I am still haunted by this moment.

By articulating this concept of an epiphanic moment through Gordon's (2008) work on haunting, I seek to broaden the meaning I make of this epiphany to include the seen and unseen forces, powers, and *invisible hands* that push, pull, and intertwine our lived experiences with the residual effects of historical and present-day systems of power, privilege, and oppression. Knowing that my memory of *The Shining*, the gender and sexual representation it portrays, and the internalized and externalized realities that manifested as a result are indeed haunted by "a repressed or unresolved social violence" that is demanding to "make itself known" (Gordon, 2008, p. xvi), it is necessary that I explore this epiphany recognizing that past, present, and future are *not* separate entities but rather flow together within my bodymind (Gordon, 2008; Smith 2012). When dealing with ghosts, Gordon (2008) reminds us that they appear with the most intensity when the "trouble they represent and symptomize" can no longer be suppressed or ignored (p. xvi). I am particularly drawn to Gordon's (2008)

---

2   I further expand on this concept of epiphanic haunting in the context of my Buddhist spiritual practice and my development and implementation of a Mad, trans, mindful dialogic pedagogy in the article *The possibilities of an anti-oppression mindful dialogic pedagogy in the intergroup dialogue classroom: An autoethnographic exploration* (Cosantino, 2021, *Western Journal of Communication*).

use of the word "symptomize" to describe the felt sense of haunting. It not only seems to imply haunting's physical manifestations within the bodymind but also it articulates a connection between haunting and various diagnostic criteria used by the medical industrial complex3 to, as I will later explore, heal and/or harm nonnormative bodyminds - individuals whose lived experiences, orientations, worldviews, presentations, and expressions directly challenge the status quo, otherwise known as the norm.

The medical model of disability, which focuses heavily on cure and the "illness" of the individual as opposed to the larger social structures that create disabling environments and deny disabled bodyminds access to services and supports, is laced with its own haunting, with the remnants of abusive power structures seeping through ideologies and theories that claim to cure (Clare, 2017). By confronting these specters head-on, unearthing their stories and moments of origin, and connecting these points to their future manifestations, it is my hope that the ghosts' "reason for being and their power to haunt are severely restricted" (Gordon, 2008, p. xvii and xix). Only time will tell how successful this enterprise will be, but, for now, it is clear that the only way to move forward is to return to the beginning.

---

3  As Mingus (2015) describes, "The Medical Industrial Complex is an enormous system with tentacles that reach beyond simply doctors, nurses, clinics, and hospitals. It is a system about profit, first and foremost, rather than 'health,' wellbeing and care. Its roots run deep and its history and present are connected to everything including eugenics, capitalism, colonization, slavery, immigration, war, prisons, and reproductive oppression. It is not just a major piece of the history of ableism, but all systems of oppression."

## *Deviance and Delusion*

By placing my first memory of gender nonconformity and queer sexuality from Kubrick's film within a historical, political, social, and embodied context (Durham, 2014; Haraway, 1988), this epiphanic moment transforms into an epiphanic haunting. The Overlook Hotel, which is the key setting of *The Shining*, is a place that is implied to be quite *literally* haunted. However, drawing from the literary world crafted by Stephen King, Kubrick leaves the audience wondering about the degree to which this hotel's haunting is a manifestation of the residual effects of horrific crimes past and/ or the byproduct of Jack Torrance's increasingly delusional mind and his violence towards his wife, Wendy, and child, Danny (Hornbeck, 2016).

Although Jack's murderous madness4 is central to the film's plot, Jack's son, Danny, also sees various ghosts and grotesque acts of violence during the family's stay at the hotel. Additionally, Jack's wife, Wendy, sees an image that unsettles her of a man in a bear costume performing oral sex on a man in a suit in one of the guest rooms. It is uncertain if

---

4   Although I will capitalize Madness in this essay when referring to
    Mad Studies, Madness frameworks, and my own Mad identity, I am
    intentionally choosing not to capitalize madness here. This is so be-
    cause Madness, as a reclaimed term and justice movement originally
    led by psychiatric survivors against the medical industrial complex,
    embraces a capital letter "M" as a symbol of pride and reclamation of
    linguistic power and mental and bodily autonomy (Menzies, Le-
    Francois, & Reaume, 2013). When referring to Kubrick's intentions
    in *The Shining*, I am arguing that the madness that is represented
    can further the painful and harmful stigma of Mad individuals by
    portraying them as murderers, abusers, and criminals, thus meaning
    that Kubrick's version of madness must remain in lower case here.

Wendy's sighting is supernatural or the product of Wendy's mad mind. Regardless, this scene, ending with Wendy running and screaming in fright, is an example of how Kubrick problematically associates nonnormative sexuality with horror, delusion, and repulsion. We, as viewers, are meant to be disturbed by this scene. Ultimately, the Torrance family's sightings at the Overlook Hotel blur the lines between reality and imagination, the "natural" and the supernatural, the socially acceptable and the deviant, and can be attributed both to the haunting of the hotel and/or to each family member's experience of trauma and madness.

Within this context, my young mind understood gender and sexual nonnormativity to be associated with terror, madness, and violence. This representation was complicated in that it paradoxically gave me an understanding of gender and sexuality that seemed oddly both "against [my] will" and also, equally, a "transformative recognition" (Gordon, 2008, p. 8) of the possible identities that exist. As many critical scenes of the film were portrayed through Jack's, Danny's, and/or Wendy's white, heterosexual, cisgender, middle class perspectives, I, as the viewer, took on the role of voyeur, desperately seeking access to a world that frightened me, enticed me, and that I, ultimately, remained distanced from (Denzin, 2003, p. 61). Returning to the scene where Jack peeks behind the door of a hotel room and meets the lingering eyes and flirtatious smiles of queer and gender fluid ghostly guests, I found these nonverbal acts to be invitations to this cinematic world. I, however, did not understand how to connect my reality with theirs, solidifying my role as the longing spectator for years to come.

Reflecting on my experience of this film as a young child assigned female at birth, decades away from coming out as queer, genderqueer, then trans and nonbinary with a masculine gender expression, I find it curious that my obsession (a word that I use intentionally since my obsessive-compulsive "disorder" began as a child) with memories of *The Shining* has always been centered on Jack's experiences at the Overlook Hotel. Consistently desiring to understand how adult masculinity operated in all of its forms and manifestations, I found myself drawn almost exclusively to Jack's perspective in ways that hauntingly and complicatedly illuminate my far too long suppressed internal desire to transition.

Witnessing the possibilities for other forms of sexuality and gender identity and expression for the first time through the lens of Jack, a mad, violently abusive character, I could not help but associate gender nonconformity and queer sexuality with the madness and domestic violence perpetually on display in my childhood home. I made it my life's goal to never become my parents. What aspect of them *must* I take on to gain access to the world that allows for expansive gender and sexual identity, to see it again, to even possibly *become* part of it? And, what meaning do I make of a childhood spent desperately grasping for ways to express a gender identity that always eluded me due to the enforcement of binaries and imposition of the sex I was assigned at birth? In what ways did my experience of Jack's version of masculinity as something to be feared, especially since it so closely resembled my father's violence, foster my terror of my own trans masculine-presenting identity, which I spent much of my life repressing? With my longing poised on the borders of madness and sanity, illusion and reality, nonnormativity and normativity, my young self unsurprisingly attempted to adhere to the latter of each, since I had not been offered a model for madness, illusion, and nonnormativity that did not also imply violence, trauma, and fear.

## Madness
### *The Shining (as Reality)*

*Performance ethnography answers Trinh's (1991:162) call for works that seek the truth of life's fictions and in which experiences are evoked, not explained. The performer seeks a presentation that, like good fiction, is true in experience, but not necessarily true to experience (Lockford 1998:216). Whether the events presented actually occurred is [secondary] to the larger project (Lockford 1998:216).*
-Norman K. Denzin, *Performance Ethnography: Critical Pedagogy and the Politics of Culture*, 2003, pp. 36-37

By attempting to shine light on the nonnormative identities and experiences that a heteropatriarchal, cis-normative, ableist, white settler colonial society has historically cast into the shadows (Khubchandani, 2020, p. 4), I hope to embrace this haunting "in the name of a will to heal" thus allowing "the ghost to help [me] imagine what was lost that never even existed, *really*" (Gordon, 2003, p. 57, emphasis mine). Seeking to engage directly with these ghosts, I recently returned to *The Shining* as a site of cultural and personal meaning making, revisiting "those embodied, sensuous experiences that create the conditions for understanding" (Denzin, 2003, p. 13). Shockingly, after hours of scrolling through the film's footage, I discovered that the scene that defined my foundational gender identity-related epiphanic haunting never *really* existed.

In the midst of frantically searching for *where* this memory came from, a mysterious internal pull, a provoking *invisible hand,* if you will, encouraged me to explore Madonna's music videos from the early 90's. Low and behold, the 1990 video for "Justify My Love" contained all of my memory's key visual elements, but lacked the felt-sense (Madison, 2020, p. 8) of horror that this memory took on after I had linked it to my experience of watching *The Shining* (Pink, 2012, p. 122). Fascinatingly, shortly after this discovery, a friend who had been helping me research texted that someone in an online forum had suggested this same music video. As members of forums that I posted on hauntingly confirmed my memory, saying they *absolutely* recalled this scene in *The Shining,* others challenged the definitive nature of my gender and Madness origin story by pointing out that memories can be fragmented and can encompass reality *and* delusion.

The beauty of defining this memory as an epiphanic haunting and "reliv[ing]" (Denzin, 2014, p. 52) it through autoethnography (writing about personal experiences to understand larger social meanings) is that meaning can and *should* be made from how an event is experienced, as opposed to necessarily "depict[ing] experience exactly as it was lived (Bochner, 2000, p. 270)" (Adams & Holman Jones, 2014, p. 375). By making myself the subject of my autoethnography, I embrace the realization that I *and* my memories are "incomplete, unknown, fragmented and conflictual" (Adams & Holman Jones, 2014, p. 387) and, thus, inherently, *Mad*. This *Mad*dening of memory transforms this "life story" from factual experience into "invention" (Denzin, 2014, p. 28), disturbingly disrupting the ways in which I had previously made sense of myself and my life (Denzin, 2014, p. 52).

Until now, I had not recognized that this story I had told myself for so long manifested within a Mad, queer, and trans form of analysis that "names...what official knowledge represses" (Gordon, 2008, p. xviii) and what dominant power structures silence. By "creat[ing] new ways of performing and experiencing the past" (Denzin, 2014, p. 28), such as through this autoethnographic retelling, it is possible to refuse to "recognize it 'the way it really was' (Benjamin, 1968, p. 257)" (Denzin, 2014, p. 28). Thus, this Mad framework for interpreting memory "makes visible the processes of settler colonial knowledge" (Tuck & Yang, 2014) that are deeply invested in sanism (the privileging of individuals without mental health conditions) and "treat emotionality and intellectuality as adversaries" (Price, 2014, p. 50).

As Smith (2020) poetically describes, sanism is:

an institutionalised, ideological process / inherent in Western, Eurocentric, hegemonic culture / founded in psychiatrism (the ideology of psychiatry) / and the psy-complex (the set of practices, ideas, research, and social institu-/ tions that includes psychiatry, psychology, special education, social work, and other fields) (p. 373).

Revisiting epiphanic moments and their subsequent hauntings through a Mad framework "refigure[s] key assumptions of autobiographical discourse, including rationality, coherence, truth, and independence" (Price, 2014, p. 179), and centers the embodied experiences of an "irrational mind" (p. 179). Therefore, knowing that Mad Studies "disputes the differences / between fact/fiction / true/false / real/ imagined" (Smith, 2020, p. 372), I am able to calm the rising panic that came from learning that my long-held memory was only partially true and embrace an epiphany that is certainly "true *in* experience, but not...true *to* experience" (Denzin, 2003, p. 37).

## Grasping for Truth

As someone who excels at meeting the diagnostic criteria for obsessive-compulsive "disorder" (OCD) and bipolar II, mental health conditions that, for me, disguise the irrational as rational, I find myself on a never-ending journey for a truth that perpetually feels out of reach. "Sometimes we fear and hate and love ourselves / all at the same time" (Piepzna-Samarasinha, 2015, p. 43). Expanding my conception of truth to encompass the embodied, felt-sense of all experiences challenges rigid Western, settler colonial binaries of "inner and outer space" (Kovach, 2009, p. 57), which are constricting beliefs that I simultaneously represent and perpetuate as a white settler. It also disrupts my internalized ableist (the privileging of able-bodied/minded individuals) longings for a rational mind crafted through the lens of white supremacy (Sins Invalid, 2019, p. 111). Tapping into an "inner space" where embodied knowing, imagination, and spiritual understanding are not limited by Western constructed notions of what is real versus unreal (Kovach, 2009, p. 57) provides the anti-colonial framework to recognize the interconnectivity of my "psychobiosocialpoliticalbodymind" (Price, 2014, p. 240). This recognition upholds one of the key tenets of disability justice - that "[d]isabled people are whole people" (Sins Invalid, 2019, p. 24).

At the intersections of these frameworks, I can relax my longing for truth based on rationality and feel confident that my memory and its subsequent hauntings are, themselves, bearers of (and *witnesses* to) an embodied truth that may or may not be easily named or physically manifested but is nonetheless entirely real. This decisive act of "claim[ing] authority not in spite of, but through and because of, [my] mental disabilities" is defined by Price (2014) as a "counter-diagnostic move" (p. 179). Within autobiographical writing like autoethnography, the "counter-diagnosis...uses language...to subvert the diagnostic urge to 'explain' an irrational mind" (Price, 2014, p. 179), complicates and confuses memory (p. 179), and, ultimately, "queers" it (p. 179), a social identity that I very much embrace as someone who is trans, nonbinary, queer, *and* Mad.

Building on the notion that autoethnography is a fluid method of communicating oppressed "knowledges [and] stories that are present but disguised" (Denzin, 2014, p. 387), especially behind the veil of "White Mainstream English" that, when left unchallenged, becomes "the invisible—or better, inaudible—norm" (Baker-Bell, 2020, p. 3), we can expand the queerness of Mad writing to encompass autoethnography as a whole (p. 377). In a similar vein to an LGBTQ2IA+5 coming-out story, queer autoethnography (Denzin, 2014) defies the expectation that an epiphanic moment of self-knowing is a singular, solely linguistically definable experience (Price, 2014, p. 179). Instead, it makes space for haunting and fragmentation, allowing self-narratives to be conveyed as if one were "moving through a hall of mirrors ("Then You'll Be Straight," 98)" (Price, 2014, p. 179), confronted *with* (and possibly frightened *by*) the multiplicities of what one sees, struggling to identify the true version of self when faced with countless representations of how we perform ourselves to (and are represented by) others and society.

When considering this metaphor of a hall of mirrors, I cannot help but picture it within a "fun" house or haunted house that is so often found in small-town carnivals, spaces and places that have historically commodified individuals with nonnormative, marginalized identities, labeling those who were not white, of particular European origin, middle class, cisgender, heterosexual, and able-bodied/minded as *freaks* (Clare, 2009, p. 85). The freak show:

---

5  LGBTQ2IA+ stands for Lesbian, Gay, Bisexual, Transgender, Queer/Questioning, Two Spirit, Intersex, Asexual, and the ever-evolving language for nonbinary identities and expressions.

tells the story of an elaborate and calculated social construction that utilized performance and fabrication as well as deeply held cultural beliefs [to] construc[t] an exaggerated divide between "normal" and Other, sustained in turn by rubes willing to pay good money to stare (Clare, 2009, p. 86-87).

My formative memories of *The Shining* are quite literally *haunted* (Gordon, 2008) by these histories and the ways in which my own privileged and oppressed identities have, at various points in my life depending on my ability to "pass" (*as sane, as heterosexual, as cisgender*), caused me to assume the role of the voyeur *and* the freak.

## At the Intersections

Within an anti-colonial framework, "revelations comprise various sources, including 'dreams, visions, cellular memory, and intuition' (quoted in E. Steinhauer, 2002, p. 74)" (Kovach, 2009, p. 57). Challenging the coloniality of my memory structures makes valid the "insight [that] comes... inwardly and intuitively" (Kovach, 2009, p. 57) and embraces a "partial quality of knowledge" (Johnson & McRuer, 2014, p. 142). This knowledge contains a "slipperiness" and holds many "clouds of meaning" (McRuer & Johnson, 2014, p. 151). "So even though experience is not necessarily a way to authentic knowledge, is it a way to slide at the edges, inhabit the clouds?" (McRuer & Johnson, 2014, p. 151). Additionally, to fully challenge the superiority of rationality requires illuminating the ways in which it has been "idealized...through the intersections of race, gender, class, and sexuality" (Ferguson, 2004, p. 83), acting as the seemingly objective (Haraway, 1988), ableist glue that holds together "normative assumptions about citizenship and humanity" (Ferguson, 2004, p. 83).

This grappling with an epiphanic haunting that seeps into every aspect of one's "complex personhood" (Gordon, 2008, p. 4) must be located within the realm of shadows of what "has been lost[,]...marginali[zed], excluded, or repressed" (p. viii) by historical and present-day systems of oppression. Such hauntings are relational and, when located within a decolonizing Black and transnational feminist framework, that which dominant power structures attempted to make *invisible* (in order to solidify the myth of their superiority) become *visible* (Durham, 2014, p. 7):

> Suppressing the knowledge produced by any oppressed group makes it easier for dominant groups to rule because the seeming absence of dissent suggests that subordinating groups willingly collaborate in their own victimization (Scott, 1985)... [which] has been critical in maintaining social inequalities (Collins, 2000, p. 3).

At the meeting of Mad Studies, Trans Studies, and Black, decolonizing, and transnational feminist theory, autoethnographic stories can be told that reclaim and honor marginalized knowledges (Collins, 2000, p. 13), locate all forms of representation within "systems of domination" (Durham, 2014, p. 7; Collins, 2000), and "entangl[e] and weave between what is immediately available as a story and what...imaginations are reaching toward" (Gordon, 2008, p. 4).

This space of complex personhood is one of remembering and forgetting, understanding and misunderstanding self and *other*, that sees all lives, privileges, and oppressions as haunted by that which can be named and that which defies restrictive categories of sanist language production (Gordon, 2008, pp. 4-5). My epiphanic haunting that originated in brief, mediated, and *Madd*eningly interwoven displays of gender and sexual nonnormativity was never mine alone, but rather interconnected within a deeply embodied and relational experience that reinforces the notion that "life and people's lives are simultaneously straightforward and full of enormously subtle meaning" (Gordon, 2008, p. 5). It is by revisiting this origin story and its resulting traces that I attempt to "bring a new awareness of life into previously forgotten, silenced, or deadened areas of the body" (Minh-ha, 1989, p. 40), giving in to the "ongoing unsettling process" (p. 40) of making meaning of experiences that, ultimately, "leads no more to openings than to closures" (p. 40).

**Longing**6 *(a Poetic Transcription (Durham, 2014, p. 103))*7

*When something happens it can leave a trace of itself behind...*
*Maybe things that happen leave other kinds of traces behind.*
-Richard Hallorann, Head Chef at the Overlook Hotel, from
*The Shining*, Stanley Kubrick, 1980

---

6   This Poetic Transcription was originally published in *Disability Studies Quarterly* on June 15, 2021, under the title *Hauntings of Longing: A Mad Autoethnographic Poetic Transcription,* available online here: https://dsq-sds.org/article/view/7669/5951

7   The inspiration for this chapter comes from Mad scholar, Phil Smith's (2020) essay, entitled "[R]evolving Towards Mad: Spinning Away from the Psy/Spy-Complex Through Auto/Biography," where poetry is used as a tool to convey the inner workings of a Mad mind. Smith's (2020) piece, when read alongside texts such as Durham's (2014) Home with Hip Hop Feminism, Denzin's (2003) Performance Ethnography: Critical Pedagogy and the Politics of Culture, Piepzna-Samarasinha's (2015) Bodymap, and Smith's (1993) Fires in the Mirror, proves the power of poetry to "hint at possibility made real. Our poems formulate the implications of ourselves, what we feel within and dare make real (or bring action into accordance with), our fears, our hopes, our most cherished terrors" (Lorde, 1984, p. 39). Given this context, when engaging in a fully embodied autoethnographic reflective process that explores the hidden crevices of my Mad and trans identities, I found myself, as researcher, uncovering my fears, hopes, and terrors in ways that defy the boundaries of sanist forms of knowledge production and narration. Thus, I consider this culminating chapter a form of poetic transcription for it presents my self-interviews utilizing "[t]he malleability of language...to carve interpretive space and us[ing] literary tools to craft a concrete, embodied text grounded in lived experience" (Durham, 2014, p. 105) that continuously "moves back and forth...between the public and private realms" (Denzin, 2003, p. 88) in an attempt to convey the illusive intricacies and hauntings (Gordon, 2008) of my situated Mad and trans felt-sense experiences.

1. *Traces*

My first experience in a mental health facility

was in college

not as a patient

but as a visitor

a *voyeur*

a participant in a medical model of disability

wherein *"All of our bodyminds are judged*

*in one way or another,*

*found to be normal and abnormal,*

*valuable or disposable,*

*healthy or unhealthy." (Clare, 2017, p. 69)*

No one is spared this judgment.

We do it to one another,

to ourselves,

in desperate attempts to adhere to normative notions of

    rationality,

acceptability,

performativity,

that govern our lives

our bodies,

our "body*minds*" (*Price, 2014, p. 240*),

and some,

    (intentionally)

*very* much more so than others.

*"Across the centuries, how many communities have been declared*

    *defective*

*by white people, rich people, nondisabled people, men backed by*
*    medical,*

*scientific,*

*academic,*

*and state authority?" (Clare, 2017, p. 24)*

This single label

*defective*

is never

was never

*"innocent" (Burstow, 2013, p. 81)*

for, *"as a species,*

*we live in and through words...words matter" (Burstow, 2013, p.*
*    79).*

They hold centuries of hauntings,

representing, symbolizing, epitomizing,

*symptomizing*

*"not the invisible or some ineffable excess" (Gordon, 2008, p. xvi)*

but rather

*"[t]he whole essence" (Gordon, 2008, p. xvi)*

of that which has been concealed by abusive power struc-
    tures

and, due to its living, breathing, animated existence within
    each of us,

in every space and place we occupy,

  (or has been violently occupied),

*"makes itself known or apparent to us" (Gordon, 2008, p. 8).*

It is in these *seemingly* un*assuming* moments

*"when home becomes unfamiliar,*

*when your bearings on the world lose direction,*

*when the over-and-done-with comes alive,*
*when what's been in your blind spot*
*comes into view,"*
*demanding "your attention,"*
*"demand[ing] its due" (Gordon, 2008, p. xvi).*

*2. Pieces*
As I sat across the table from you
forcing small talk,
pleasantries,
scattered puzzle pieces
helped me focus my attention
and put to use my jittery, nervous hands
whose shaking physically manifested
the terror I held inside of *becoming*
one of you,
one of *them.*
You frustratingly told us how
fucked up it was that you were here.
Sitting across the desk of your
on-campus therapist one minute
then put into an ambulance the next,
whisked away to a psychiatric hospital
that I am sure you didn't have penciled in
to your agenda for today.
*"What a bitch."*
Rolling your eyes, like you usually do,
you warned us to never tell the *actual*

truth when asked, *"Do you have thoughts of taking your own
    life?"*
because, when you said, *"Of course I fucking do! Who
    doesn't?!"*
you earned yourself a two week hold in a locked facility
when all you wanted was a routine refill of your SSRIs.
*Damn.*
My mind flooded with every suicidal ideation I ever had
including the year, yes full year,
during high school when my parents stopped talking to me
and, to comfort myself, I would play on loop
all of the ways that I could end it all
if I didn't get a sports scholarship or academic scholarship
to anywhere but here.
*Did that make me crazy?*
What separated me from *you?*
What did I do that kept me
on the other side of the locked doors
that kept you "safe" here
and me "free"
out there?
*"there is a moral to this tale, and you |*
*were born to tell it |*
*safe and free are not the same thing |*
*living and alive are not the same thing"* (Thom, 2019, p. 153).
Since then, I bore your warning like an omen
refusing to ever, ever tell my therapist the truth
the whole truth
so help us god,

because, if anyone knew what *really* happened
inside my mind
I would be locked away so long that
there would be no way in *hell* that I would
*ever* get out.
*"your crazy is beloved genius art when you're not standing |*
*on the tracks trying not to jump, and when you are...that's |*
*different." (Piepzna-Samarasinha, 2015, p. 42)*
So, I smiled, you smiled.
I faked sanity.
I *fake* sanity.


*3. Diagnosis*
I came to your office after weeks of reaching out to
therapist after therapist who took sliding scale
payments
and stated having *some* competency around trans issues
and trans people
like me.
I, honestly, just wanted you to sign my letter
that proved, according to the WPATH8 Standards of Care,
that I was *sane, competent, and capable*
of making the decision all  by  *myself*
to chop off parts of my chest that
were undesired "freebies"

---

8   WPATH stands for the World Professional Association for Transgen-
    der Health. Their complete guide to standards of care for medical
    professionals who are working with "transexual, transgender, and
    gender nonconforming people" can be found here: https://www.
    wpath.org/publications/soc.

on an AFAB body that desperately wanted to be cut loose
of excess baggage.
You told me that it would take at least 3 sessions (*300
   bucks!*)
to get my letter.
I told myself, that's 3 fucking weeks where you better not
sound crazy
say *anything* crazy
*or* tell the truth.
It was pretty clear from the start
that the truth would not set me free
but rather would keep me locked in a cage
to which, unfortunately, only you
held the key.
After two years of working together,
gender affirmation surgery and countless bottles
of hormone gel later,
I finally let you in,
opening the door to my mind
ever  so  slightly
to let you peak, only as a guest
and perpetually as a voyeur
into the inner workings of, what I would consider,
a "*Mad Mad Mad Mad Mad Mad world*" (*Smith, 2020, p. 377*).
Ironically, I have to pause here
because it's time for our weekly phone session
where I still pick and choose how much to say,
how much to let on to.
Never, ever, ever will

I tell you about the intrusive thoughts,
*those* intrusive thoughts
that I learned while being a call operator
for a crisis lifeline
are a *normal, reasonable, and understandable*
form of harm reduction
used to cope
with a society that never envisioned me part of it.
Those thoughts,
        I'd rather keep them to myself...


*"if your bones should start to murmur and hiss |*
*in a language that is not safe to know, then leave...|*
*if you should start to think forbidden thoughts |*
*then come for me ||*
*the end of ever after is the beginning of the truth"* (Thom, 2019,
        *p. 40-41)*


*4. Access*
Standing outside of the LGBTQIA+ mental health facility
in the outskirts of Boston,
a few minutes before I was due for my intake appointment,
I couldn't help but stop and stare
at the juxtaposition of the rather quaint,
New England-style house
turned facility for the crazy *and* queer
situated next to the gray warehouse-looking,
locked-down institution for those who,
unlike me, would not be allowed out each night.

I had spent years avoiding *this* exact place,

*this* exact situation,

*this* exact mind.

But for all of my running,

*what was it? 6 marathons now?*

and all of my numbing,

the ghosts kept surfacing

and could be pushed down no longer.

It's wild to me that the very thing that I feared for so long

became the *only* thing that I felt could save me

hold me

protect me

in the midst of this darkness.

*"I claim brokenness to make this irrevocable shattering visible"*

     *(Clare, 2017, p. 160).*

The *"twisted genius"* *(Dyson, 2018, p. ix)*

of the medical industrial complex is that

*that* which we need

so often perpetuates our dependency,

harming and haunting

with remarkable intentionality and precision:

> *The Medical Industrial Complex is an enormous system with tentacles that reach beyond simply doctors, nurses, clinics, and hospitals. It is a system about profit, first and foremost, rather than "health," wellbeing and care. Its roots run deep and its history and present are connected to everything including eugenics, capitalism, colonization, slavery, immigration, war, prisons, and reproductive oppression. It is not just a major piece*

*of the history of ableism, but all systems of oppression.*
(*Mingus, 2015*)

To walk through the doors of this facility,
to receive care,
and walk back out,
day in and day out,
was a privilege reflective of my whiteness,
my class, my citizenship status,
my job, my access to health care...
"*...as a widespread ideology centered on eradication, cure always
operates in relationship to violence*" (Clare, 2017, p. 28),
It is my privilege that opens the doors to 'treatment'
from a "*debilitating*" (Puar, 2017, p. 16) system
that constructs and *re*constructs
ableist notions of normativity and
curative ideology that ensures that "*access to
the identity of disability*" remains
"*a function, result, and reclamation of
white privilege*" (Puar, 2017, p. 15).
My longing for the *exact* space
that haunted me for so long
was, thus, saturated with linguistic and systemic structures
designed to further the lives of some
and enact a "*slow death*" (Puar, 2017, p. 12)
on those bodyminds for whom survival
remains contingent upon the denial of
debility (Puar, 2017, p. 15).

In the fine print, just below the line
where I signed my name
that first day
on the facility's intake form,
it read...

> *There is always a cost to getting better (Puar, 2017, p. 1).*
> *What price are you willing to pay?*

*5. Release*
To kick off group therapy,
we were asked to draw our
dysphoria.
Scanning a table full of
miscellaneous art supplies,
I couldn't help but chuckle to myself
at the absurdity of constructing
a thing that has caused me
so much pain,
so much suffering,
so much confusion,
out of pipe cleaners, markers, glitter, and glue.
*You gotta be fucking kidding me.*
Sitting there in frustration, silence, *and* bemusement,
I began to realize that this task was so hard
so difficult
so damn unfathomable to me
because my dysphoria has always remained

*illusive, slippery, slimy,*
perpetually just out of reach.
As I picked up my pen and began to draw,
I looked at my arm
and remembered the satisfaction,
the relief,
the *release,*
of getting two dark, solid bands of ink
etched deep, deep under my skin.
The pain *was   beautiful*
because, for the first time,
I felt like I could tap into you,
know you, even briefly,
by inviting you up to the surface,
to my level, to live, breathe, and manifest
in a way that bore some semblance of reality,
rationality,
*truth.*
You were never something that I could describe
easily,
but your name, the ability to be named,
granted to us by the indefatigable medical industrial com-
    plex,
remarkably and hauntingly,
offered a small, illuminated pathway
through years and years of darkness.
It's so fucked to think of you as
both an identity and a diagnosis,

a *"trans diagnosis"* imbued with *"standards*
*that are embedded with racist, ableist, classist, and heterosexist*
*expectations"* (Lair, 2016, p. 171),
hinged on our experience of *"distress"* and
*"impairment"* (American Psychiatric Association, 2013),
and fully couched within the "Diagnostic and Statistical
    Manual
of Mental Disorders - *5th Edition"*.
Progress has *attempted* to be made
to distance our "treatment" today
from the medicalized horrors of the past

    (a distancing that tries to erase culpability, forgetting
    transness'
    *"transitive"* quality to always refer back to an action
    *"that requires a direct object to complete its sense of meaning"*
    (Snorton, 2017, p. 6)).

This past (and present), based on the principles of eugenics
    and
the *"perpetuation of white racial superiority"*,
sought out the complete and utter *"elimination of those*
*deemed 'unfit'"* based on labels,
diagnoses,
*"notions of degeneracy, criminality, perversion,*
*and disability"* (Lair, 2016, p. 20):

*"Simply put, diagnosis wields immense power. It can provide us*
    *access to vital medical technology or shame us, reveal a path*
    *toward less pain or get us locked up. It opens doors and slams*

*them shut."* (Clare, 2017, p. 41)

The thing though about the past is that it haunts,
it demands to be known, and refuses to be ignored.
And when you say that you're "doing better"
by establishing a *"current term [that] is more descriptive*
*than the previous DSM-IV term gender identity disorder"*
because this term *"focuses on dysphoria as the clinical problem,*
*not identity per se"* (American Psychiatric Association, 2013),
you fail to recognize that you *still* label us as problems
to be fixed,
to be healed,
to be cured,
forced to meet the expectations of a *"white, able-minded,*
*and heterosexual definition for*
... *'normality'"* (Lair, 2016, p. 23).
So, as I draw you, dysphoria,
I cannot separate you from the past, from the present,
from the future,
from the systems that are purportedly designed to
"cure":

> *"Cure promises wholeness even as the world pokes and*
> *prods, reverberating beneath our skin, a broken world*
> *giving rise to broken selves....The ideology of cure would*
> *have us believe that whole and broken are opposites and*
> *that the latter has no value."* (Clare, 2017, p. 158-159)

Is my testosterone a cure, a tool to force my bodymind
into the rigid, binary definitions of cisnormativity?

As I rub gel into my skin each morning, I hold these ques-
    tions,

these notions,

these hauntings,

in the same hand that grips a bottle of $300 medicine

that quiets my dysphoria,

my distress,

my impairment,

lulling it back to sleep deep within the recesses

of an embodied sense of self

that I desperately want to

call home.

> *"how can i feel homesick /*
> > *if i've never been home?"* (*Thom, 2019, p. 100*)

## References

Adams, T. E., & S. L. Holman Jones. (2008). Autoethnography is queer. In N. K. Denzin, Y. S. Lincoln, & L. T. Smith
(Eds.), *Handbook of critical and indigenous methodologies*
(373-390). SAGE.

American Psychiatric Association. (2013). Gender Dysphoria.
In Diagnostic and statistical manual of mental disorders
(5th ed.). Washington, DC: Author. https://doi-org.libez-
proxy2.syr.edu/10.1176/appi.books.9780890425596.dsm14

Baker-Bell, A. (2020). *Linguistic justice: Black languages, literacy, identity, and pedagogy.* Routledge.

Burstow, B. (2013). A rose by any other name: Naming and the battle against psychiatry. In B. A. L., R. M., & G. R. (Eds.), *Mad matters: A critical reader in Canadian Mad Studies* (pp. 79-90). Canadian Scholars' Press Inc.

Clare, E. (2015). *Exile and pride: Disability, queerness, and liberation.* Duke University Press.

Clare, E. (2017). *Brilliant imperfection: Grappling with cure.* Duke University Press.

Collins, P. H. (2002). *Black feminist thought: Knowledge, consciousness, and the politics of empowerment.* Routledge.

Denzin, N. K. (2003). *Performance ethnography: Critical pedagogy and the politics of culture.* SAGE.

Denzin, N. K. (2014). *Interpretive autoethnography* (2nd ed.). SAGE.

Durham, A. (2014). *At Home with Hip Hop Feminism: Performances in Communication and Culture.* Peter Lang Publishing Group.

Dyson, M. E. (2018). Keyser Söze, Beyoncé, and the whiteness protection program. In DiAngelo, R., *White fragility: Why it's so hard for white people to talk about racism* (ix-xii) [Foreword]. Beacon Press.

Ferguson, R. A. (2004). *Aberrations in black: Toward a queer of color critique.* University of Minnesota Press.

Gordon, A. F. (2008). *Ghostly matters: Haunting and the sociological imagination.* University of Minnesota Press.

Haraway, D. (1988). Situated knowledges: The science question in feminism and the privilege of partial perspective. *Feminist studies, 14*(3), 575 599. doi:10.2307/3178066

Hornbeck, E. J. (2016). Who's afraid of the big bad wolf?: Domestic violence in The Shining. *Feminist Studies, 42*(3), 689-719, 769-770.

Johnson, E. P. (2011). *Sweet tea: Black gay men of the south.* University of North Carolina Press.

Johnson, M., & McRuer, R. (2014). Cripistemologies: Introduction. Journal of Literary & *Cultural Disability Studies, 8*(2), 127-148. doi:10.3828/jlcds.2014.12

Khubchandani, K. (2020). Dance Floor Divas: Fieldwork, Fabulating and Fathoming in Queer Bangalore. *South Asia: Journal of South Asian Studies,* (43)2, 1-12.

Kovach, M. E. (2010). *Indigenous methodologies: Characteristics, conversations, and*

*contexts.* University of Toronto Press.

Kubrick, S. (Producer/Director). (1980). *The Shining* [Motion picture]. United States: Warner Bros.

Lair, L. O. (2016). *Disciplining diagnoses: Sexology, eugenics, and trans\* subjectivities* (Order No. 10129514). Available from GenderWatch; ProQuest Dissertations & Theses Global. (1799673978). Retrieved from https://search-proquest-com.libezproxy2.syr.edu/docview/1799673978

Lorde, A. (1984). "Poetry is Not a Luxury." In *Sister outsider: essays and speeches by Audre Lorde.* Crossing Press. 36-39.

Madison, D. S. (2005). *Critical ethnography: Method, ethics, and performance.* SAGE.

McRuer, R., Johnson, M. L., Davis, L., Serlin, D., Kivisild, E., Nash, J., . . . Sandahl, C. (2014). Proliferating cripiste-mologies: A virtual roundtable. *Journal of Literary and Cultural Disability Studies, 8*(2), 149-170. doi:10.3828/jlcds.2014.13

Menzies, R. J., Reaume, G., & LeFrançois, B. A. (2013). *Mad matters: A critical reader in Canadian mad studies.* Canadian Scholars' Press Inc.

Mingus, Mia. "Medical Industrial Complex Visual." *Leaving Evidence* (blog), February 6, 2015. https://leavingevidence.wordpress.com/2015/02/06/medical-industrial-complex-visual/.

Minh-Ha, T. T. (2009). *Woman, native, other: Writing postco-loniality and feminism.*

Indiana University Press.

Piepzna-Samarasinha, L. L. (2015). *Bodymap.* Mawenzi House.

Pink, S. (2012). *Doing Sensory Ethnography.* SAGE.

Price, M. (2014). *Mad at school: Rhetorics of mental disability and academic life.* The University of Michigan Press.

Puar, J. K., 1967. (2017). *The right to maim: Debility, capacity, disability.* Duke University Press.

Sins Invalid. (2019). *Skin, tooth, and bone: The basis of move-ment is our people a disability justice primer* (2nd ed.). Sins Invalid.

Smith, A. D. (2015). *Fires in the Mirror.* Anchor.

Smith, L. T. (2012). *Decolonizing methodologies: Research and Indigenous peoples.* Zed Books.

Smith, P. (2020) [R]evolving towards Mad: Spinning away from the psy/spy-complex through auto/biography. In Parsons J., Chappell A. (eds) *The Palgrave Handbook of Auto/Biography.* Palgrave Macmillan, Cham.

Snorton, C. R. (2017). *Black on both sides: A racial history of trans identity.* University of Minnesota Press. http://dx. doi.org/10.5749/minnesota/9781517901721.001.0001

Thom, K. C. (2019). I hope we choose love: A trans girl's notes from the end of the world. Arsenal Pulp Press.

Tuck, E. & Yang, K.W. (2014). R-words: Refusing research. In D. Paris & M. T. Winn (Eds.), *Humanizing research: Decolonizing qualitative inquiry with youth and communities.* (pp. 223-248). SAGE.

# Maddening moments

## Or how I came to trust myself

*Adam W.J. Davies*

Notions of madness are intricately connected to societal fears of violence, excessive affect, and dangerousness (Aho, Ben-Moshe, & Hilton, 2017). Modern society's focus on rationality continues to only conceptualize madness through pathology, fear, and illness (Gomory & Dunleavy, 2017). While moments of rupture and disruption can be disorienting, there are also important learnings that can be gleaned from being disoriented and allowing ourselves to be affected. I hope to emphasize these learnings in this chapter and reflect on how what I term *maddening moments* have played into my research and teaching (Davies, 2022). I aim in this chapter to note how, by paying attention to embodied feelings, sensations, and moments of madness, I am able to remain curious and rethink my own relationship with madness. Ahmed (2016) theorizes noticing as a political act in terms of how some forms of injustices and violence affect us, while others go unnoticed. How we allow certain kinds of inequities to impact and affect us is illuminating of what we pay attention to and what we value (Ahmed, 2016). However, for

Mad people who are constantly questioned about their/our understandings and interpretations of the world, paying attention to self-knowledge and embodied sensations can be difficult, especially when dominant constructions of mental illness only consider our feelings and sensations as pathology. Through biomedical and psychiatric apparatuses and interventions, we – Mad people – learn to distrust our intuition and inner knowing. Throughout this chapter, I use the term Mad to indicate people who have experiences with psychiatric violence, and who identify as consumers/survivors/ activists. As such, I am using it as an umbrella term for people with a variety of experiences, acknowledging that while I identify with this term, not all who are under this umbrella term might necessarily do so.

Madness can be unsettling for many who are invested in bio-medical approaches to mental illness and who might be uneasy when Mad people honour their/our own experiences, affective responses, and hermeneutic resources (Snyder et al., 2019). Through rationalist and biomedical knowledges, Mad people are subjugated, discredited, and gaslit, which as Bruce (2017) notes, can lead to going mad with "*good reason*" (emphasis in original). Going mad with "good reason" entails a justifiable response to experiences of structural oppression and harm (Bruce, 2017) and listening to embodied, gut feelings that arise. Ahmed (2016) describes such gut feelings by theorizing how "a gut has its own intelligence. A feminist gut might sense something is amiss. You have to get closer to the feeling; but once you try to think about a feeling, how quickly it can recede" (p. 27). However, it has not always been easy for me to listen to my gut feelings and embodied responses due to learning to separate my thoughts, cognitions, and interpretations from any embodied anxiety, sensations, and feelings that would emerge. As I describe in this chapter, I essentially learned to ignore when my body was communicating that a situation was not right or even when I felt a reasonable amount of anxiety.

LeFrançois and Voronka (2022) note in their work on mad methodologies how the mental health industry is sanist in its epistemic ignorance and discrediting of Mad people's thoughts, behaviours, and feelings. Mad people are taught to distrust their/our own gut reactions, feelings, sensations, and emotions, and to even deem our feelings untrue, unrealistic, or false through mental health interventions, such as Cognitive Behavioural Therapy (CBT), for example (S. Smith, 2022). Such forms of self-distrust reach into the very soul of Mad people and Mad researchers, who are often trained in higher education to only count knowledge and sensations that can be measured and accounted for through scientific processes. In particular, it is positivist approaches to research and knowledge production that forward worldviews that can only conceptualize Mad people and madness as psychopathology in need of intervention (LeFrançois & Voronka, 2022). How can mad knowledge, mad feelings, and mad sensations become involved in research processes? How can Mad researchers come to trust their/our own embodied sensations and reactions while analyzing data? In this, I turn to post-qualitative research9 (St. Pierre, 2021) and combine such theorizations with maddening research approaches (e.g., LeFrançois & Voronka, 2022) to begin the work of describing *maddening moments* (Davies, 2022) as an explicitly mad research approach that emphasizes mad feelings, sensations, and emotions within the research process.

I will start by describing how I came to theorize such *maddening moments* in research and teaching and what such moments entail. I will then provide a background in Mad studies and post-qualitative research, which both inform my theorizing of *maddening moments*. I will follow with a description of affect theory and specifically affects that are deemed Mad. I then turn to mad methodologies and how mad methodologies inform my theorizing of *maddening moments*. I finish with some further description of how I came into *maddening moments* in my teaching and research, and how I learned to honour inner feelings, curiosities, and wonderings, and embodied affective responses within academic work.

## Becoming Mad: Entering Mad Studies

I start this chapter and my theorizing as someone who has experienced immense trauma within my life that has impacted my ability to stay grounded within bodily sensations,

---

9  Post-qualitative research is an onto-epistemological stance that almost escapes definition. Drawing from poststructuralist thought, post-qualitative work challenges positivist notions of "methods" and methodologies by working with embodied techniques to approaching research that break down divides between the discursive/material and mind/body. Post-qualitative approaches are experimental approaches to research (St. Pierre, 2021).

feelings, and emotions. In essence, I disassociate quickly. As such, my body can become numb quite quickly as a way of dissociating from the overwhelming emotions, thoughts, and feelings running through my bodymind system. Here, I use the phrase bodymind following Margaret Price (2015) to indicate the interconnected nature of the mind and body and to challenge Cartesian notions that the mind and mental/psychological processes are separate from our embodied subjectivities. It is important to note this since this numbness has impacted my levels of trust in myself – trust in myself as a theorist, researcher, academic, and even as a person with my own independent thoughts and opinions.

As Burstow (2003) notes, trauma is intricately connected to experiences of dissociation, memory loss, and disconnection, which involve embodied attempts to separate thoughts (cognitions) from feelings:

> with individuals and communities dissociating from aspects of the past that are associated with the trauma; with people and communities fleeing events, history, or memory; with people dissociated from all or parts of their traumatized bodies; with thought separating from feeling; with people disconnecting from others; and with the ties that bind a community coming asunder (Burstow, 2003, p. 1303).

My history with school as a site of trauma has emerged through intense pressures to achieve that I have experienced throughout my schooling endeavours. Schooling and higher education have been places of trauma for me as a Mad student, researcher, and academic, which has been true for as long as I can remember. Even as a student in elementary school, I struggled with anxiety over grades, being a good student, and desiring to perform. I used to ask teachers continuously for my grades and felt shame about presenting any grades to my parents if they were not an A. Such anxiety impacted me physiologically as I would experience stomach aches, headaches, and fast heartbeats, which even impacted my ability to sleep. I knew something was wrong, but I never considered that, perhaps, my body was communicating a message to me regarding my stress surrounding school. I did not learn to listen to my body and instead sought to ignore my embodied sensations and anxieties.

Upon entering my undergraduate degree in music education, I started experiencing anxiety attacks and panic over school that felt unbearable. As a music student, performance was a large part of my program; yet, performing elicited a lot of anxiety in my system that became overwhelming for my body to process. While working on managing such anxiety and panic when performing on my saxophone, which was my main instrument of study in my undergraduate degree, I struggled with singing and doing ear and sight training tests in front of my peers and professors in my courses. My voice would crack, my pitch would waver, and I even failed my introductory ear and sight training course in my first year due to my intense anxiety surrounding performing in front of others. While discussing this anxiety during counseling, I was often reminded that "feelings are just feelings" and that "feelings are not facts." My counselor told me to breathe deeply and learn to separate my anxious embodied feelings from the task at hand in the moment, which was performing. This seemed to work well for me. I retook my ear and sight training course and did well in the course upon repeating it. While I was still anxious about singing in front of my peers, I began learning to separate my embodied feelings of anxiety and unease from my thoughts and actions. I eventually was able to move through my ear and sight training courses. Applying this to other contexts, I learned to distrust and second guess my embodied feelings of anxiety and sensations or even deem them wrong and potentially pathological.

However, in my last year of undergraduate training, I started feeling the anxiety again during my final ear and sight training courses. My instructor explicitly refused my accommodation request to have my tests in his office instead of singing in front of my peers, which increased the knots in my stomach, feelings of tension, and embodied anxiety. During a session with my counselor, who was a different person at this point than my previous counselor, I mentioned my inability to ignore or overcome my anxious feelings during my tests. "Why would you want to ignore these feelings?" asked my new counselor. "These feelings are telling you something. It might be inconvenient, but they are speaking to you, and you could benefit from listening to them." I thought I understood this message at the time, but I continued trying to ignore my anxious feelings, such as the gut feelings within the pits in my stomach, disorientation, dizziness, headaches, and fast-beating heart. I continued to feel that there was something wrong with me as I fumbled through this course. I only considered my embodied feelings a result of my mental illnesses.

As I entered graduate study in education and pre-service teacher education, I increased the amount of anti-anxiety medication I was taking, the frequency of my therapy visits, and even the number of trips to the emergency room and hospital for mental health-related treatment. I felt constantly tense, queasy, and experienced stomach pains and constant headaches. I did not really wish to become a schoolteacher but thought of pre-service teacher education as the natural next step after my undergraduate degree in music education. As such, I was busy in placements, trying to present myself as a happy and effervescent teacher, while feeling numb on the inside due to how disconnected I was (or felt) between my overstimulated and overanxious body and what I was (or was not) actually processing. Working from auto-pilot mode, I was more focused on handing in the next class assignment, writing my lesson plans, showing up with a positive attitude for placement than actually sitting with my anxiety. Increasing my frequency of psychiatric visits, I eventually reached a breaking point and was feeling suicidal without even being fully aware of my own suicidal thoughts and emotions. My stomach was in knots, but I was not sure why. Upon realizing I was suicidal, I had already been accepted into my doctoral program, was preparing to finish my masters and teacher education program and had committed to dozens of research and teaching opportunities. I was in such a daze that I even printed the wrong slides for my presentation at the annual American

Educational Research Association conference and was mostly unable to complete any tasks or focus on work of any kind. I felt so disconnected with and dissociated from my embodied self that I was unable to notice or sense when my body was reacting, responding, or warning me in any way. I was afraid of becoming overwhelmed, so I instead became numb. My body might have been trying to tell me that I was on a path that was unsustainable and not what I wanted. Ignoring my body's reaction to situations, people, and places where I felt unsafe, anxious, or responsive, I had trained myself to question and doubt my body's sensations and emotions.

Eventually, I was hired as a tenure-track faculty in a post-secondary pre-service education program in early childhood education (Child Studies). While teaching, I experienced growing anxiety over the epistemological incommensurability between the queer and disability studies frameworks I used in my academic work and the mandated developmental and psychoeducational frameworks entrenched in pre-service early childhood education programs (Ontario Ministry of Training, Colleges, and Universities, 2018). I could no longer ignore my body's sensations, which I had started to be able to listen to through exploring post-qualitative research (e.g., Ahmed, 2016; MacLure, 2013; Ringrose & Renold, 2014) during my dissertation work (Davies, 2021). However, I had not yet theorized the relationship between my anxious and embodied feelings and emotions and my history with Madness and psychiatrization. While teaching in undergraduate classes, I would encounter madness through sinking feelings in my stomach, frustration, embodied anxiety, and other signs that I did not feel right about what I was teaching. Finally, I was able to feel the sensations in my body that something was not right with my courses and the mandated developmental and psychoeducational content, but I still tried to continue forwards by ignoring these feelings.

At times, I would take an Ativan after teaching my lectures to calm my body down due to the stress I felt at disseminating knowledge that I did not agree with. I often felt out of place in my home department and that my critical theory and cultural studies teachings were not welcome in relationship with the dominant biopsychosocial and developmental models that my colleagues were using (Davies, 2022; Davies & Neustifter, 2022; Davies & Joy, 2022). Moreover, I felt surveilled through provincial early childhood education accreditation standards, which many of my colleagues used to shape and mould my teachings (Ontario Ministry of Training, Colleges, and Universities, 2018). Together, these pressures produced feelings of dis-ease in me. Here I use the phrase, dis-ease to emphasize the discomfort, anxiety, and unease I felt in my teaching situations delivering content that I felt was potentially harmful. I refuse the assignment of a diagnostic category to these feelings and the construction of them as a medical problem. Instead, I relate this to the stress and discomfort that my body was communicating in relation to the knowledge that I was being asked to disseminate.

I start with these vignettes from my early experiences in higher education to explain the importance of embodied feelings and sensations that are typically deemed nonsensical at minimum, or a nuisance, by biomedical and psychiatric approaches to madness. In my early stages of higher education, I learned to disassociate my feelings of anxiety, uncertainty, and distress and to separate them neatly from experiences in the moment. Although madness is often associated with angry feelings and emotions (Chapman, 2013), *maddening moments* can be any feelings which bring about discomfort, unease, uncertainty, confusion, or disorientation and create some form of rupture through embodied responses (Davies, 2022). Despite my training throughout my PhD in critical theory and critical and post-qualitative approaches, the early words of counselors echoed, encouraging me to disconnect embodied sensations and feelings from self-knowledge (Haraway, 1988).

In her work on peer support workers in the mental health industry, Voronka (2017) asks: "to what effect are we deploying our work to orient clients toward feelings and responses that actually encourage compliance and cooperation with dominant conceptual models of mental illness?" (p. 335). Reflecting on my experiences learning to question my embodied sensations and anxieties, I came to realize that while my counselors were attempting to assist me in regulating my emotions and being able to successfully perform in front of my instructor and peers, this also prevented me from listening to my embodied sensations, feelings, and emotions, and only allowed them to be understood as a barrier, pathology, or hindrance. I considered the anxiety that resonated throughout my body as a nuisance and something to be rid of; I had never considered the potential that it offered me or where and how I could listen to such anxiety.

## Mad affects

Seigworth and Gregg (2010) theorize how affect, as an intense force and capacity, "accumulates across both relatedness and interruptions in relatedness" (p. 2), meaning that some affects are interrelational and connective and some are disruptive. This diversity in affect is important to note in how madness is inherently associated with disruptive affects and emotions, leaving others in a state of concern, confusion, or unease towards madness and Mad people. Within helping or social service professions, such as education, early childhood education, social work, and nursing, madness can only be imagined through the potential for emotional and mental disruption, dysregulation, or violence (Davies et al., 2022; Davies, 2022; Poole et al., 2021). Whatever madness is, it certainly is considered non-normative, affective, and emotional. As I have noted in other work, the connection between emotions, sensations, feelings, and thoughts that are uncomfortable and the potential for violence has become an anchoring point for the regulation of Mad professionals and practitioners in various fields and disciplines (Chapman et al., 2016; Davies et al., 2022; Poole et al., 2021). Emotions and feelings that are deemed unreasonable, scary, or potentially even violent in their expression, such as rage, anger, frustration, are notably disavowed in the helping professions, leaving emotional regulation as a key tenet of engaging with social service and care work (Davies et al., 2022). However, as noted by Snyder et al. (2019), "Mad Studies is a reminder that we must consider the dialectical and affective intensifications that make up any experience" (p. 488). Whether teaching in front of a classroom of students, performing in front of an instructor for a grade, interacting with a small child, or a patient as a medical practitioner, there are certainly emotions and mental states that are deemed desirable and even normal for given situations (Hochschild, 1979). Yet, when the emotional and mental states and expressions that are deemed undesirable present themselves – and are even tapped into or felt in an embodied way to the fullest degree – there can be forms of radical opportunities and self-honouring (Lorde, 1978). This is where Mad Studies (LeFrançois et al., 2013) and Mad methodologies (LeFrançois & Voronka, 2022) offer learnings and potentiality.

Madness and emotionality are interconnected – when I have felt my madness presenting itself is often in situations where my emotions and feelings have felt unmanageable or that I have been unable to control my emotions, feelings, thoughts, and even behaviours (Davies, 2022, 2023). Bruce (2017) describes four productions of madness within modernity, including: (1) phenomenal madness; (2) clinical and medicalized madness; (3) madness as anger and intensity; and (4) psychosocial madness, which includes mental states outside normalcy in different contexts, which could potentially mark the individual as mad or crazy (p. 308). In particular, Bruce describes how Black people have continually had to experience phenomenal madness, or "radical crises of perception, emotion, meaning, and selfhood" (p. 305) throughout their time within modernity due to ongoing legacies of slavery, anti-Black racism, and forced displacement and enslavement. It is necessary to note these connections between anti-Black racism and sanism and the necessity of maintaining intersectional Mad analytics (Gorman & LeFrançois, 2017).

These different iterations of madness are interconnected, which is important in the context of this chapter and theorizing of *maddening moments*. *Maddening moments* certainly can involve anger and intensity, although it is important not to equate madness with anger or to assume that madness is necessarily the only emotion that can arise in *maddening moments* (Chapman, 2013; Davies, 2022). Bruce's description of psychosocial madness is particularly helpful in its delineation of emotional and mental states that are outside of normalcy, or what is constructed as normal in a given context. In Davies (2022), I described the feeling of experiencing emotional distress and dysregulation while teaching in pre-service ECEC classrooms. My emotional expressivity in front of my students, in particular, my expression of frustration, sadness, even anger, at the mandated course materials that I was expected to disseminate to my students, presented itself as emotional dysregulation (Davies, 2022). Instead of considering these moments through a frame of pathology, I wondered about what these moments offered pedagogically and how such moments where I felt like my madness became visible potentially provided opportunities for reflection (Davies, 2023). This is where I turn to mad methodologies.

## Mad methodologies

Mad methodologies embrace dysregulation, emotional unease, disturbance, and instability while connecting such feelings and emotional states to greater socio-political and cultural politics. As described by Bruce (2021), Mad methodologies:

> cultivates critical ambivalence to reckon with the
> simultaneous harm and benefit that may accompany
> madness. It respects and sometimes harnesses "mad"
> feelings like obsession and rage as stimulus for radical
> thought and action. Whereas rationalism roundly
> discredits madpersons, mad methodology recognizes
> madpersons as critical theorists and decisive protagonists
> in struggles for liberation (Bruce, 2021, p. 9).

In this, I bring forward my theorization of *maddening
moments* by drawing from Mad studies and post-qualitative
approaches (Davies, 2022). I must be clear that this chapter
is not a roadmap; that is, I am not offering a step-by-step
guide on how to enact *maddening moments* within your own
research. I am theorizing and describing how *maddening
moments* emerged in my research; yet, it will look different
each time. As St. Pierre (2021) notes about post-qualitative research, "it must be invented, created differently each
time" (p. 6), which means that traditional positivist notions
of "data collection" do not resonate in this chapter. Instead
of turning to measurement, extraction, and representation,
*maddening moments* follow Ringrose and Renold (2014) in
being "a moment of rupture co-constructed through our

feminist research assemblage" (p. 776). Such "moments of rupture" are where "affective intensities happen and are made meaning of in live research encounters" (Ringrose & Renold, 2014, p. 776). What this means is that *maddening moments* are lived, often jarring or unsettling in many ways, and evoke critical questions in the moment that are guided and led by bodymind reactions and gut responses that escape linguistic description in the moment (Davies, 2022; MacLure, 2013; Ringrose & Renold, 2014).

In particular, for me as a researcher-teacher who teaches in a pre-service Early Childhood Education and Care (ECEC) program, embodied responses, anxiety, and madness often present themselves in the middle of my classroom teachings where I am left wondering what Pickens (2019) articulates as "the vagueness and insult mad bring" (p. 4). As someone who experiences high levels of anxiety, who is known by my students to be "quirky" and "off-center," madness presents itself in my teachings in terms of both mental distress and also behaviours, expressions, teachings, that are known as "mad" in their rejection of traditional, technocratic knowledges and pedagogies. smith (2017) describes mad methodologies and approaches as "anti-methodologies" that are "crazy as a motherfucker":

*a Mad poesis*
*a Mad Turn*
*that offers a way outta*
*the dead-end of academic logical positivizm*
*anti-founded instead*

*on/in/through/out/about*

*a Turn towards the*  *irrational*

*unreasonable*

*surreal*

*inappropriate*

*unmanageable*

*incredible*

*illegitimate.*

*an anti-methodology that is crazy as a motherfucker.*

(smith, 2017)

Certainly, my students, colleagues, and others at the university might believe this about me in how my approaches tend to embrace the nonsensical, the mad or the impossible (Davies, 2022). Turning away from pathology and turning towards the irrational (smith, 2017) is "a method of navigating discursive deconstructions and embodied experiences of mental illness" (Johnson, 2021, p. 649), or a methodology of listening to all of us who live within the borderline of methods, methodologies, pedagogies, and normative approaches. Such borderline approaches (Johnson, 2021) include *maddening moments* of disorientation, disarray, or where words escape but the body reacts. Within my current field of early childhood education, I occupy the fringes of respectability, the shadows of normativity, whereby my scholarship and teachings evoke questions about the current state of the field in its emphasis on developmentalism, normative images of children and educators, and the maintenance of the status quo (Davies et al., 2022). Yet, as I have written about before (Davies, 2022, 2023), I am often constrained by both ideas of accreditation in pre-service early childhood education, which tend to emphasize normative notions of child development, ages and stages approaches to understanding children, and Enlightenment-based philosophies and developmentalist theorists, who are emphasized as the cornerstone and foundational theorists of ECEC.

Upon being hired and arriving in pre-service ECEC, I found the textbooks and works passed on to me to teach emphasized the theories of Jean Piaget, Erik Erikson, B.F. Skinner, and Lee Vygotsky – all prominent developmental psychologists and emphasized notions of child-centered pedagogies. Despite teaching contractually in pre-service ECEC previously, my doctoral training in education was in cultural studies, and as such, I began integrating critical theory and cultural studies into my courses. While engaging with the course textbooks from previous years, I began reacting physically to some of the core developmental content in the textbooks associated with my courses, including content that emphasized Applied Behavioural Analysis (ABA) interventions and approaches (Davies, 2022). Such moments elicited physical reactions in my body and moments where my madness became visible as I taught in front of my students. As such, I started journaling about these moments and taking note of how I was incorporating madness into my teachings as I was navigating teaching materials that I did not agree with and felt often forced to teach (Davies, 2022). In particular, I received reminders often from my department regarding the mandatory accreditation standards for our program to continue providing our students with their eligibility to register with the Ontario College of Early Childhood Educators (Ontario Ministry of Training, Colleges, and Universities, 2018). However, I realized how maddening this content was for me to teach and felt my embodied reactions had to be important pedagogically. I wanted to continue to investigate how I could incorporate madness and Mad methodologies and pedagogies into my teaching and research (Davies, 2022).

Eventually, I started rebuilding my courses from scratch and incorporating content from my own educational background and epistemologies (Davies, 2022). I began to use moments of rupture or expressions of madness as a curiosity (Davies, 2023) and started to consider, following MacLure (2013) "the capacity for wonder that resides and radiates in data, or rather in the entangled relation of data-and-researcher" (p. 228). These notes emphasized my own reactions, responses, and feelings while teaching certain texts and emphasized how madness may have presented itself in specific moments. These notes emphasized the curiosity or wonder (MacLure, 2013; Titchkosky, 2011) elicited when taken-for-granted ideas and truths bring about embodied reactions and responses. I delineated this process and reflections in Davies (2022). I truly believe that considering madness in research and teaching can bring a generative orientation towards re-examining common unquestioned ideas, such as developmentalist narratives (Davies et al., 2022). As LeFrançois (2020) describes, developmentalism can only imagine madness as in need of intervention and mad childhoods as a problem in need of psychiatric cure. When reflecting on moments where I felt discomfort and embodied anxiety, I aimed to theorize how these moments might be generative. Seigworth and Gregg (2010) note how moments of affective disruption can be "a generative, pedagogic nudge aimed toward a body's becoming an ever more worldly sensitive interface, toward a style of being present to the struggles of our time" (Seigworth & Gregg, 2010, p. 12). Without paying attention to moments when my body felt anxious, uneasy, disrupted, I would not have been able to tune into my concerns and questions about the content I was teaching future practitioners.

## This is not a roadmap: Finding my way to Mad Studies

Again, I repeat, this is not a roadmap. I used to find comfort in roadmaps by looking at how to get from A to B; however, somewhere along the path between A and B, I'd still not quite follow the directions properly. Roadmaps are supposed to be as easy as a recipe! I joke with people in my life that if they give me a recipe, the food might not turn out as expected due to my own propensity for "getting lost" (Lather, 2012) somewhere along the way. I even think that when we get lost when trying to follow our roadmaps precisely, there can be fun learning, stressful learning, maddening learning, joyous learning that takes place. I certainly did not think I would end up where I am currently, writing this chapter for you... that is not a roadmap. My original roadmap for my academic trajectory did not even include Mad studies... yet. However, I found Mad studies (or Mad studies found me) and I am here now, writing this chapter for you that is not a roadmap.

I am not providing the reader with a how-to-do *maddening moments*; this is a chapter about my embodied experiences with madness and how such moments have played into my research and teaching. Even attempting to describe such maddening feelings, behaviours, potentials, and reactions relies on the connection between language, cognition, and meaning (Gibbs, 2010), which *maddening moments* escape. Whatever madness is, it is beyond signification, yet still known as outside the realm of reason, rationality, and procedure. Positivist approaches to research lean into notions of validity, reliability, and measurement. Positivism wants to make sense of the mind, to create universalizable truths, and use positivist procedures (O'Leary, 2007). But I'm not interested in that. Who gets to decide what *my* truth is? My truth isn't your truth, which isn't their truth, which isn't anyone else's truth! My feelings are not your feelings, which are not anyone else's feelings! Positivist approaches to knowing expect us to separate our thinking (cognition) and our feeling (emotion). Fuck, no! What we feel is what we know and what we know is what and how we feel (Lorde, 1978).

## Epistemic injustice: Self-listening in *maddening moments*

*What we know*
*depends on*
*who does the knowing.*
*Because Mad people are crazy*
*they are by definition*
*unreliable knowers.*
(smith, 2020, p. 371)

Mad methodologies inherently validate Mad people's knowledges, understandings, and experiences, conceptualizing mad personal experiences as beginning places to theorize (smith, 2017; LeFrançois & Voronka, 2022). *Maddening moments* share autoethnography's interest in "seek to produc[ing] aesthetic and evocative thick descriptions of personal and interpersonal experience" (Ellis et al., 2011, p. 5); however, of particular relevance is "the exploration of self in relation to other and the space created between them" (Starr, 2010, p. 4). If Mad people are inherently constructed as "unreliable knowers" (smith, 2020), how does one become a reliable knower? What makes up the space between reliable and unreliable and how can such binaries be unmade? As described by Fricker (2007), epistemic injustice occurs when individuals' truths, experiences, or testimonies are discredited, misinterpreted, left unheard, or distrusted, which, in particular, happens when Mad people are discredited through the propagation of psychologized or psychiatric explanations (LeBlanc & Kinsella, 2016). For many people who are invested in the psy-disciplines and industrial medical complexes, it can be maddening to think that Mad people's testimonies and truths might lead to alternative explanations than the hegemonic order (Davies, 2022; Davies et al., 2022). Honouring Mad truths and Mad experiences is a vital component of taking note of such *maddening moments*.

Spear (2019) writes how gaslighting, or the distortion and undermining of one's independent thoughts and interpretations of the world, have significant epistemic consequences, including influencing one's self-trust. While being a Mad student and faculty member in higher education, I distrusted my embodied reactions to situations that elicited emotions, sensations, and expressions that seemed to be out of place or potentially unreasonable for the situation. Was the intense heart racing I was feeling unreasonable and therefore, something to ignore? Should I just take a Tylenol to ignore the headache that was emerging continually as I was teaching? I knew that these physiological experiences were not just me being irrational or responding inappropriately to content that I did not agree with; yet, I still ignored the sense within my body that these feelings were not just an illness.

## *Maddening moments*: moments of curiosity and wonder

What has kept me going in all my degrees and now as a faculty and researcher in higher education is my curiosity about the world, my experiences, and trying to reimagine the taken-for-granted order of society (Davies, 2023). I have never been interested in taking any experiences or ideas at face value, and it is this curiosity and wonder (Titchkosky, 2011) about the world that has brought me to Critical Disability Studies and Mad studies (Davies, 2022, 2023). In my work regarding Mad studies in early childhood education and care (Davies, 2022, 2023; Davies et al., 2022), I have theorized how the field of early childhood education tries to fix madness as pathology, the potential for violence, and push out Mad educators. While I have described anxiety throughout this chapter, there are of course many other emotions and forms of emotional expression that are commonly constructed as mad and therefore signs of mental unwellness. While teaching, my passion for critiquing the medical model can potentially present itself as madness, or visible signifiers of sadness that might seem out-of-place or odd for a course instructor to express in front of students (Davies, 2022). These expressions are *affecting* in how they both affect me, as an instructor, and affect my students within the classroom environment (Massumi, 1995). The disorientation involved in such moments can be confusing but also lead to new learnings and reflections.

Following MacLure (2013), *maddening moments* are certainly filled with wonder and can be enacted during data analysis. While reviewing data, there is always data that affects us in a certain way, or that can seem absolutely maddening, or promote wonder (Davies, 2022). MacLure (2013) notes how wonder "insists in bodies as well as minds" and is "not necessarily a safe, comforting, or uncomplicatedly positive affect. It shades into curiosity, horror, fascination, disgust, and monstrosity" (p. 229). For Mad folks, such feelings of horror or monstrosity hold particular meanings given the medicalization and pathologization of Mad people and their emotional expressions. In particular, Mad researchers might have learned to disconnect themselves from their embodied affects, feelings, and emotions, meaning that it could even be difficult to pay attention to embodied responses to data. It is important to note this because in my experiences, I was used to dissociating myself from my embodied reactions and feelings as a way of trying to cope with mental and emotional distress. However, upon reflecting on moments where I intentionally brought my madness into my classroom pedagogies, I also began to note my body's differential reactions to such written reflections. Listening to my body as an anchor for my analysis (MacLure, 2013; Ringrose & Renold, 2014), I began paying attention to the emotional and affective responses I was experiencing while reviewing these written reflections (see Davies, 2022).

To be clear, again, this is not stating that *maddening moments* will be the same in my work as it might be in another researcher's work. However, by listening to and honouring moments of emotional and mental distress that felt embodied in some way, I began to pay attention to distress in a way that guided data analysis work in a non-positivist and non-hierarchical manner (Davies, 2021, 2022). What I am offering here is a consideration of what embodied experiences with madness might bring research, particularly as a challenge to positivist, linear approaches to research methodologies.

This also turns the attention away from Mad people's experiences as only pathology, illness, or deviance and honours the inner knowing of Mad truths within research.

It was through my post-secondary teaching and the experiences of homing in on my embodied feelings and reactions to course materials and content pathologizing mental diversity and madness that I began to reconceptualize my relationship with madness. I became curious about how else madness could be constructed and even theorized within research. Whether through gut reactions (Ahmed, 2016) to mandated course and accreditation content (Ontario Ministry of Training, Colleges, & Universities, 2018), or embodied tension due to frustration, or even anger, feelings and emotions are embodied and provide helpful analytic information. I encourage the reader to go from here into their own theorizing of *maddening moments* and thus do not provide a template – just a reflection and a starting point. However, every starting point is different and as such, where each person will begin with madness will be different.

## In conclusion: It's only the beginning

In this chapter, I have not provided a reflection on my overcoming dysregulated feelings, emotions, and embodied sensations, nor have I discussed how I was able to teach and research *despite* my madness. I have instead taken note of different occasions when my madness and embodied feelings of distress have presented themselves, whether teaching, or analyzing data, and noted how such moments have guided how

I have moved forward in my work (Davies, 2022). Madness evokes wonder and curiosity (Davies 2023), which in and of itself, can be disorienting and unnerving (MacLure, 2013). *Maddening moments* are not always positive, or immediately illuminating, but they are moments when the unease, discomfort, anxiety, or frustration we feel is honed into instead of disassociated from. While dominant biomedical and psychiatric frameworks might wish to encourage Mad people to regulate any emotional dysregulation or separate themselves from any embodied feelings that could be deemed impediments to daily functioning, instead, I offer these feelings of dis-ease and discomfort as potential learning opportunities and a way to even consider maddening higher education on my journey to trusting myself and my madness.

## References

Ahmed, S. (2016). *Living a feminist life*. Duke University Press.

Aho, T., Ben-Moshe, L., & Hilton, L. J. (2017). Mad futures: Affect/theory/violence. *American Quarterly*, *69*(2), 291-302.

Bruce, L. M. J. (2017). Interludes in Madtime: Black music, Madness, and metaphysical syncopation. *Social Text*, *35*(4), 1-31.

Bruce, L. M. J. (2021). *How to go mad without losing your mind: Madness and black radical creativity*. Duke University Press.

Burstow, B. (2003). Toward a radical understanding of trauma and trauma work. *Violence Against Women*, *9*(11), 1293-1317.

Chapman, C. (2013). Cultivating a troubled consciousness: Compulsory sound-mindedness and complicity in oppression. *Health, Culture and Society, 5*(1), 182-198.

Chapman, C., Azevedo, J., Ballen, R., & Poole, J. (2016). A kind of collective freezing-out: How helping professionals' regulatory bodies create "incompetence" and increase distress. In *Psychiatry interrogated* (pp. 41-61). Palgrave Macmillan, Cham.

Davies, A. W. (2021). *Queering App-propriate Behaviours: The Affective Politics of Gay Social- Sexual Applications in Toronto, Canada* [Doctoral dissertation, University of Toronto].

Davies, A. (2022). Professional ruptures in pre-service ECEC: Maddening early childhood education and care. *Curriculum Inquiry*, 1-22.

Davies, A. (2023). Teaching with madness in pre-service Early Childhood Education and Care (ECEC): Bringing autobiographical mad subjectivities and promoting curiosity. In P. Trifonas & S. Jagger (Eds.), *International handbook of curriculum theory, research, and practice*. Springer.

Davies, A. W., & Neustifter, R. (2021). Heteroprofessionalism in the academy: The surveillance and regulation of queer faculty in higher education. *Journal of Homosexuality*, 1-25.

Davies, A. W., & Joy, P. (2022). Queerness and queer subjectivities in Home Economics: Navigating and disrupting the helping professions in higher education. *Equity & Excellence in Education*, 1-16.

Davies, A., Brewer, K., & Shay, B. (2022). Sanism in early childhood education and care: Cultivating space for madness and mad educators. *EceLINK, 6*(1), 18–30.

https://assets. nationbuilder.com/aeceo/pages/2524/attachments/original/1655592321/Sanism_in_Early_Childhood_Education_ and_Care.pdf?1655592321

Ellis, C., Adams, T. E., & Bochner, A. P. (2011). Autoethnography: an overview. *Historical social research/Historische sozialforschung*, 273-290.

Fricker, M. (2007). *Epistemic injustice: Power and the ethics of knowing*. Oxford University Press.

Gibbs, A. (2010). Sympathy, Synchrony, and Mimetic Communication. In M. Gregg & G. J. Seigworth (Eds.), *The affect theory reader*. Durham: Duke University Press. pp. 186–205.

Gorman, R., & LeFrançois, B. A. (2017). Mad studies. In *Routledge international handbook of critical mental health* (pp. 107-114). Routledge.

Haraway, D. (1988). Situated knowledges: The science question in feminism and the privilege of partial perspective. *Feminist Studies, 14*(3), 575–599.

Hochschild, A. R. (1979). Emotion work, feeling rules, and social structure. *American Journal of Sociology, 85*(3), 551-575.

Johnson, M. L. (2021). Neuroqueer feminism: turning with tenderness toward borderline personality disorder. *Signs: Journal of Women in Culture and Society, 46*(3), 635-662.

Lather, P. (2012). *Getting lost: Feminist efforts toward a double(d) science*. Suny Press.

Leblanc, S., & Kinsella, E. A. (2016). Toward epistemic justice: A critically reflexive examination of 'sanism' and implications for knowledge generation. *Studies in Social Justice, 10*(1), 59-78.

LeFrançois, B. A. (2020). Psychiatrising children. In V. Cooper & N. Holford (Eds.), *Exploring childhood and youth* (pp. 177–190). Routledge.

LeFrançois, B. A., & Voronka, J. (2022). Mad epistemologies and Maddening the ethics of knowledge production. *Un/Ethical Un/Knowing: Ethical Reflections on Methodology and Politics in Social Science Research.* Canadian Scholars Press Inc.

LeFrançois, B. A., Menzies, R., & Reaume, G. (Eds.). (2013). *Mad matters: A critical reader in Canadian mad studies.* Canadian Scholars Press.

Lorde, Audre (1978/2000). "The Uses of the Erotic." *The Uses of the Erotic: The Erotic as Power.*Tucson: Kore Press.

Massumi, B. (1995). The autonomy of affect. *Cultural Critique, (31)*, 83-109.

O'Leary, Z. (2007). *The social science jargon buster.* London: Sage.

Ontario Ministry of Training, Colleges, and Universities. (2018). Early Childhood Education    Program Standard. http://www.tcu.gov.on.ca/pepg/audiences/colleges/progstan/humserv/51211-early-childhood-education.pdf.

Pickens, T. A. (2019). *Black madness: Mad blackness.* Duke University Press.

Poole, J., Chapman, C., Meerai, S., Azevedo, J., Gebara, A., Hussaini, N., & Ballen, R. (2021). The professional regulation of madness in nursing and social work. In *The Routledge International Handbook of Mad Studies* (pp. 177-189). Routledge.

Price, M. (2015). The bodymind problem and the possibilities of pain. *Hypatia, 30*(1), 268-284.

Smith, P. (2017). Defining disability studies and its intersection with madness. *Disability Studies Quarterly, 37*(3).

Smith, P. (2020). [R]evolving towards Mad: Spinning away from the psy/spy-complex through auto/biography. In *The Palgrave Handbook of Auto/Biography* (pp. 369-388). Palgrave Macmillan, Cham.

Smith, S. (2022). Neoliberalism and mental health care in Ontario: A critique of internet-based cognitive behavioural therapy. *Canadian Journal of Disability Studies, 11*(1), 1-25.

Snyder, S. N., Pitt, K. A., Shanouda, F., Voronka, J., Reid, J., & Landry, D. (2019). Unlearning through Mad studies: Disruptive pedagogical praxis. *Curriculum Inquiry, 49*(4), 485-502.

Spear, A. D. (2019). Epistemic dimensions of gaslighting: Peer-disagreement, self-trust, and epistemic injustice. *Inquiry*, 1-24.

Starr, L. J. (2010). The use of autoethnography in educational research: Locating who we are in what we do. *Canadian Journal for New Scholars in Education/Revue canadienne des jeunes chercheures et chercheurs en éducation, 3*(1).

St. Pierre, E. A. (2021). Post qualitative inquiry, the refusal of method, and the risk of the new. *Qualitative Inquiry, 27*(1), 3-9.

Titchkosky, T. (2011). *The question of access: Disability, space, meaning.* University of Toronto Press.

Voronka, J. (2017). Turning mad knowledge into affective labor: the case of the peer support worker. *American Quarterly*, 69(2), 333-338.

# Knitting Like Mad

*Rebecca-Eli M. Long*

Knitting is the opposite of unraveling, a bringing together, connecting. Knitting provides form, a structure to keep yourself from falling apart. I knit to keep myself safe, treating the yarn as though it is a lifeline, refusing to set it down even when my wrists and shoulders ache from the repetitive motions. I find myself turning to knitting especially in times of distress, which has turned me into a prolific knitter, and I am rarely without at least one work in progress, if not more. The combination of the needles rubbing against each other, the yarn sliding through my hands, and the texture of the fabric slowly taking shape builds a sensory environment, one which holds my experiences in ways different from anything else I have ever found.

I'm not one of those people who learned knitting from an older relative at an early age, though a grandmother did gift me her old knitting needles after I learned. I started knitting by chance, thanks to a housemate who taught me the summer before I started graduate school. By the time the semester started, I had made two hats, a shawl, and was working on my first sweater, which eventually unraveled in the wash. Undeterred, my knitting only escalated. I found myself entranced by the rhythm of stitch after stitch, row after row.

My knitting accompanied me almost everywhere: meetings, classes, conferences.

When I brought knitting to my ethnographic field site at the local senior center, it also became a helpful way of connecting to people. I found that it supported my neurodivergent communication style. Rather than me having to initiate conversations directly, people would ask about my knitting, and I would ask if they knew how to knit, and we'd be well on our way to a conversation without any of the awkward precursors. Once I realized that knitting was something that helped me communicate, I started to wonder what the knitting itself might be able to communicate as a broader way of storying research interactions. Recognizing the importance of research that consists of stories (Smith, 2013), I wanted new methods for telling those stories.

As an anthropologist, my discipline sometimes presumes a certain amount of conversational dexterity on the part of the researcher, expecting a certain level of sociality. My methods classes were based on the assumption that we'd be socially outgoing, eager to strike up conversations, have bodyminds that would be capable of staying up late into the night to take copious amounts of notes. While the myth of the lone anthropologist going off to some exotic field site is criticized and outdated, the ablebodied and ablemindedness inherent in that construction usually goes unquestioned, except by disabled anthropologists (Colligan, 2001; Raphael et al., 2001), though recent calls for a disability anthropology have called for methodological interventions alongside theoretical commitments (Hartblay, 2020).

For a discipline that is fairly open to reflexivity, I've found the lack of consideration of the anthropologist's own body-mind strangely absent, as well as alienating. Yet when disability becomes centered in our fieldwork and other research interactions, it provides a chance for interviewing "sideways, crooked, and crip" (Price & Kerschbaum, 2016). In considering Mad methods across disciplinary spaces, it is necessary to reconsider what the space of research interactions look like, not only for participants who may have access needs, but for the researcher as well. I was never formally taught research methods that centered my access needs, but eventually I turned to my knitting as a way to disrupt normative sanist assumptions about what research, and by extension, what a researcher, should look like.

Knitting existed consistently in the background of my academic life throughout graduate school. Despite its persistence, I didn't think of it as a potential academic activity until after I had finished my Master's degree and had started towards doctoral work. At first bringing knitting into my research was a joke until one day I got the crazy [sic] idea to actually do it. The idea of knitting as Mad method arose out of asking *what if I showed up fully in my academic life? What if I stopped shoving this piece of who I am to the side? What does it mean to insist on more diverse ways of "doing research?" Is this a way to chip away, bit by bit, stitch by stitch, at the sanism and ableism of academic spaces?*

Knitting provides a methodological intervention that supports my Mad, neurodivergent bodymind, through reshaping the social space involved in conducting research. I connect this approach both with histories of craftivism (activism through crafting) as well as the challenges to self-narration and expression I experience as an autistic grad student. Through enabling new ways of taking up physical space, whether in the classroom or research site, and more expansive forms of communication, knitting as a method gives material form to a commitment to revisioning interactions. Though anthropologists have long been concerned with practices of representation through writing (Clifford & Marcus, 1986), I consider knitting to be an example of "needlework as productive practice that yields ethnographic possibilities quite different from writing, that is, needlework as knowledge production" (Chin, 2020, p. 7).

Specifically, I think knitting has the potential to reflect the knowledge production arising from autistic echophenomena to refute the epistemic violence of actions that might otherwise be thought of as meaningless. Echophenomena are a range of rhetorical practices consisting of repetition of spoken words, drawn shapes, physical motion and the like that are frequently dismissed as noncommunicative (Yergeau, 2018), and epistemic violence is the harm done through the ways that knowledge gets produced and when certain types of knowledge are considered illegitimate. Disregarding echophenomena is just one example of autistic people being seen as unable to use rhetoric, despite the richness of autistic life writing (Van Goidsenhoven, 2017). Autism has "been crafted as a disorder of neurological queerness," with autistic rhetoric in need of straightening and correcting (Yergeau, 2018, p. 184). In counter to this, I craft with my neurological queerness, rather than straightening anything, I twist the yarn, making loop after interlocking loop.

## (K)neurodivergent Knitting

I feel fairly confident that there are certain aspects of my bodymind that made me more prone to take knitting up with an uninhibited enthusiasm. The friend who taught me later remarked that I was the only person she had taught that ever got much further into knitting besides the first hat or scarf. Despite my initial trepidation about my lack of skill in picking up physical motions and the slight tremor in my hands, knitting came to me fairly easily. At the time, I was working as a home health aide and spent many hours keeping people company in their homes, often not engaged in any particular task besides providing companionship. I found myself with ample time to practice my knitting while at work and ample space in the pockets of my scrubs to hold a ball of yarn. Clients didn't mind if I knitted on the job. In fact, it gave us something to talk about. Knitting helped me fit into the role of a domestic caregiver. I like to think it also helped distinguish me from the other aides, as clients would often be faced with an unpredictable schedule of workers coming in and out of their house.

Knitting is generally thought of as a relaxing activity, beneficial for wellbeing (Corkhill et al., 2014). But what I noticed was more specific: knitting supported my wellbeing in particularly autistic ways. Knitting presented itself as an ideal stim. More than that though, it is a type of echopraxia, a repeated movement, almost involuntary at times. Indeed, I am grappling with the urge to pick up my knitting even as I try to write this. [And again, as I go back to edit this.] Echophenomena, such as repeated words and motions, are an autistic communication tactic. In reclaiming knitting as an autistic motion, I am suggesting that autistic stims are communicative and that, as Remi Yergeau asserts, there are resonances of rhetoricity in autistic echoes. I am telling a story not only about knitting and autism, but of different ways to tell stories.

Textile and text have a shared etymology. Both words come from the Latin word for "to weave," which makes me think of Mel Baggs, who wrote, "And when I crochet, I can feel the way the world is woven together, weaves itself together, with every movement" (2018). Knitting can be understood as a narrative practice, part of a long history of using textiles as a way of communicating stories. As one book on textiles and narrative asserts in its opening chapter: stories are an inherent part of being human (Prain, 2014, p. 15). But to be Mad and autistic is to have one's narrative ability called into question. If storytelling is part of being human, and autistic people can't tell stories, where does that leave the neurodivergent knitter? Knitting provides a queer way to story autism, which is itself a collection of narratives, some given more legitimacy than others (Orsini & Davidson, 2013).

I've always been the type of autistic with loud hands, ranging from excited flapping to nervous skin picking. In the context of autism, "loud hands" means finding ways to communicate in the ways that we want to (Sequenzia, 2012). But more than just keeping my hands occupied, my entire body gets wrapped up in my knitting, as it creates a subtle rhythm that I settle into. Elements of sound and touch create a rich sensory experience. If whatever knitting I've brought along is too complicated to tackle at the moment, I draw satisfaction from simply rubbing my fingers along the textured material, feeling the ridges and bumps. And I got the satisfaction of seeing something gradually take shape on my knitting needles, giving form to my experiences, a way of keeping track of time. My memories now are often organized along with what I was knitting at the time. Knitting becomes an organizational schema, for charting memories, for interacting with people, for stimming in autistic defiance.

Perhaps I am driven to knit by a neuroqueer (Walker, 2021) narrative failure. In insisting that knitting tells a story about autism, I am also insisting that I am capable of telling stories about my autism, even if they are outside of the form that people expect. Knitting neuroqueers communication, disrupting and subverting how I express myself and connect with others. If knitting translated into words, I would rarely be quiet. The repetition of stitches would be echolalic, a form of communication that makes use of repeated words and phrases. Perhaps a ribbing, which is knit and purl stitches over and over, with a smattering of lace for punctuation. Or cables, making a bold sweeping statement. I've recently taken up something called double knitting, which creates two layers of fabric simultaneously in communicative excess. When I knit, I have loud hands, extending a metaphorical middle finger to those who say autistics cannot communicate.

As knitting solidified its place as my go-to stim, I wanted to learn more, and soon it fell into another site of autistic wellbeing, the special interest. At first, I was interested in learning new skills and finding new patterns, building my expertise as a knitter. Then I moved into learning more about the history of knitting itself. I also eventually started learning about the ways knitting had been used as a form of communication throughout history, as secret code, as artful protest, as a way of resisting violence. I now consider my knitting to be in conversation with various forms of anti-violence actions around the world that make use of textiles as a form of resistance.

## Crafty activism

Knitting, along other forms of textile work and crafting more broadly, can be a political act, even if it is often dismissed as insignificant or simply a way to pass time. Craft is frequently denigrated as low art or women's work, a position that has been subversively reclaimed (Parker, 2010). Julia Bryan-Wilson highlights what she terms "textile politics," by which she means not only "how textiles have been used to advance political agendas but also to indicate a procedure of making politics material: textile as a transitive verb" (2017, p. 7).

Popularized by Betsy Greer in response to increased violence and militarization following 9/11, craftivism, or activism through craft, takes many different forms, with Greer encouraging crafting as a meditative way to channel one's anger into a visual statement (Greer, 2011). Other craftivists include artists who expand the boundaries of the art world through creating politically-engaged art both inside and outside established institutions. Knitting is among some of the most prominent craftivism efforts, described as "willful" (Clarke, 2016) and "radical" (Robertson, 2011). While knitted objects are often analyzed after they are made, the process of making can be equally or more important than the finished product. In considering knitting as a methodology, I am most interested in forms of craftivism that bring attention to space in new ways, whether through installations or knitting in public.

Yarn bombing, sometimes known as "knit graffiti" or "yarn storming" to disrupt associations between bombing and violence, involves attaching handmade fiber items to public infrastructure with various degrees of stealth. By placing knit or crochet fabric into the urban landscape, craftivists can share a message or encourage people to interact with the space in new ways (McGovern, 2019). These installations can take place on a variety of scales, sometimes being "just for fun" and other times being an explicit form of protest. Even yarn bombing done for whimsical reasons can be a form of "micro-politics" (Mann, 2015). However, yarn bombing can also function at the macro scale to demonstrate a collective commitment to a cause, with knitters coming together to create impressively large works, such as the Cast Off Knitters' project *Pink Tank* (2006), where individual squares were pieced together into a cozy covering a tank in a public square. This project's "dramatic use of the crafted object to call attention to what is underneath creates a rupture in the ways in which the public interacts with the tank as a public war monument" (Black & Burisch, 2011, p. 208).

Knitting in public is seen as out of place and even uncanny because of the ways in which it transgresses the boundaries between public and private (Bratich & Brush, 2011, p. 237). While this applies to the individual knitter, sometimes this is mobilized by a group of knitters in a "knit in." For example, in 1982, a group of knitters formed the Women's Peace Camp outside the Greenham Royal Air Force Base in England as an antinuclear protest. The group leveraged knitting's domesticity and softness as a form of protest in opposition to more violent forms of activism (Robertson, 2011). Similar tactics have been carried out over the past several decades by the Australian group Knitting Nannas Against Gas, in environmental justice and anti-militarization protests, who use the grandmotherly connotations of knitting as a way to occupy space, bear witness, and offer protection to those who are participating in riskier activisms (Clarke, 2016). Public knitting is therefore not necessarily about the object that is produced, but about the process of making. In fact, some forms of knitting as performance may involve intentional unraveling or destruction of the knitted piece (Hemmings, 2019).

Certainly, craftivism is not without its criticisms. Knitting may often be political, but it is not inherently liberatory. For example, one could just as easily knit items to be gifted to members of the military as one could knit in protest of war. There is a long history of knitting during wartime as an expression of patriotism (MacDonald, 1988). Knitting's association with gender and domesticity can give it a deeply conservative edge (Pentney, 2008). Further, knitting communities may be exclusionary, and protests using knitting may fail to substantively consider racial politics (Close, 2018). While knitting is often presented as an anti-capitalist activity, with its slower tempo challenging fast fashion, knitting involves its own forms of consumption and could be seen as a demand to constantly produce something, even during "leisure" time.

In addition to sometimes assuming a participant of a certain financial standing, able to buy yarn and other knitting supplies, today's version of craftivism often invokes a break with an imagined past, in which knitting is something that can now be reclaimed from the dusty domestic realm of grandmothers who would never think of knitting as political. Such "claims of inventiveness in reviving the lost rewards of handicraft demonstrate a collective amnesia about the enduring paradoxes of craft, since handmaking, a site of perpetual struggle in our relation to the past, frequently oscillates between being forgotten, then reclaimed, then denigrated, and then once again vaunted within the churning cycles of taste and trend" (Bryan-Wilson, 2017, p. 32). This is perhaps part of craftivism's appeal, that it is seen as a site of constant invention and refusal of past attitudes (Robertson, 2011). Rather than see craftivism as a rupture with the past, it can be framed as resurgence or recomposition, never a complete split with the past, but a separation opening up to a new future (Bratich & Brush, 2011, p. 256).

Crafting presents a material intervention toward ideological ends, quite literally giving form to a set of ideas. "Leaning on the objectness of craft orients our thinking to the spatial and temporal landscape of embodiment" (Vaccaro, 2015, p. 276). Knitting is a not only making something ourselves; it is a way of *making our selves,* of crafting our lives. It is also a way of situating ourselves in relation with the place around us and making visible a political commitment. Frequently theorized in relationship to gender, knitting's connections with disability (Gotfrid et al., 2021) or Madness have been underexplored; however, knitting's subversive, crafty methods can be employed for neurodivergent critiques of academic spaces, an all too literal interpretation of Rosemarie Garland-Thomson's call to "knit disability as a category of analysis into all of the courses in which we examine the workings of culture, especially courses that address issues of representation, identity, subjectivity" (Garland-Thomson, 1995, p. 16).

## Meaning and Meaninglessness

The knitting project sitting next to me as I write this is a tank top, to be made from one continuous cake of yarn, shifting colors gradually from lime green to navy blue. It's knitting that is simple enough that I can do it while I read, but the yarn keeps tangling as I pull from the center of the cake, prompting distractions and interruptions from the narrative flow. As an autistic person, I'm told I fail at understanding narrative, which is quite an interesting thing to have to write about. How can I tell a narrative of my own failure to make meaning? I'm caught in the web of epistemic violence that denies Mad people the ability to be seen as legitimate knowers (Lieggho, 2013). I knit through this tangle by picking apart the diagnostic criteria that would classify knitting as a "restrictive and repetitive behavior."

As both a stim and a special interest, knitting holds a particular connection to the neurodivergent community for me. Yet clinically, special interests are described as "highly restricted, fixated interests that are abnormal in intensity or focus (e.g., strong attachment to or preoccupation with unusual objects, excessively circumscribed or perseverative interests)" (American Psychiatric Association, 2013). Some clinicians and educators have begun to see special interests as an autistic strength, but behavioral therapists have mobilized special interests to modify and control behaviors (Boyd et al., 2007), turning them into yet another site of intervention.

A common trope in behaviorist writings is to "proclaim that autistic speech acts and gestures [are] behaviors lacking in meaning, purpose, or social value" (Yergeau, 2018, p. 15). Autistic people don't get to *communicate*; we only get to have *behaviors* that supposedly require intervention. Knitting is not a failure to communicate; it is a way to quite literally make connections, a social fabric of a different sort. When I knit, I practice autistic agency (Williams, 2018). I often knit alone, but even when I am in isolation, the knitting bears traces of the environment in which it was made, whether that's cat hair, dust, or bits of fuzz from yarn from a concurrent knitting project. I like to have two knitting projects at a time, one that requires more intense focus, and one that is fairly straightforward. That way I can match the complexity of my knitting to whatever task I may be doing in the moment. Knitting also reflects my mental state, in terms of how tightly I am holding the yarn and the evenness of the stitches.

While I'm knitting almost all the time, I notice I'm more likely to knit for hours on end when I'm stressed or having a hard time figuring out how to express myself. While I often knit when I'm uncomfortable, the practice of knitting is itself an act of autistic joy, a term that became popular as a hashtag on Twitter in 2018 and is associated with the artwork of Jennifer White-Johnson of her autistic son, Knox. White-Johnson focused on Knox's joy as a way to counter narratives of pity and needing a cure, and specifically to highlight Black autistic joy (White-Johnson, 2019). Joy, in this formulation, is an act of resistance, found in playing and art and dance. Thus, I think of knitting as a way to move beyond "damage-centered research" (Tuck, 2009), research that asks us to "only speak from that space in the margin that is a sign of deprivation, a wound, an unfulfilled longing. Only speak your pain" (Hooks, 1990, p. 152). Particularly in academia, I am asked to narrate my own discomfort for the sake of representing an institutional commitment to diversity. Rather than focus on the painful experience of academic ableism, as I have elsewhere (Long & Stabler, 2021), knitting provides a counterpoint rooted in joy. I find immense meaning in knitting, even though it is a practice that is often overlooked.

Knitting may get some of its power precisely because it is so easily trivialized as hobby or feminized labor. While knitting cannot be read as an entirely subversive act, I find it interesting to think with how this practice, sometimes assumed to have little meaning because of the gender of people who take it up, can be used in service of countering autistic meaninglessness. As Simone de Beauvoir wrote in 1949, "With the needle or the crochet hook, woman sadly weaves the very nothingness of her days" (quoted in Bryan-Wilson, 2017, p. 20). While knitting is clearly not nothingness, the idea of knitting as a meaningless action is perhaps in line with dominant conceptions of stims and special interests, as a nonexpressive failure to engage in neurotypical worlds. I could imagine a clinician perhaps writing about me, "With their needles, the autistic sadly knits the very nothingness of their days. They pay no attention to the social world and prefer to engage in such a restrictive behavior. They have no imaginative capabilities."

Yet, I imagine knitting as a form of reshaping the social landscape, of resisting a compulsory ablemindedness that dictates how we should occupy space, what our research should look like. I've never been scolded for knitting in public, but I get the impression that it is considered a somewhat unusual way to occupy space. Knitting is actually a cinematic trope for madness, with knitting in public, particularly alone, being a cinematic harbinger of catastrophe (Faiers, 2014).

Sometimes my presence feels like an impending catastrophe. Knitting has been explored as an autoethnographic method for tracing the tensions of neoliberal academia (Jubas & Seidel, 2016), tensions that can be especially pronounced for Mad academics. Kairotic spaces, as discussed by

Margaret Price, are high-stakes spaces of social interaction that are laden with power imbalances, placing marginalized folks at a disadvantage (Price, 2011, p. 61). Kairotic spaces often have an element of time pressure, in requiring quick response times and processing information at a normative speed. Intervening in kairotic space involves rethinking what participation and engagement look like. Knitting in class can be seen as not participating. Knitting while conducting an interview might be perceived as rude and disinvested from the research. However, knitting is also a chance to consider how these spaces might be different.

As an intervention into research, knitting reshapes the possible social relationships through insisting on the creative possibilities of Madness. Perhaps a little too enthusiastically sometimes, an eager "hey, want to see what I've knitted?!" in the middle of the conversation. Knitting makes interactions seem just a little more flexible, reshaping what engagement looks like. In this way, knitting is a bit of an assistive technology, helping my brain reach just the right amount of input, a clever way of avoiding eye contact, a roundabout way of starting a conversation. It is also a way to stim in public and to make visible a practice of autistic joy. This perhaps begins to reshape the kairotic space, as I keep myself "in the loop" through knitting.

## Neuroqueer Narrativity

Ultimately, I see knitting as a way to create more nuanced storying of Mad bodyminds, both for myself and for those with whom I am in relation. While textile practices are too diverse to make sweeping statements, textiles are sometimes analyzed as queer, destabilizing the boundaries between art and design, body and society. Positioning craft as "queer" could "relocate craft as an aesthetic category that embraces an enormous range of multiple and seemingly contradictory practices, as well as an agent to challenge existing systems that define materiality and makers" (Roberts, 2011, p. 248). Because of craft's association with various marginalized groups of people, including women, queer folk, and people of color, it frequently takes on a subversive role, and has been well suited to be analyzed from the positions of otherness, though Mad studies is thread that has not been taken up.

By moving textiles to the domain of the neuroqueer, I think of knitted objects as having a powerful politics of making and representation that are in tension with the challenges of representing autism. Indeed, when I tell people my research is on knitting and autism, a number of assumptions get made: that I am working with autistic children, that I am teaching them how to knit, that knitting will somehow be "good for them," with "good for them" being code for "less autistic." The logics of normative violence say that the autistic child is a threat, a site in need of intervention as soon as possible (McGuire, 2016). Instead, I position myself against the need to intervene or cure autism. While I found knitting to have beneficial effects, it most certainly did not cure my autism. In fact, I it helped me embrace my stims and special interests, letting them guide my academic activities. Neuroqueer knitting asks us to consider wellbeing outside of the curative impulse.

I am against the sort of institutional knitting described by a mental healthcare worker as "ordinary and bland and not beautiful," where "the patients felt that this was all they were worth – dishcloths" (Turney, 2009, pp. 158–159). Additionally, special interests should not be leveraged as a means of behavioral control over autistic people. I think of knitting as a way to challenge disciplinary and institutional norms, not to conform to them. Of course, knitting is not for everyone, and I do not expect everyone to pick up a pair of knitting needles (though I do suggest you give it a try). Rather, knitting is just one a constellation of methods that refute epistemic violence by establishing new ways of transmitting meaning. In finding meaning in what might otherwise be taken as meaningless, I am suggesting that we can be authors of our experiences.

As the history of craftivism shows, there's a tendency to claim fiber-based protests as novel, despite their long transnational history. Thus, I am cautious to position ethnographic knitting as a new research method, though I do think it innovates the kairotic spaces of research and academic life. I think of knitting as institutional critique as well, believing that "when the dialogic and pedagogical start to be used as artistic *material,* the university becomes both a site of institutional critique and exploratory playground" (Loveless, 2019, pp. 9-10, emphasis in original). The university becomes my knitting laboratory and art studio, generating new creative potentials that exceed the way that space was intended to be used. I story autism in ways that contradict institutionalized knowledges about autism, instead creating a narrative with a genealogy based in autistic self-advocacy and craftivism. There's no way of knowing how many stitches I knit in a year, tens of thousands, at least, making use of miles of yarn. Each stitch is a testament to reclaiming the narrative practices of autism, of finding new ways to mark Mad experiences.

Knitting captures meanings in a way that exceeds the bounds of written or spoken language, allowing for storying outside of neurotypical narrative forms that privilege verbal agility. Considering knitting as a Mad method means focusing on the relations that knitting can foster, even if one is sitting alone. Even solitary knitting connects with others: pattern designers, yarn dyers, various organisms from which the fibers come. In the future, I hope to incorporate knitting with other Mad folks in forms of collaboration, building on work done in participatory textile making (Shercliff & Holroyd, 2020). In the meantime, I collaborate at the level of pattern design, thinking about how knitting patterns can represent autistic experiences. I ask people what symbols they think represent their experiences and about their own special interests, in direct defiance of claims that autistic people have "deficits in social-emotional reciprocity, ranging, for example, from abnormal social approach and failure of normal back-and-forth conversation; to reduced sharing of interests, emotions, or affect; to failure to initiate or respond to social interactions" (American Psychiatric Association, 2013).

People will often tell me that knitting is complicated, a compliment I tend to brush aside by telling them that no matter how complicated a piece of knitting is, it is based on variations of the same stitch. Knitting, to me, is a way of bringing together endless variation of ways to exist into new and exciting patterns. I think it's a nice metaphor for neurodiversity, though metaphor is among the rhetorical things autistic people aren't supposed to understand, so maybe it's a terrible metaphor. Nevertheless, knitting is fundamentally interconnected; it is a series of loops pulled through other loops to create an elastic, expansive fabric of the different threads of our experiences.

## References

American Psychiatric Association. 2013. *Diagnostic and statistical manual of mental disorders (DSM-V)*. Washington, DC: American Psychiatric Association Publishing.

Baggs, M. (2018, August 16). The things that really matter. *Cussin' and Discussin'*. https://cussinanddiscussin.wordpress.com/2018/08/16/the-things-that-really-matter/

Black, A., & Burisch, N. (2011). Craft hard die free: Radical curatorial strategies for craftivism. In M. E. Buszek (Ed.), *Extra/ordinary: Craft and contemporary art* (pp. 204–221). Duke University Press.

Boyd, B. A., Conroy, M. A., Mancil, G. R., Nakao, T., & Alter, P. J. (2007). Effects of circumscribed interests on the social behaviors of children with autism spectrum disorders. *Journal of Autism and Developmental Disorders*, 37(8), 1550–1561. https://doi.org/10.1007/s10803-006-0286-8

Bratich, J. Z., & Brush, H. M. (2011). Fabricating activism: *Utopian Studies*, 22(2), 233–260. https://doi.org/10.5325/utopianstudies.22.2.0233

Bryan-Wilson, J. (2017). *Fray: Art + textile politics*. The University of Chicago Press.

Chin, E. (2020). Needlework. *Feminist Anthropology*, 1(1), 7–13. https://doi.org/10.1002/fea2.12009

Clarke, K. (2016). Willful knitting? Contemporary Australian craftivism and feminist histories. *Continuum*, 30(3), 298–306. https://doi.org/10.1080/10304312.2016.1166557

Clifford, J., & Marcus, G. E. (Eds.). (1986). *Writing culture: The poetics and politics of ethnography*. University of California Press.

Close, S. (2018). Knitting activism, knitting gender, knitting race. *International Journal of Communication*, 12, 23.

Colligan, S. (2001). The ethnographer's body as text and context: Revisiting and revisioning the body through anthropology and disability studies. *Disability Studies Quarterly*, 21(3). https://doi.org/10.18061/dsq.v21i3.298

Corkhill, B., Hemmings, J., Maddock, A., & Riley, J. (2014). Knitting and well-being. *Textile*, 12(1), 34–57. https://doi.org/10.2752/175183514x13916051793433

Faiers, J. (2014). Knitting and catastrophe. *Textile, 12*(1), 100–109. https://doi.org/10.2752/17518351 4X13916051793596

Garland-Thomson, R. (1995). Integrating disability studies into the existing curriculum: The example of "Women and Literature" at Howard University. *The Radical Teacher, 47,* 15–21.

Gotfrid, T., Mack, K., Lum, K. J., Yang, E., Hodgins, J., Hudson, S. E., & Mankoff, J. (2021). Stitching together the experiences of disabled knitters. *Proceedings of the 2021 CHI Conference on Human Factors in Computing Systems,* 1–14. https://doi.org/10.1145/3411764.3445521

Greer, B. (2011). Craftivist history. In M. E. Buszek (Ed.), *Extra/ordinary: Craft and contemporary art* (pp. 175–183). Duke University Press.

Hartblay, C. (2020). Disability expertise: Claiming disability anthropology. *Current Anthropology, 61*(S21), S26–S36. https://doi.org/10.1086/705781

Hemmings, J. (2019). Knitting after making: What we do with what we make. In J. Gilson & N. Moffat (Eds.), *Textiles, community, and controversy: The knitting map* (pp. 77–94). Bloomsbury Visual Arts.

Hooks, B. (1990). *Yearning: Race, gender, and cultural politics.* South End Press.

Jubas, K., & Seidel, J. (2016). Knitting as metaphor for work: An institutional autoethnography to surface tensions of visibility and invisibility in the neoliberal academy. *Journal of Contemporary Ethnography, 45*(1), 60–84. https://doi.org/10.1177/0891241614550200

Lieggho, M. (2013). A denial of being: Psychaitrization as epistemic violence. In B. A.

LeFrancois, R. Menzies, & G. Reaume (Eds.), *Mad matters: A critical reader in Canadian mad studies* (pp. 122–129). Canadian Scholar's Press.

Long, R.-E. M., & Stabler, A. (2021). "This is NOT okay:" Building a creative collective against academic ableism. *Journal of Curriculum and Pedagogy*, 1–27. https://doi.org/1 0.1080/15505170.2021.1926374

MacDonald, A. L. (1988). No *idle hands: The social history of American knitting.* Ballantine.

McGovern, A. (2019). *Craftivism and yarn bombing: a criminological exploration.* Palgrave

Macmillan UK. https://doi.org/10.1057/978-1-137-57991-1

McGuire, A. (2016). *War on Autism: On the Cultural Logic of Normative Violence.* University of

Michigan Press.

Orsini, M., & Davidson, J. (2013). Critical autism studies: Notes on an emerging field. In J. Davidson & M. Orsini (Eds.), *Worlds of autism: Across the spectrum of neurological difference* (pp. 1–28). University of Minnesota Press.

Parker, R. (2010). *The subversive Stitch: Embroidery and the making of the feminine* (New Edition). I. B. Taurus.

Pentney, B. A. (2008). Feminism, activism, and knitting: Are the fibre arts a viable mode for feminist political action? *Thirdspace: A Journal of Feminist Theory & Culture*, 8(1), n. p. https://journals.sfu.ca/thirdspace/index.php/journal/article/view/pentney

Prain, L. (2014). *Strange material: Storytelling through textiles.* Arsenal Pulp Press.

Price, M. (2011). *Mad at school: Rhetorics of mental disability and academic life.* University of Michigan Press.

Price, M., & Kerschbaum, S. L. (2016). Stories of methodology: Interviewing sideways, crooked and crip. *Canadian Journal of Disability Studies, 5*(3), 18–56. https://doi.org/10.15353/cjds.v5i3.295

Raphael, D., Salovesh, M., & Laclave, M. (2001). The world in 3D: Dyslexia, dysgraphia, dysnumia. *Disability Studies Quarterly, 21*(3), 152–160. https://doi.org/10.18061/dsq.v21i3.301

Roberts, L. J. (2011). Put Your Thing Down, Flip It, and Reverse It. In M. E. Buszek (Ed.), *Extra/ordinary: Craft and contemporary art* (pp. 243–259). Duke University Press.

Robertson, K. (2011). Rebellious doilies and subversive stitches. In M. E. Buszek (Ed.), *Extra/ordinary: Craft and contemporary art* (pp. 184–203). Duke University Press.

Sequenzia, A. (2012). Loud hands: I speak up with my fingers. In J. Bascom (Ed.), *Loud hands: Autistic people, speaking* (pp. 346–351). Autistic Self Advocacy Network.

Shercliff, E., & Holroyd, A. T. (2020). Stitching together: Participatory textile making as an emerging methodological approach to research. *Journal of Arts & Communities, 10*(1/2), 5–18. https://doi.org/10.1386/jaac_00002_1

Smith, P. (2013). "Why Autoethnography?" In P. Smith (Ed.), *Both sides of the table: Autoethnographies of educators learning and teaching with/in [dis]ability* (pp. 15-33). Peter Lang.

Tuck, E. (2009). Suspending damage: A letter to communities. *Harvard Educational Review, 79*(3), 409–428. https://doi.org/10.17763/haer.79.3.n0016675661t3n15

Turney, J. (2009). *The culture of knitting*. Berg.

Vaccaro, J. (2015). Feelings and fractals: Woolly ecologies of transgender matter. *GLQ: A Journal of Lesbian and Gay Studies, 21*(2–3), 273–293. https://doi.org/10.1215/10642684-2843347

Van Goidsenhoven, L. (2017). 'Autie-biographies:' Life writing genres and strategies from an autistic perspective. *Journal of Language, Literature and Culture, 64*(2), 79–95. https://doi.org/10.1080/20512856.2017.1348054

Walker, N. (2021). Neuroqueer: An introduction. *Neuroqueer.* https://neuroqueer.com/neuroqueer-an-introduction/

White-Johnson, J. (2019, October 25). Autistic joy as an act of resistance. *Thinking Person's Guide to Autism.* http://www.thinkingautismguide.com/2019/10/autistic-joy-as-act-of- resistance.html

Williams, R. M. (2018). Autonomously autistic: Exposing the locus of autistic pathology. *Canadian Journal of Disability Studies, 7*(2), 60–82. https://doi.org/10.15353/cjds.v7i2.423

Yergeau, Remi M. (2018). *Authoring autism: On rhetoric and neurological queerness*. Duke University Press.

# Paranoia & Reliably Unreliable Narrators

*Samuel Z. Shelton*

People scare me, and for good reason. I am more familiar with exclusion, ridicule, rejection, and other relational
harms than I am with some of my closest friends. The experiences that led me to fear people have been present in and
affected all parts of my life, but for the moment, I want to
focus on academia. The academy is a hostile place for people
who do not fit into what Audre Lorde (1984, 116) describes as
"the mythical norm." This hostility assumes varying degrees
and forms, but it has a singular purpose: hoarding power and
control – of resources, of policies, of ideas, of networks – by
forcing people out. In other words, academic hostility allows
for elitism to continue without formally excluding uninvited
people – sure, anyone can come into the ivory tower, but for
most of us, staying inside is going to be exhausting and quite
often traumatic.

Mad people have rarely been welcomed into academic institutions as intellectuals. More often, we are and have been
the subjects of academic curiosity – the things knowledge is
produced about instead of recognized as knowledge creators

ourselves. This disempowerment has a lot to do with the ideo-logical dominance of psychology and its related disciplines, which have historically worked to medicalize and pathologize non-normative mental states. My acceptance in academia has often hinged on the silencing of my Madness, on me doing the labor of passing for "sane" by concealing my mental differenc-es and conforming to the norms of scholarly thought. There are certain things that I feel I cannot speak/write about with-out overly exposing myself as an intellectual outsider – things which have been so impactful to my experience / understand-ing of the world around me that I long to bring them into the open air (*\*cough\* critical thoughts about suicide and self-harm \*cough\**). But doing so remains problematic and perilous, even in my chosen disciplines of Women, Gender, and Sexuality Studies, Queer Studies, and Disability Studies.

Even now, as I compose this short chapter for an edited collection about Madness, I am anxious about its repercus-sions. (How) will people see me differently? Will they dislike and distrust me even more than I feel like they already do? Will I become even more isolated and vulnerable? Will I lose what little support I currently have? The compulsory silence I have felt in academia has shown up in most other parts of my life as well, and it often seems as if I move through my days partially, largely, shrouding myself to avoid undue sus-picion. But I would be remiss to say that this passing work is just about Madness, for my tendencies to conceal myself are also the artifacts of growing up in a persistently queerphobic and transphobic society. In academia and elsewhere, I am put into positions where I have to make difficult decisions about if, when, and how I will resist other people's attempts to normatively gender/sexualize my bodymind. These situations can become all the more confusing or arduous because of the historical entanglements between queerness, transness, and Madness, such as the reality of how many trans folks have had to subject ourselves to pathologization (i.e. establish ourselves as "mentally ill / disordered") in order to access recognition and resources. I have also often betrayed my Madness to legitimize my gender and sexuality – after all, a queer, trans, and Mad person is an easy target, and I refuse to be easy.

## Reliable Unreliability

From the perspective of literary analysis, I am an unreliable narrator. The two classic instances of unreliable narrators: they're either lying, or insane... In empirical research, reliable refers to the ability of an experiment to be repeated consistently, that is, to yield the same results under the same conditions. This sort of reliability is relatively easy to define in quantitative or experimental research; it generally means replicability. The term gets more complicated in qualitative research, comes to mean something more like trust. Does the audience trust the researcher—the narrator of the study? Do they believe his/her/hir account of what's happened? Reliability in that sense can get philosophical, start to scrape against concepts like truth, sometimes even justice. – Margaret Price (2011, 3)

What does it mean to be unreliable? Some of us are rarely if ever seen as reliable while others seem to be born with "reliable" stamped on their foreheads. Sometimes, the differentiating factor is our actions – how predictably we show up for each other and how often we follow through with our promises or stay true to our words. Much of the time, however, a determination of un/reliability precedes evidence, and any subsequent actions become measured against already formed perceptions. Internalized beliefs about race, class, gender, age, dis/ability, and other sites of power and difference, particularly mental difference and Madness, lead people to make judgements first; they lead us to prejudice. And reliability is tangled up with a whole mess of other things from how predisposed we are to see others as criminals, to how un/comfortable we are conditioned to feel around other people, to how deserving of kindness we believe others to be.

In a sanist world that readily hates, fears, pities, and mocks most forms of neurodivergence, the never-simple act of reclaiming Madness often makes me out to be an unreliable narrator, a voice too unstable and deceitful to follow through the pages of a story. If this were a novel, I would most certainly be up to something nefarious. Maybe I killed my sibling or parent. If so, I probably started out with animals and buried them in the back yard. Or, maybe I've lied about all the events leading up to this point and you can't believe a word I write, for Madness isn't seen as trustworthy or credible because it has been made into a spectacle. In books and television shows, Mad people eat up the lives of others until they are vanquished or until there's nothing left to consume. Sometimes, consumption comes in the form of slowly sucking away a neuro-normie's life down to last drop – and being so emptied often causes them to break. Sometimes, consumption is a straight-up blood show, like all those horror flicks or gritty superhero movies where the villain busts out of some "asylum for the criminally insane" and gets high on life by gluttonously snorting it away from everyone else.

In either case, the oppressive spectacle of Madness primes people to doubt, question, and refuse Mad-centered stories because we cannot possibly be reliable narrators; because Mad folks are too often not "in our right minds" and always driven by some unfamiliar, unscrupulous, and/or outright destructive motive. This problematic representation is all the more damaging for queer and trans folks, people of color, poor people, and others who are, in their own unique ways, perpetually rendered dishonest and guilty until proven exceptional (i.e., not like one of *those* people). Venturing into Madness, for me, has been made all the more complicated and challenging by my queerness and transness. No, that's wrong, that's a lie – my queerness and transness aren't the culprits here; they are just interconnected pieces of myself. What gets in the way, what makes things messy, is all the vulnerabilities I am made to bear in a society that refuses to accept and honor my queer, trans, Mad bodymind.

Because the last thing I want is for people to see me as an unreliable narrator about my own gender and sexuality. I spend enough time dealing with people misgendering me day in and day out or making wrong assumptions about who

I am, and should be, getting it on with. I've spent so much time and effort working to establish myself as the only authority about my identities that I have to be careful with anything that might bring that authority into question. Authority contradicts Madness in a sanest world: Mad people supposedly aren't in control but have control exerted over us. Other people determine who we are through observations that lead to diagnosis and "treatment," which may include coercive / involuntary medication. Other people typically get to determine what is best for us, and it becomes socially acceptable for them to doubt or question everything about us. Claiming Madness publicly threatens to open up space for my gender and sexuality to be invalidated, reduced to symptoms of a misguided mental illness, and this loss is something I fear greatly. I am already on such unsteady ground, and I am afraid of permanently losing my balance.

Learning to bring myself fully and wholly into the world as a simultaneously queer, trans, Mad person, especially the academic world where I am trying my best to build a home on what I am discovering is more like gravel than an ivory tower, has been an ongoing and exhausting task. Gender has been a site where people have routinely lain claim to intimate knowledge about my body – everything from what it should do, to how it should look, to who it should be attracted to or involved with. Defining gender and sexuality on my own terms remains a constant battle, and one which has often depleted the energy I require to hold space for the complex realities of my Madness. I have often been reluctant to engage openly with Madness because of how frequently others act like my bodymind is not my own. I've been afraid that, just like with my gender and sexuality, people will try to steal my Madness by forcing their own labels and explanations and "cures" onto me – and I just do not want those things. I much prefer solitude and silence.

At the same, however, my experiences with gender and sexuality have opened up incredible intellectual spaces in which to be swallowed up by Madness and to reclaim it for myself. Finding ways to tune out the hateful messages and oppressive ideologies so that I might genuinely listen to my queer non-binary body has been personally transformative, and it was within this transformation that I realized my mind, like my body, was not the property of other people. For if I could resist the pressure to accept a mode of embodiment that felt inauthentic and gross, then so too could I find methods for releasing the need to think and express myself in prescribed, normative manners. Expecting people to use my pronouns, refusing to allow people to gloss over or invalidate my queerness, not suppressing my ticks and talking honestly about my sensations/perceptions/feelings – these and related acts of resistance and radical self-care together constitute a practice of narrative reclamation through which I alter the reality around me and demand accountability.

In this sense, refusing to suppress my queerness, transness, and Madness have all become practices of unreliable narration – practices which tell people that the narratives they assign to my life are inaccurate and unwelcome. That if they want to make sense of me, they will have to undergo a profound narrative shift and, in so doing, arrive at more expansive, less predictable concepts of sexual, gender, and mental difference. My life's work is that of authentic, unapologetic expression, and their work is to become capable of receiving that expression with openness and curiosity. As much as I am able, I strive to live in such a way that I become *reliably unreliable*, but more on this later – we're not quite there yet. For now, I just hope it is clear that I am building up to a different interpretation and application of un/reliability that can empower Mad people instead of undermining us.

•

Assumptions of unreliability take many different forms. They may manifest informally during everyday social interactions, and they can also be codified into laws, policies, and procedures. As an example of the former, I will always remember the cold, Autumn day when I went to an advisor for help accessing resources to speak with professors about social anxiety disorder and her main input was, "No one will believe you." With those five words, she communicated her unwillingness to support me, and she also instructed me about my systemic / structural unreliability as a "mentally ill" student within a neoliberal, sanist university – though, of course, not in such language. Since long before then, but especially since that day, I have found it difficult to truly accept that anyone in academia has my best interests in mind. They have become unreliable to me. Few things are more devastating for students than the corrosive belief that their teachers do not trust them or care about their well-being. Even now in my graduate program, I feel isolated, like I am pushing through while always having to watch my back. Most days, I struggle to find the motivation I need to keep going. I have nearly dropped out several times.

As an example of the latter – of codified unreliability – think about what the need for "documentation" communicates to students or others expected to provide "proof" of ourselves and our intentions. Compulsory documentation is an assertion of distrust and un-credibility. It comes from an oppressive belief that ordinary people are not capable of correctly making sense out of our experiences and/or being honest about our needs; it makes us out to be both unqualified and untrustworthy. The act of requiring documentation indicates that someone or something is not willing to believe me without the support of an "authority," whether that be a person, an institution, or a government. Inevitably, my agency is undercut, and my power is transferred somewhere else, which exposes me, leaves me vulnerable to different sorts of violence and exclusion. All expectations of documentation keep this pattern, whether they are for accommodations, right of presence (e.g., to not be deported/removed from premises), access to resources (e.g., for trans people to access hormones/surgeries), or for anything else. There is room for solidarity to grow in the naming of this pattern.

They follow this pattern because documentation is and has only ever been about one thing: the refusal of recognition and belonging. How often can White people at the U.S.-Mexico border get by without citizenship papers? How easily can cis people get access to hormones without "proof" of their gender? How quickly did accommodations for remote teaching / learning become available when the COVID-19 pandemic began to impact able-bodied / able-minded students? The expectation of documentation undermines recognition and belonging so that marginalized and oppressed peoples have to fight for things that are readily given to others. And, once again, belonging is about un/reliability: it separates the "we" from the "them" – the upright, good, decent, welcome from the immoral, bad, strange, uninvited. The need for documentation in academia, which can be particularly hard to get for intellectual, emotional, or mental differences, is ultimately about protecting the sanist elitism of intellectual spaces.

I am reminded here of an article by Bonnie Tucker (2017), who asks that we "[c]onsider the differences between the questions, 'Are your classrooms inaccessible?' and 'Do you discriminate against disabled students?'" She was writing about the ways that technology often gets confused with social justice (i.e., how tech is presented as a solution for accessibility but fails to actually respond to discrimination and inequity). But I think her questions are meaningful in a broader sense too. In particular, documentation establishes expectations for which students teachers have to make their classrooms accessible for and which students teachers are allowed to discriminate against. Again, this goes back to how belonging is mediated by documentation, how it constructs an "us" and a "them." And how painful it is to be kept on the outside, to be told by our institutions that our needs are unimportant, neglect-able, or too much.

At the same time as it marks people as unreliable, documentation (re)produces unreliability by reducing access to needed resources and support. After my advisor told me that no one would believe me about my social anxiety, which comes from traumatic experiences, I had to make the hard decision about whether maybe receiving access to accommodations was worth the potential harm of subjecting myself to psychological evaluations. The thing about documentation most people do not think about, or maybe they do, is its impact on identity or sense of self. Seeking out diagnosis required relinquishing a part of my acceptance and love for who I am – instead of just being neurodivergent or queerly Mad, I now carry a *pathology*, a medicalized disorder deserving of "treatment." So, to get the documentation I needed to prove that I belonged in academia but just with a few minor accommodations, I could no longer belong fully to myself – I had to become an unreliable narrator in my own story. And, since I had to speak with professors individually about accommodations, they each came to view me through that pathology that was not my own, and of course they treated me differently because of it.

I want to recognize here that, for many people, diagnoses can be generative and open up opportunities for healing/ restoration and transformation. I have, in some ways, gained reassurance and grown from my diagnoses, but at a cost. I was forced to seek out therapists when I was not mentally or emotionally prepared to do so, and when they were least accessible to me. As a student, I had to search and search to find a psychologist that I could afford, which ended up being counseling students in training. And they only provided free or reduced cost services for a few hours a week during business days, so I was lucky to be able to see them at all. The labor and cost of getting documented is an especially important intersection of sanism, ableism, and classism, and it is yet another way that disadvantaged or oppressed people are made out to be unreliable.

For those who choose not to undergo the process of documentation, who choose to retain their sense of self instead of accepting the terms of power that seek to penetrate our lives, there is perhaps greater agency and control, but they often lack professorial or institutional support. And, without this support, making it through inaccessible, ableist, sanist programs is challenging. Much of the time, these students actually do become unreliable, not because of a deficit within them but rather because learning spaces are not set up to meet their needs and make them feel welcome or capable of success. There have been classes where I just stopped showing up because the professor failed to center inclusivity and access in their pedagogical approach. When I could tell that a professor was not receptive to the needs of disabled and Mad students, which was often, I did not feel comfortable talking to them about my access needs, and so I often chose to drop out of their classes instead. Similar sorts of experiences have occurred in relation to my queerness and transness, such as the lingering fear that a teacher would force me to misgender myself or make a scene in front of the whole class.

A particularly harmful double-bind is at play here through which unreliability becomes a self-fulfilling prophecy and predictably results in othering, exclusion, violence, and other sorts of harm. Whether or not I willingly subject myself to psychology's hegemonic power, the pervasive, authoritative normalcy of documentation traps me in a difficult position. I am made to feel like I must either compromise my narration by letting someone else set the terms of my story or struggle to exist in spaces that refuse to meet me where I am at. There is no clear middle ground, except among those professors who sought to work around the system by finding creative ways to promote access for all students all of the time, which is the kind of scholar and educator I have striven to become.

●

So far in this first section, I have been writing a lot about un/reliability as it relates to Madness. Much of the time, unreliability is described in negative terms as something that is unwanted and undesirable. By association, people and things determined to be unreliable are subjected to power in a number of different ways – sometimes in ways that compel us to become more "reliable" by looking, being, acting more like people in power expect us to, and sometimes in ways that punish us or seek to get rid of us entirely. But now, I want to question if, in a Mad world, in a world liberated from sanism, unreliability might be transformed according to our individual or collective needs? What if instead of always hating on unreliability, we sought to make space for it? Or even to build our worlds around it?

As a student and a teacher, I have come to understand that unreliability isn't always a bad thing because it can be a vital component of critical thinking. By encouraging us to seek out and listen to subjugated knowledges, Madness teaches us that critical thinking might be described a practice of approaching all sources of information with hesitation – as if they must always be doubted, questioned, and validated before they can be trusted because knowledge itself is unreliable, and that's ok. In one sense, redefining un/reliability through a Mad perspective involves breaking down the sanist ideologies that render Mad people untrustworthy for the wrong reasons, like simply because we have been categorized as "crazy," "unstable," or "mentally ill." For example, we might instead name and explore how sanist institutions are unreliable in their care and support for Mad students, which in turns makes us less willing and able to show up. But that's just the start; there's even more we can do.

Earlier in this section, I also brought up the concept of being *reliably unreliable*, which I want to bring back into this conversation – now is time, we have arrived. Acting from an acceptance that people are reliably unreliable means a couple of things. First, that we build relationships and expectations around people's needs instead of pressuring people to suppress or sideline those needs. If someone struggles to leave their home or be out in public (especially during a pandemic), we find ways of including them from the spaces where they feel safe and comfortable. If someone gets overwhelmed by certain sights, sounds, smells, textures, etc., we find ways of changing the environment to make it work for everyone. Doing these things recognizes that un/reliability is a socially produced reality instead of simply a deficit in some people. It allows us to start from an assumption that all people are unreliable when their needs are not being met, and so finding ways of meeting needs becomes a standard relational practice.

Second, reliably unreliable centers the wisdom that knowledge is always partial, situational, fluctuating, and political – that knowledge itself is reliably unreliable. Viewing knowledge in this way helps people to accept that learning must happen again and again all throughout our lives if we are to keep up with the world and be in right relationship with the people around us. People change, environments change, times change. Each of us only has access to one tiny sliver of reality, and we need other people to help fill in the missing bits. So, whenever people fail to live up to our expectations, we can practice kindness by reevaluating. Perhaps we don't have the full story. Perhaps we missed something. Perhaps we were not clear about our expectations. Or, perhaps our expectations were not set to the right frequencies / in the right places. Maybe people have shown up for us in the ways that truly matter, but we are getting stuck on the ways they haven't.

The question I'm getting at here is, "What would happen if we all sought to make a collective habit of interpreting the world through this lens of reliable unreliability? Could it serve as a proper foundation of freedom and community?" Johanna Hedva's article, "Sick Woman Theory" (2016), opens with this powerful story of them not being able to attend a Black Lives Matter protest because of their sickness. Their story has resonated with me ever since I first read the article because of how many events I have not been able to participate in despite wanting to be there in solidarity. I strive to practice solidarity in all the ways I can, but large marches, protests, and other, similar events are usually too much for my bodymind to handle. So, I want to offer this idea: making space for unreliability is a practice of access, of making space for difference, so long as we are creatively and collectively imagining alternative ways of showing up for one another in defiance of White supremacy and other systems of dominance.

Bringing unreliability into my life has at times worsened the sense of "imposter syndrome" that plagues countless scholars and academics. Sometimes, it feels as though being unreliable is "proof" that I am not capable of making it, that I don't belong. But, at the same time, embracing unreliability has enabled me to let go of the "hero" mentality – the problematic idea that people who make it big are exceptional or flawless. In reality, success tends to come from one of three things: privilege, care, or luck combined with an overwhelming, often soul-crushing amount of stubbornness. Hard work matters, of course – you just can't get anywhere without it – but the fact remains that systems were set in place to advantage some people and disadvantage others. Yet, if I am only as unreliable as my environment has made me, then failure and struggle have much less to do with who I am and there is a lot more space for changing things.

## The Virtue of Paranoia

Embracing Madness can be a lot like putting on a tinfoil hat. Sometimes it literally requires putting on a hat made out of tinfoil. Or rubbing up against specific textures. Or talking to yourselves. Embracing Madness means shuffling through the entryway to a different reality, recognizing that you crossed over that threshold some time ago, or acknowledging that you have always been there despite other people's efforts to convince you that you were somewhere else. In many ways, my experience of Madness has been similar to my experience of transness in the sense that people had systematically conditioned me to believe I was a hetero guy/boy/man, which I am quite happily not. I have always been a queer and non-binary, for at least as long I can/care to remember, and people should have known that a long time ago given how often I wore my mom's dresses and high heels. My grandma bought me a life-size fairy doll when I was a kid and I wore her sparkly wings everywhere I went, for fuck's sake. Likewise, I do not know if I ever crossed through that entryway of Madness so much as I have forever existed in here. Have I always been wearing a tinfoil hat? Did someone slip it on me when I wasn't looking?

What is the purpose of a wearing a tinfoil hat? Tinfoil hats block stuff out; they act like textured, silver shields against unwanted intrusions and the intruders sneaking them in. Wearing tinfoil hats reflects a paranoid perception, a belief that there are indeed things needing to be blocked out because there are indeed things trying to force their way in. But here is the thing about paranoia: it is a well-loaded term. A political term. A term for surveilling, disciplining, and punishing. It is only paranoia when the people around you are not wearing tinfoil hats, too. Or locking themselves in-doors and drawing the curtains. Or keeping track of the goings-on around them. Police do not get labeled paranoid for stalking around Black and Brown neighborhoods or for mistaking children's toys for guns, but you can bet that people of color have been mocked, assaulted, institutionalized, and incarcerated for being suspicious / fearful whenever a red and blue siren sounds off around them. Cishet people are not labelled as paranoid for worrying that queer and trans folks are out to get them (as if they are sexy enough for us), despite the fact that violence overwhelmingly moves in the opposite direction.

Yeah, sometimes paranoia might legitimately describe an experience of the world that is out of touch with other people's sense of reality, but a lot of time, describing experiences or perceptions as paranoia is a convenient tool for discrediting people's critical awareness of systems or structures of power. Like other psychological/psychiatric labels, diagnoses of paranoia can operate as a method of marking people as unreliable in order to subject them to "therapies" that alter their perspectives and worldviews. When I underwent psychological evaluation, I took a number of tests to measure my outlook. Several of the questions on these tests were designed to assess my beliefs about other people's intentions, specifically if they were "out to get me." At the time, I was deeply engaged with queer feminist thought and activism, as I also am today, so I answered the questions from a critical consciousness perspective. Being a queer feminist and not-quite-but-soon-to-emerge disability justice advocate, the results indicated that I had a paranoia complex. Go figure.

So, maybe tinfoil hats really do keep things out, even if the people wearing them are labelled paranoid. Perhaps the paranoid among us have an awareness that others haven't yet accessed or have suppressed. Maybe, just maybe, tinfoil hats are indicators of intellect and clever devices to stop others from taking that intellect away. But what else are they good for, exactly? If they keep intruding things out, do they also hold other stuff inside? Maybe tinfoil hats provide all around good insulation. Maybe tinfoil hats lock the Madness in, protecting us from the humiliatingly devastating violence of a sanist world.

Some of the most excruciating experiences of my life have come from people who made me feel safe and comfortable enough to go out without my tinfoil hat on. And isn't that always when the shit seems to hit the fan? For example, I don't have many friends, which is both by choice and not by choice. In those few periods of my life when I have opened myself up to friend groups, it has always come back to bite me in the ass. They pretend or maybe even try to like me right up to the point when I drop my guard and become unsuspecting, which is another word for defenseless and vulnerable. At that point, I am almost immediately shut out and ridiculed or verbally assaulted. I am shown to the door, treated as if I never was welcome in the first place, like I never belonged to begin with. How do I not interpret such experiences as evidence that my tinfoil hat boasts a high armor rating?

So, I know that wearing a tinfoil hat might not actually insulate me head (and also it might), but maybe wearing it is a sort of symbolic act, a ritual of vigilance and remembrance that keeps the paranoia alive. That helps us keep our shield arms raised and our horns ready for blowing. There is power in symbolic acts. When I am around other people, I often intentionally wear feminine clothes because, even though it can magnify the queerphobia / transphobia directed against me, it reminds me that my body belongs to no one else, and that knowledge gives me more courage to fight back against the hatred. Sometimes, I wear clothes that show off my fat stomach, clothes that people tell me either were not made for me or make me look ugly, because I love the feel of fresh air against my belly and that feeling reminds to honor my body for all the joy and pleasure it brings me. Who's to say that equipping a tinfoil hat can't also be a symbolic act of loving a Mad, paranoid mind?

And maybe there is something to learn from paranoia. When balanced with a longing to trust and love those who show up for us and who invite us to show up for them in return, paranoia has an instructive quality. It has a place in the reliable unreliability that I wrote about earlier, for being a little bit paranoid means constantly asking questions, exploring doubts, and finding ways to inhabit an unpredictable or uncertain world. The challenge is recognizing that the reasons people become suspect often have more to do with the ways they have been raised than intrinsic qualities about them. My inability to make or sustain friends has a lot to do with how they were raised to accept beliefs systems that marginalize and harm crip, Mad, and sick folks. I cannot believe that they would humiliate me because that's just who they are – I have to believe that they have been made complicit in my suffering, that something big is acting on them, because then there is space for us all to be freed.

My intense, at times overwhelming social anxiety is the manifestation of a paranoia that is rooted deep down in the crevices of my soul with octopus-like tentacles suction-cupped around my core memories. Paranoia is in some ways an innate aspect of who I am, and in other ways, a prolonged trauma response that wounds me as it keeps me safe – like an abusive relationship with a resentful caretaker. One day I may be able to let it go, but for now I think I will keep it because it has been proven right a few times too many.

Until that day comes, if it ever does, I want to advocate for the urgency of empathizing with paranoia / paranoid people instead of simply discounting our perceptions and interpretations of reality. Sure, you can offer us your take on things, help us to see another side of the story, but you can also support us. Listen to us. Take notes with us. Become aware of things with us. Make your own tinfoil hats. Accept that we all know and don't know things, and the only thing we can be absolutely sure about is the love and kindness we show to ourselves and to others. Whether someone is right or wrong is less important than how we make one another feel safe and cared for as part of the process of building communities together. I think it's always helpful to step back and make sure we are focusing on the right things, on what really matters. If paranoia really is a political construct as I have argued here, then we must all be aware of how we contribute to each other's uncertainty and fear.

## References

Hedva, J. (2016). sick woman theory. *Mask Magazine.*

Lorde, A. (1984). *Sister outsider: Essays and speeches.* Ten Speed Press.

Price, M. (2011). Cripping revolution: A crazed essay. Plenary. *Society for Disability Studies.* San Jose, CA.

Tucker, B. (2017). Technocapitalist disability rhetoric: When technology is confused with social justice." *Enculturation.* http://dnculturation.net/technocapitalist-disability-rhetoric

# What Came After the Jungle

*Monica K. Shields*

I see cockroaches. Everywhere. The dark spots on the wood floor. The hair and lint balls from clean laundry. The cable tie on the cord to my laptop charger. They are everywhere. I think it's because I caught them and ate them for so many years. Bigger was better—you need to eat less. But their legs scrape more going down and were more difficult to chew. Never cooked. Always raw. Preserve freshness.

## Failed Performance

I spent some time in the jungle. Forty years, give or take. There were no other people with me— except for a few visitors there only to do me harm. I sustained myself on cockroaches, mostly. Some pineapples and avocados. A few plantains. But mostly cockroaches.

You see, this was shortly after the devastation of hurricane Maria, and the trees and shrubs hadn't recovered enough to bear fruit. I had rain water to drink, but that wasn't very much. I kept active with hiking and safety drills. I walked around as much as I could at night. I needed to learn the terrain so I could use my home advantage and escape when a threat emerged. I practiced getting into small dirty spaces fast and quietly. I practiced these drills to escape the Chinese snipers that were after me. They hunted me on foot in the jungle and overhead with helicopters. I was a human anomaly. My existence was not normal and I was the perfect specimen to capture and study, which undoubtedly meant experimentation. The Chinese assassins hacked the protective Faraday shield I kept over my thoughts and aura. They somehow learned that if they studied me they could get an advantage over the US in medical advances.

I eventually found other humans, some Puertorriqueños and some Americans. They insisted I leave the jungle, the place I had called home for so many years. They said I was better off with doctors and nurses (I think I was better off in the jungle, but that is a different story). I survived and learned some stuff all those years, like the visceral satisfaction of living close to the land. I honed trapping skills, and I learned to enjoy food raw. I learned the importance of tracking patterns and paying attention to small details like what happens before rain showers. I learned that the largest palm fronds weren't the easiest to drink from but could be used to transfer water. I learned how to skillfully open a coconut so I could drink the water, eat the white flesh, and preserve the husk to hold rain water. I learned how sparse water can become and how to ration the tiny amount I collected. A rain shower taught me resourcefulness; it was a gift from Gaia. I learned to navigate my terrain in the dark guided by shadows and smells. The shadows changed, but certain places had specific smells that indicated a turn. I also learned that I preferred garden-to-table over ground-to-mouth and filtering rain water has definite benefits. I discovered an ease and comfort I hadn't otherwise experienced when allowing the rhythms of insects, animals, stars, moon, and sunlight to structure my day.

I haven't told many people about my forty-year long jungle experience. I don't think they would believe me. One reason they might not believe it is because I think time works differently for them than it does me. I came out of the jungle in 2021. I was 41 years old in 2021, according to my driver's license. When the ambulance driver secured me into the ambulance, I told him that I was in jungle for 40 years. He didn't say anything. He just stared into my eyes for an uncomfortable amount of time. I knew I was filthy and needed a shower but I figured I just looked good for my age since, based on my calculations, I was about 80 years old. The ambulance driver was with a group of police officers. They asked me basic questions like my name, address, and date of birth. I didn't tell the police about the jungle. I told them what was on my driver's license. I didn't want them to stare at me like that first guy—it scared me, and they also had guns.

Another reason they might not believe is because it sounds insane.

Is insane.

Crazy. Mad.

They put me in a psych hospital anyway.

## Performing Normal

When my time in the jungle came to an end, I was filled with more questions than answers. Everywhere I looked things were different—literally, sometimes brighter or duller. They also looked different metaphorically. I began to see clearly the power relations and politics in everything. Theories and ideas that I read about in school now overlaid the way I saw the world. I questioned the social effects of everything I did. I questioned the ethics of other people's behaviors. I traced transactional exchanges to figure out who benefited. I was hyper-aware of waste and could see opportunities for conservation everywhere. I was surrounded by and could no longer tolerate the activists who seemed more interested in social media opportunities than helping people. I saw myself differently. I was not a person separate from the world around me; rather, I was a person woven into a network of relationships. I realized that I could not separate who I was from what I did, and I needed to be the change I wanted to see in the world.

I felt hope when I remembered the false dichotomy between epistemology (ways of knowing and knowledge) and ontology (ways of being). I remembered my intrigue as a student learning about these ideas, but it wasn't until I experienced 40 years alone in the jungle—hunted by the Chinese government, surviving off cockroaches—did those ideas begin to alter my thinking. I came to see past the confines of knowing and understanding with certainty, and began to embrace the unknown. I eventually found comfort in uncertainty. This was different than approaching problems, situations, and life knowing what to do in advance (St. Pierre, 2023). As a student, I tried to think differently, but I never felt like I was hitting the mark. It wasn't until I realized that my habitual ways of thinking were normalized in patriarchal logic did I start to live differently.

Patriarchal logic is top down, depends on a value hierarchy, and binary thinking (Shields, 2019). This creates hyper-separation where differences are mutually exclusive. When being and doing are polarized, thinking is limited to what has been normalized (St. Pierre, 2000). Normal science assumes that the positivist scientific community knows what the world is like (Kuhn, 1962/2012). Normal humans assume the mind and body are a certain way (Chapman, 2023). Normal schooling trains teachers on speaking, acting, and assuming norms of pedagogy and curriculum. A normal life assumes getting a job, paying a mortgage, getting married, and consuming (Prakash & Esteva, 2008). How a person views themself has been normalized, too.

I can clearly see how the life I was living before my time in the jungle was an attempt to be normal. In all the ways. I say attempt because even at its best, I was never normal. I had the mortgage, the cis-het marriage, the job, the debit card. In spite of it, I was still the weird one. The one who packed my lunch instead of bought. I carried a reusable water bottle everywhere. I used a reusable coffee cup on the days I purchased coffee. I ate until I was satisfied, not full. I picked up cigarette butts, cardboard, beer and soda cans, and plastic off the sidewalk, carried them around until I could find appropriate recycling. I bought used clothes. I fed stray animals. I unplugged cords after use. I used public transportation. I looked for ways to use less, waste less, or recycle. This is not the way of the dominant normal culture, where waste is assumed, bigger is better, and consumerism is expected. I saw the looks of disgust from others when I would get off the bus. I heard the exasperated, "Why are you carrying around trash?" I saw the confused looks on people's faces and their eye rolls when I got excited about something beautiful I found at a second hand store. Fortunately, many of these behaviors have become more common and not so weird, but that wasn't always the case.

I learned to interpret the whispers of dislike, the eye rolls, the overt aggression, as indicators of my abnormality. I was afraid of myself and afraid of what would happen to me if others saw my deep and profound weirdnesses. I tempered myself around others so I could blend in, so I could pass. It didn't work. I never blended in. All I did was suppress and exhaust myself, in all the ways. I don't get most jokes, especially the ones steeped in sarcasm. I think I'm hilarious and laugh at my own jokes. I get overstimulated at the library and by my teeth. I don't like to shop or eat at restaurants. I cry for other's pain. I feel deep sadness for injustice and advocate for the oppressed. I ask, "Why?" a lot. I hate violence and war. I believe in non-violent conflict resolution. I don't believe humans are more important than nature. I tend not to be too talkative unless I can obsess endlessly about things I'm interested in. I clap my hands when I'm excited. I eat the same food day after day. I struggle with change, even good change. These are not the ways of doing and being of someone who is normal.

After I got out of the jungle, and began healing and detoxing from the psych hospital stay, I tried to go back to the habits, activities, and ways of interacting that I always used to do. I met people for brunch at restaurants. I exhausted myself listening to them and filtering out the noisy background. I smiled at the right times. I laughed when they laughed. I answered questions briefly and didn't bring up my opinions or thoughts. I went shopping and accumulated stuff that I didn't really want or need. I did all the things a normal person does—and hated it. I felt bad because I hated it. I missed my time in the jungle. I felt bad for that too.

I began to take a close look at myself and my relationships to people, places, and things. I wanted to pinpoint what brought me joy. Sadly, there wasn't much. I was a stranger to myself. I began a friendship a few months before I went into the jungle. This person and I shared our vulnerabilities, talked about politics. I took a chance that the friendship could tolerate me and all my oddities, and I shared the discontent and disconnection I felt to everything in my life. One of his first responses were, "What are you reading?" This simple question reminded me that I love to read and I hadn't read a book since before I went into the jungle. I said, "Well, short answer, nothing. I didn't have books in the jungle. All the books in the hospital were in Spanish. And all the books in my library are, well, boring." He tossed me a purple paperback and said, "Here, read this." The book was *Neuroqueer Heresies* by Nick Walker. I said, "Hey, you told me about her blog; I read that a while ago."

Walker's book grabbed me from the beginning and I read every word. I experienced a combination of self-discovery and intellectual stimulation. She explained how neuroessentialism creates false limitations and normalizes normality. I began to think about the normality of being. What was normal for me? Why was it normal? I examined my relationship to myself. I realized that, for most of my life, I was trying to pass as normal. First, trying to pass was a result of the way my parents and church punished or rewarded me for race and gender-appropriate performances, behaviors, and interests. A normal girl wore dresses, behaved nice and sweet, did what she was told. A normal girl was also colorblind and didn't ask questions about the differences in skin color. Then trying to pass grew from self-imposed ideas of success and failure based on White, neoliberal, neurotypical accomplishments like university degrees, leadership roles, committee positions, stamps on a passport, and being busy. Walker's stories helped me see how I understood myself and how my relationship to my life had been socially constructed. Her stories helped me reframe what I understood as my personal failures into Neuroqueer, an intentional noncompliance with the demands of normality.

## Meeting my Bodymind

Neuroessentialism is steeped in positivism. Positivism polarizes differences, creating binaries of value and political hierarchies. It oversimplifies ethics and limits knowing to knowing with certainty. Ideas and research based in positivism are almost guaranteed to simply repeat existing knowledge. At minimum it might add a small piece of knowledge, one that hardly matters, to fill a gap that barely exists (St. Pierre, 2017). A neuroessentialist understanding of a human separates the mind and the body. It reduces the human experience to being psychological and occurring in the brain through brain activity. A neuroessentialist understanding of the self, others, and relationships is problematic because it places limits on the full range of neurocognitive possibilities (Walker, 2021). It doesn't have space for people, relationships, and thing that are unique. The crux of Neuroqueer theory is to break away from neuroessentialism.

When I was in the jungle, I got to know myself. I learned how to push myself past what I thought I could or would do. I learned to take care of myself and survive without the conveniences of consumer culture. I didn't have the pressures to conform to standards —all kinds of standards. I wore the same clothes day after day. I didn't shower regularly. I ate what was available. I slept when I felt like it. I cried when I was overwhelmed and yelled when I was afraid. I didn't have relationships to maintain or community standards to uphold. My days were not beholden to time on a clock. Early morning was when the sunlight just started to highlight the thick jungle foliage and insects and amphibians hissed and buzzed. Middle of the day was when the sun was directly overhead bringing the most light and heat of the day. The sun kept the animals and birds sheltered, making this part of the day the quietest and loneliest part, too. Daytime ended

when sunlight faded and the sounds of the insects and amphibians returned. I learned quickly that the sun sets fast.
Once the light starts to fade, darkness quickly follows. I slept
during the hottest and darkest parts of the day. I ate, whenever I could, typically when there was little sunlight.

After I came out of the jungle, I began to see life differently. I realized that I experienced my bodymind as a single
thing. In the jungle, there was no end in sight to my terror
and panic. I had to protect myself and take care of myself
among never-ending, unknown dangers. When I couldn't
form thoughts or use my mind and reason, as I had in the
past, my bodymind guided me to food, shelter, water, and
safety. There was clearly a knowing that I was not previously
aware of. This knowing is unconventional and doesn't fit in
a positivist world where a bodymind does not exist. In a positivist world, essentialist assumptions set the standard for a
normal body and a normal mind. Assumptions of normality
make the ways for how things get evaluated, and deficits in
normality are problematic and pathological. The separated
body and mind each must function like a well-oiled machine
that is balanced, energetic, and calm. It is not supposed to be
unruly. Neuroqueer theory aims to create spaces where all
bodyminds are accepted and differences are assumed.

## Questioning the Binary

I am clearly not sane. According to patriarchal logic, I am insane—Mad. Insanity in a positivist world carries moral judgment. The insane are considered dangerous, unpredictable,

incompetent, unstable, irresponsible, and irrational (Kafai, 2021). Where is the line between sane and insane? Who decides on the line? My bodymind is antithetical to the normative neuroessentialist framings of a human. My identity, my reputation, my words and ideas are discounted and dismissed. I perform sanity for my survival to avoid being patronized, shamed, excluded, and exploited. If I sound insane then I risk losing my moral integrity—my perceived normality. Until I lived in the jungle for 40 years I didn't realize how much performing normality harmed me. Until then, I didn't recognize my performance or the politics of normality. It didn't feel insane to live in the jungle for 40 years; it felt insane to bottle that experience up and not share it with everyone.

Seeing differently led me to begin thinking differently. I began to wonder about changes that seemed unchangeable. Like was I living a life that made the world a better place? Were my relationships with others an ebb and flow of meaningful exchanges? Did I feel safe to be vulnerable with the people I called friends? I also started to think about questions, like how do I exist? How was I different from other people? How did I need to live in order to feel good about being alive? I could no longer deny that I was different and could not tolerate performing normality, as I had in the past. My bodymind was different and the way I experienced the world was different. What does it mean to be bodymind and not a body and a mind?

## Questioning the Subject

I cannot separate what I do from what I am. The way I perform my politics represents how I experience the world. My mind and body are not separate, in the same way I am embedded in my environment and with others. I am not a self separate from and looking out at others. I am part of a collective. I am in relation with my family, my home, and my community. I am also part of the natural world. I do not understand humans to have central importance or value. I understand humans to be in relationships of reciprocity with people, nature, and material things. These relationships are limitless and are always changing. My experience in the jungle and my understanding of myself in the world is contrary to the humanistic understanding of the self and the positivist assumptions of how knowledge works.

For the humanist individual, self is separate from the other. This separation creates assumptions of sameness rather than assumptions of difference. Humanism is difficult to escape because the effects of humanism have been operating for centuries, envelope us in every moment, and have become natural (St. Pierre, 2000). This sets up a particular kind of human and individual that does not interrogate the self, how the self is produced as a subject, or how in relations we produce the other (St. Pierre, 2011). Because the humanist individual is so natural, it's difficult to see and work with. St Pierre (2011) describes it as the, "air we breathe, the language we speak, the shape of the homes we live in, the relations we are able to have with others, the politics we practice, the map that locates us on the earth, the futures we can imagine, [and] the limits of our pleasures" (p. 478). A person that organizes and structures their world with these concepts also limits their understanding of the related concepts such as truth, reality, experience, and freedom. These limitations are why Neuroqueer theory is needed. A person that refuses to repeat the essentialist individual is enacting an ethic and taking responsibility for producing themselves as an individual and how they create subjects of others.

## Self and Knowledge

Humanism has a variety of knowledge projects, including positivism, which has incredible longevity despite centuries of critiques (St. Pierre, 2000). Positivism is historically linked to Descartes, the method of systematic doubt, and the master binary self/other, as well as its offshoots mind/body and identity/difference. Within this epistemology, the mind is the superior sense and reason is the grand narrative and standard of rationality. Thought is independent of its object. The knower is separate from the known. Since the self is separate from the world around it, there is a reality "out there" that a mind can discover, describe, and know (St. Pierre, 2000). An individual is generally understood to be rational, knowing, ahistoric, stable, and coherent. This kind of individual is a thinking subject and the author of knowledge. This kind of individual constructs knowledge from the bottom up, understands that truths can be discovered through the minds of "men," and truths can be logically linked together. The weakness with this way of understanding knowledge is it sets foundational boundaries, limits, and creates a grid of normalcy (St. Pierre, 2000). It depends on the humanistic definition of self that holds individuals apart from others and the environment.

Alternatively, the self could be considered a construction, something created in the ongoing effects of relations and responses to experiences. A primary focus in Neuroqueer theory is to actively subvert and intentionally not comply with the demands of normality. The subject is an effect of practice, an ongoing activity, an innovation (St. Pierre, 2000).

To the neuroessentialist, it would be natural to dismiss me and my experience in the jungle as nonsense. I don't see it as nonsense. I see it as a gateway to thinking differently and the beginning of questioning what I know about knowing. It's an opportunity to exercise my skepticism about neuroessentialism and expose the limits of normalcy.

## Curtain Call

In the jungle I experienced an exception to logic. I met my bodymind and I saw the politics around my lifelong performance of normality. How do you stop performing? Can I stop performing in the middle of a performance? I gave my final and best performance of noir-mal while in the psych hos-pee-tal. That's how I got out. I was the model patient. I was polite, quiet, punctual, did what I was told, didn't ask questions, didn't make waves. I needed to convince the staff that I was not a danger to myself or others and most importantly that I was normal—so I could go home.

The schedule for the ward was posted in the room with the television. It was about 8 feet long and 4 feet tall. The words were in Spanish and, lucky for me, it also had pictures. The only clock was in the ward hall. I needed to be aware of the time but not appear to obsess over it. I made sure I was where I was supposed to be at all times. I checked the time regularly and I paid attention to what others were doing. I promptly packed up my crayons and coloring pages when group art therapy was over. I came in promptly when the whistle blew ending outside time. I waited patiently in line for medication, three times a day. I waited 30-45 minutes to politely make eye contact with the nurse and say, with a smile, "no, gracias." The nurse would take my blood pressure, mark my chart, point at the door, and say, "próximo." I walked slowly to meal lines and waited quietly for my turn. I made eye contact and smiled at the cook staff and said, "arroz, por favor. Sin cane, por favor. ¿Tienes frijoles? Gracia, gracia." They filled my plate with chicken and rice, a carton of milk, a bread roll, two tiny plastic tubs of a butter-like substance, a tiny paper package of salt and two packages of pepper, and a plastic sleeve of cookies. A plastic spoon—no knife or fork, of course—and a plastic container of something labeled *jugo*. The *jugo* tasted like sugar water. I thought it must be radioactive because of the unnaturally bright color. I also thought they were slipping medication into the food and drink. All of this food violated my dietary needs in several ways. Meat grosses me out and violates my ethics. I'm allergic to dairy, peanuts, and gluten. Refined sugars upset my stomach and make me crazy(-er). But the show must go on; I had to convince the staff I was normal. I picked around the chicken as much as I could and told myself it was better than cockroaches... but was it?

I had daily meetings with a social worker and other staff. They asked me questions like, "Do you see or hear things that nobody else does?" and "Do you want to harm yourself or anyone else?" and "Do you know why you are here?" I made eye contact and answered "no" to each question. One day I was particularly hungry and frustrated with the lack of vegetable and bean options at meal time. I missed being in the natural world and I was irritated with the repetition of these meetings and their questions. This day the social worker was a man; he asked me different questions: "How do you feel being here?" I said, "I like the people, the staff is wonderful. The other patients are kind. But I'm bored. And hungry. I eat a vegan and gluten-free diet and there aren't many options for me to eat at meal times and I can only color so many coloring pages a day." After he wrote a bunch of notes on his clipboard, he asked me another question, "IF you get out of here what is the first thing you're going to do when you get home?" Oh shit, I thought to myself. Monica, you better get this right. I took a minute to think and replied, "Bake a loaf of bread." He wrote more stuff on my chart and told me I could go.

Later that day, group art time was replaced with group therapy on nutrition. The group was led by two nurses who spoke only Spanish. They repeated with emphasis, "proteína como en carne." They used a Powerpoint presentation projected on a piece of paper at the front of the room. The paper was white and about 3 feet wide and 2 feet tall. I couldn't see much of it from where I was seated, and they talked so fast I couldn't pick out the words I knew. All the information was in Spanish. There were some pictures of chicken legs, steaks, and fish. A picture of a pineapple, a bunch of broccoli, and cartoon pictures of smiling faces. At the end of the therapy session the nurses passed around a handout that, was, again, all in Spanish. It was a breakdown of the different food groups, a picture of the food pyramid, and some pictures of meat, vegetables and fruit. I felt bad for everyone on the ward that day. I suspected the group therapy on nutrition was probably because of me. I was the one who told the social worker I was vegan and needed different food. OOOOPSY. I messed up. This performance was the most important one of my life and I lost my cool with that interview. After that, all I wanted to do was crawl in bed under the covers and cry.

As the saying goes, the show must go on. I went back to the ward and asked to go into my room. I looked at my bed and took a few deep breaths. I looked at my stuff piled in the cubbies against the wall. A black crayon lay next to my night clothes. Contraband. Other patients slipped me black and brown crayons in the hall after art therapy. They would look me in the eyes, give me a kind smile, and say, "regalo." I took them, smiled back, and said, "gracias." I also disposed of them as soon as I could; most of the time that meant tucking them between the cushions in the tv room or tossing them in the trash with my napkin at meal time. I wanted the writing utensil. I appreciated the gesture, but I didn't want a crayon to keep me from going home. I didn't know where this one came from. I looked in the shower/toilet room and noticed that the shower was recently used. I didn't have a roommate and I showered hours prior. Tears filled my eyes, I felt a knot in my stomach, and heard the sounds of a hungry bodymind. I looked again at the bed and felt the ache in my heart. If I didn't get out of this room I was going to be engulfed by my emotions—fear and uncertainty. I needed to keep it together, get back out there, and convince the staff that I didn't need to be there.

## Clipboards

The clipboards also came out at regular intervals, maybe 5 times a day. The staff would stand together with their clipboards and pens and look out at the sea of crazy people on the ward. I was careful to not be caught staring but could see them checking boxes, turning the sheet over, checking more boxes and moving that sheet to the end of the stack. When the clipboards came out, I was careful to be social. Or as social as I could be. Many of the other patients on the ward had more English than I had Spanish. So they would talk to me with their best English and I would talk to them in my best Spanish. At best, it was bad Spanglish. Often they would switch to Spanish and not realize; I wouldn't have any idea what they were talking about. BUT I still gave all the nonverbal signs that I was engaged and listening. Sometimes they were pouring their hearts out and I had no idea what they were saying. I also knew that I didn't need to know what they were saying to connect with them and hold a space for their emotions. It distracted me from my pain and what I really wanted to be doing—yoga or sleeping or crying. But that would be antisocial and not help me convince my audience of normality.

## Becoming

The clipboards were predictable. Normality and predictability go hand in hand. Predictability is related to power and control. Power and control are key features of normalcy because those who are predictable can be controlled (Merchant, 1980). The dominant paradigm is for neurotypicals. It assumes linearity, essentialism, and sees difference as pathology. Neuroqueer theory calls for a shift to a neurodiversity paradigm where people get to choose who they want to be and how they want to be it. A paradigm that embraces differences will inherently cause tensions and contradictions. These are the sweet spots for new and creative ideas and opportunities for change.

Paradigm shifts happen when the effects of power relations are inadequate, ineffectual, and unable to respond to new sets of problems (Kuhn 1962/2012; Lather, 2006). The pathology paradigm problematizes emotions, people, behaviors, and ideas that are not normal. Within this paradigm, people who are not normal need to change or be changed. A new paradigm is needed for understanding and classifying research and researchers (Lather, 2000). New paradigms also need to be loose frameworks giving care to not stifle creative potential or compete with other paradigms (Lather, 2000). The process of creating a new paradigm involves unpacking and looking closely at the function, network, and non-containment of the self (Lather, 2006; St. Pierre, 2013). Mapping out a new paradigm includes identifying the different differences that interact and shape all aspects of people's lives. It also involves making spaces for the life experiences that shape people and the inevitable incompatibility that comes with the unpredictable.

Neuroqueer theory sharply departs from the artificial essentialist ideas that restrict human potential and calls for a shift to a neurodiversity paradigm (Walker, 2021). The neurodiversity paradigm rejects a pathology of being and the essentialist self. The self in the neurodiversity paradigm is understood to be constantly becoming, open to change, and continually being made, unmade and remade (Later, 2006; St. Pierre, 2013; Walker, 2021). Neurodiversity paradigm releases ties to the culture of essentialism within neoliberalism and opens to the possibility of ongoing change. It prioritizes formation and persistent efforts to live differently. It's an alternative space to make sense of the world. It operates outside the limits of binary categories. Two assumptions that are foundational to the neurodiversity paradigm are: everyone works differently to resist authority and blur genres and people have complex histories that produce unique knowledges that interrupt the familiar habits of being (Lather, 2006; Walker, 2021).

## That's a Wrap

During my adventures in the jungle, I not only met my bodymind —I met myself. Not the white, nonbinary person that has femme-presenting, cis-het, ablebodied, ableminded, and normal-passing privileges. Not the over-educated, imperialist capitalist either. But the neurodivergent and crazy person that loves to reject the status quo. After the jungle and the hos-pee-tal(s), my identity expanded to include a identity politics that resists neoliberalism and a response to my experiences—my process of becoming. Neuroqueer theory offers me an opportunity to break the restraints that come with assumptions of normality and the freedom to disorganize my bodymind. I no longer need to hide my delight in breaking the rules and subverting the norms. Nor do I need to feel embarrassed when I laugh when no one else is laughing or mute my joy and delight or sadness and despair. Rather, I need to do it loud and proud. This means seeking people, places, and ideas that help me grow who and what I am—to continue becoming. It means parting with people, places, and things that were not fulfilling or that rejected my unique way of experiencing the world. It also means asking difficult questions, like who benefits? Who benefits from rejecting essentialism? How does the neurodiversity paradigm exist?

I'm still figuring all that stuff out.

# References

Chapman, R. (2023). *Empire of normality*. Pluto Press (UK).

Kafai, S. (2021). The politics of mad femme disclosure. *Journal of Lesbian Studies*, 25(3), 182–194. https://doi.org/10.10 80/10894160.2020.1778851

Kuhn, T. S. (2012). *The structure of scientific revolutions*. The University Of Chicago Press. (Original work published 1962)

Lather, P. (1990). Postmodernism and the human sciences. *The Humanistic Psychologist*, 18(Spring), 64–84.

Lather, P. (2006). Paradigm proliferation as a good thing to think with: teaching research in education as a wild profusion. *International Journal of Qualitative Studies in Education*, 19(1), 35–57. https://doi. org/10.1080/09518390500450144

Merchant, C. (1980). *The death of Nature: Women, ecology, and the scientific revolution*. Harperone.

Prakash, M. S., & Esteva, G. (2008). *Escaping education*. Peter Lang Publishing.

Shields, M. K. (2019). *Considering EcoJustice and place-based responses to market-oriented schooling* [Dissertation]. https://commons.emich.edu/theses/976/

St. Pierre, E. A. (2000). Poststructural feminism in education: An overview. *International Journal of Qualitative Studies in Education*, 13(5), 477–515. https://doi. org/10.1080/09518390050156422

St. Pierre, E. A. (2011). Refusing human being in humanist qualitative inquiry. In N. K. Denzin & M. D. Giardina (Eds.), *Qualitative Inquiry and Global Crises* (pp. 40–55). Routledge.

St. Pierre, E. A. (2013). The posts continue: becoming. *International Journal of Qualitative Studies in Education, 26*(6), 646–657. https://doi.org/10.1080/09518398.2013.788754

St. Pierre, E. A. (2017). Haecceity: Laying out a plane for post qualitative inquiry. *Qualitative Inquiry, 23*(9), 686–698. https://doi.org/10.1177/1077800417727764

St. Pierre, E. A. (2023). Poststructuralism and post qualitative inquiry: What can and must be thought. *Qualitative Inquiry, 29*(1), 20–32. https://doi.org/10.1177/10778004221122282

Walker, N. (2021). *Neuroqueer heresies: Notes on the neurodiversity paradigm, autistic empowerment, and postnormal possibilities.* Autonomous Press.

# Reinscribing Madness through Poetry

## Irrationality and Interdependence in the Wor(l)d

*slp and Aubry Threlkeld*

"But then, what is it in the language of Madness that makes it different from the discourse of poetry? And what curious sense, perhaps revolutionary sense, can we find in this absurdity?"
(Cooper, 1978, p. 27)

"I have yet to find significant theoretical discussions occurring around the fluidity of madness in the fields of Disability Studies and Madness Studies." (Kafai, 2013, para. 2)

*21*

// I don't think he's a jerk — I
think — he's really into —
clever schemes —

He's asexual — he's kinky —
He's got issues — He only
connects to women — He's
gay — He's carrying a lot —
of something —

He dismisses — power — his
control of his situation

## Aubry: So many do; So let's undo

I always thought about suicide, but could never muster the
willingness to commit to it. Maybe it was my aunt killing
herself and regretting it as she bled out that dissuaded me.
Somehow in my own refuge from the pain of living as a Mad
Queer/Genderqueer white person of Roma(ni) descent with
occasional physical pain, I have found ways to live with it.
J. Logan Smilges (2023) reminds us that "disabled people
need more than this world has to offer" (p. 36) and perhaps
it is through a burgeoning crip negativity, I frame my understanding of madness. I seek in Madness what Smilges has
sought in crip – which perhaps so many sought in queer (myself included) – a home for bad feelings, for suicidal ideation,
for psychic pain, for dissociation, for hallucination, for the
wheel of anxiety that rolls over the soul, and for the opportunity for us to question both the flattening of the idea that
"everybody has mental illness" alongside the very real stigma
of being perceived as Mad. As a white person writing with
another white person, I also do not want Madness to be a

retreat from the privilege afforded through whiteness: These are merely a recording of our coping, our Mad process to which we invite others.

I repeatedly ask the same question. Where did Madness and art/writing begin? And in that question, I am reminded of the style of Buddhist lineages because they explain a transmission across time. Except in my Mad Lineage, there may not be explicit teaching linking each poet, and not always an acknowledgement of the madness in poetry or an origin:

## Mad Lineage

Sylvia Plath Chukwuemeka Akachi Anne Sexton
Nicolas Chamfort Sara Teasdale Karin Boye
Ingrid Jonker Alfonsina Storni Danielle Collobert
John Gould Fletcher Francesco Gaeta Xu Lizhi Hai Zi
Barcraft Boake John Berryman Les Murray
Jean Pierre Duprey René Crevel Hart Crane
Randall Jarrell Yukio Mishima Paul Celan
Qu Yuan Peyo Yavorov Laurence Hope
Marina Tsvetaeva Friedrich Hölderlin
Torquato Tasso . . .

The names blend together. I had some books that became my teachers, but they came much later than I would have liked: Eli Claire's (1999) *Exile and pride*, Leah Lakshmi Piepzna-Samarasinha's (2019) *Tonguebreaker*, and Phil Smith's (2018) *Writhing writing: Moving towards a mad poetics*. I feel bound by R.D. Laing's (1970) *Knots* in that, "I am doing it //
the it I am doing is // the I that is doing it // the I that is doing

it is // the it I am doing // it is doing the I that am doing it // I am being done by the it I am doing // it is doing it" (p. 84). But slp and I have each other. To trace ourselves we need not lines, but spirals: "knots, tangles, fankles, *impasses,* disjunctions, whirligigs (sic), binds" (Laing, 1970, I). We need time to be across time. There are post-words for these words: "an immanence, concerned not with what *is* but what is *not yet, to come*" (St. Pierre, 2021, pp. 163-164).

## "How do you live this life?": Grief and Poetry (slp)

"And then, the questions: how do we live our lives so that even if we could retrospectively eliminate any of the most anguished, painful experiences, we would choose not to? If we reach this position any future pain, without losing its character as pain, will become totally transformed in its value" (Cooper, 1978, p. 31).

In my ketamine trips, in writing, I keep seeing it, saying it: atomic—*penetrating every atomic moment of me* (profusion), mushroom clouds and hot radioactive wind (combustion). Atomic explosions, my grief and rage at the world, at me, all mixed up. I am White, from the United States, I am not hibakusha (Jp. 被爆者), not one who actually survived it. I can't write a shred about atomic weapons that approaches what's been said, unsaid, about the actual bombs. It feels somehow wrong to use atomic as a metaphor for my personal grief, but it keeps coming to me.

(ketamine log, Thursday February 25, 2021)

*where is this, this is a threnody all the time always at myself. why do I deserve to suffer* 10, 11 *? the atomic bomb and Hiroshima and Nagasaki [...] screeching anger of grief from those things. that's what I feel for the world. that's what I feel about the world. and my inability to do things about it, how do you not berate yourself for that. and then I become a microcosm of it*

I live in a world in which we do this to one another—in the country that did the doing. One empire against another, and are such atrocities ever earned? The atomic terror of humanity in the world. There is complicated grief; treatment-resistant depression and neural overload; lost love/r, depended upon, that staunched the pain. Collapse, implosion. Over the years, when it all stole my joy and reduced my nervous system to high-strung jelly, and me to a string of months in this daily reality, this daily wanting to die—I willed myself into the thing, and laid out the money for clinical ketamine12. Ketamine treatments didn't stop anything from hurting, really.

---

10 [read: anger, you ungrateful bitch, read: this is not real suffering]

11 [read: I need a Leah Piepzna-Samarsinha (2019) to tell me, "Beautiful baby crip, I come to you in your dreams" (Crip magic spells).]

12 [read: people sleep in the park across the street, read: why do you deserve to heal, read: I need a Leah Piepzna-Samarsinha (2019) to tell me "Darling, let me show you your first magic trick" (Crip magic spells).]

They didn't minimize the limits of my nervous system or bring anyone back—not even me, I'd argue, though that was the promise. But, excavated from years in its void, rising out of the dark-colorful-disembodied-psychedelic journeys, the first thing they brought back was poetry.

## Poetry as Mad Process

Poetry is, among many things, a deep process. We have found that sharing poetry is a methodology of finding joy, and erasure poetry, a process of (re-)creation and recreation.

### 22

// I'm your lukewarm —
Steadfast support beam
I'll take what I can get —

There's something relaxing about carving a poem from existing material, one that removes any pressing need of original creation, of egoic declaration, of "hark! my unique voice!" Often, for us, the goal is not the need to find or make a message. It is a reshaping of the material in front of us, in ways that might be funny, silly, joyfully nonsensical. Meaningfully useless in cathartic ways. Moving. Revealing. It is Mad practice, squeezing joy out of what's available, finding life overlooked in the seemingly inert. It is polysemous poly-seamlessness. It is an expression of our love and interdependence.

The small numbered poems included in this piece are erasures Aubry created from troves of gchat conversations we were having while both of us were in graduate school. For slp's graduation, they created a chapbook of these poems, all encoded with personal meaning. But even with the background knowledge of each allusion, a large aspect of joy in the poems comes, for us, from their approach to rationality. Which is to say, it's a joke. The most humor might come from a punchline being not so funny; conversations about pain can become poems of joy; meaning can come most from meaninglessness. Excavation and revelation from erasure poetry are an act against rationality, inscriptions of relief upon oppressively linear systems of knowledge.

20

// My therapist — started
hugging me —

I saw a Danish program —
about communes —
awesome — thought of — my
Hot gay Jewish techie — how
Race is constructed in sex
chat names — white —
Vagina

You know what makes me

Sad?

Hilarious reversal

## Madness is grief and grief is White and White is human and humanity is Madness (slp)

Among my close friends (I have more than just Aubry), there is one whose family lost aeons of knowledge in the six million exterminated in the Holocaust. When we talk of our histories, she hits a hard, blank wall, limning the horizon. Her grief is a food I cannot know, and everything I know is tinged with its flavor. Another friend's family may as well be named X, this inexpressible immensity of cultural loss in the genocide—the United States' role in the transatlantic slave trade covering the landscape of his past. His grief and rage are beyond me, and resonate in (every atomic moment of) me.

I would talk endlessly about American colonization, if anyone could stand it. About the bloody disparity of privileges and harms within a system of harm, one where I am cushioned from its immediacy, but not its ultimate cost, and how I must, *must*, feel it. How feeling it is a necessity—as Mad empathy, as humanity, as ethics demand. It's not that I'm trying to rip open old wounds. It's that those wounds are still being made, that most colonized subjects don't understand where their own values come from and what they signify and condone. And still I cannot actually talk about that overwhelming...*what-is-it*...without being overwhelmed by what-it-is.

And we are supposed to take our meds for what? So that we can go to work and fill out forms and yearly evaluations? To maintain insurance, to go to doctors? To get a paycheck to buy our meds? To go to work? And we are supposed to preserve our lives for what—to live through loss? To witness murders of whole communities, ecosystems, species, life-bloods? To see ourselves never doing enough to defend what needs to be defended? Madness and neurodivergence and, yes, mental illness, would still exist in any utopia, in some more loving or less grindingly utilitarian world. But how are we supposed to live in the world we have? Ontology seeks origins—living in this Madness demands an answer. And in some ways, life demands of us to live, and die, regardless.

## Circle One: Poetry and Rationality (slp)

Poetry has a long history of discussing rationality, at times quite explicitly, as in the work of Sufi mystics and the ghazal form. Amin Banani (1994) is concerned greatly with show-ing Rumi's consideration of the relationship between rea-son and love. In this contest between love and reason, the latter "is precisely what Rumi considers a shackle. For him, the animating force of existence is love, equated with unrea-son" (Banani, 1994, p. 30). According to Banani (1994), "No concept has been more vigorously attacked and subjected to more withering ridicule by Rumi than reason. The great-est portion of his...ghazals is a rhapsodic celebration of love, which he emphatically tells us, is a force diametrically op-posed to reason" (p. 31).13 Love, for Rumi and much Sufi ide-ology, is a representation of, an embodiment of, God, and it seems of note that the divine is also called Friend in many ghazals. Banani (1994) specifically observes that for Rumi, in

---

13  Aubry certainly loves me beyond reason.

these "endless" contests between reason and love—between systems of intellect and God—"out of the bruising encounter with love...comes the vigor" (p. 36). In other words, one needs to be broken by love to be broken open, and indeed one poem uses the shocking, striking image of how "the split tongue of the pen runs twice as smooth as it would have had it not suffered the fissure" (Banani, 1994, p. 36). It seems that reason, as much as self, must suffer if love is to thrive, if one is to transcend the mundane (or find the divine within it).

Ghalib's ghazals, often a vehicle of doubt rather than mystical states, spring nevertheless from similar philosophical, cultural, and poetic traditions. Paradox is the lynchpin of many of Ghalib's poems, and a kind of inherent critique of linear reason: "Sorrow stunned my head, so why should I feel bad about my beheading?" (Bly and Dutta, 1999, p. 16). Ghalib writes, "If it hadn't been detached, it would be resting on my knees anyway" (in Bly and Dutta, 1999, p. 16). While the poem works in metaphor—the poet is not speaking to us without his head, of course—the poetry is not using metaphor so much as conceit, allegory, to express an emotional and existential state. The poet's despair is such that he could; that beheading and sorrow are made equivalent. The loss of love, of the attention of the Beloved, is a living death. In this there is no metaphor, nor even a contradiction, simply a state of being that cannot be grasped by the reasoning mind or language that insists upon exclusionary duality. He continues, "Why shouldn't I scream? I can stop. Perhaps/ The Great One notices Ghalib only when he stops screaming" (Bly and Dutta 1999, p. 13). It is in such accretion of paradox and irony that the interminable, inalterable state of existence can reside within the poem. The poem enacts the internal, externalizes it, holds space for it. That internal state is one that cannot be flattened, mapped in two dimensions. Rather it is spherical, worldly, all-encompassing—like a crystal ball it holds the known and the unknown.14 The many conflicting feelings and possibilities of cause and effect, conjectures on how the world works, and despair over many of them.

Such work is hardly isolated to the poetry of Rumi, Ghalib, Sufi mystics, or ghazals. In a very real way, irrationality is central to the work of poetry. It is, perhaps, an extant theory of Madness already in the world. In *Touched With Fire*, psychiatrist Kay Redfield Jamison (1996), herself bipolar, draws direct connections between well-known artists (Byron, Woolf, Coleridge, Melville, Van Gogh, etc.) and diagnostic characteristics of bipolar/manic-depressive illness. In some cases she offers a sort of posthumous diagnosis via works, personal communiqués, and calendars of productivity, and in all cases she notes the influence of their mental states on their creative capacities—generally, this work shows in quantitatively measurable ways that mood fluctuations and depressed states correlate with artistic production. Though there is great debate about the value of doing this work formally through modern diagnostic tools, it gives a history—perhaps personal to Jamison—where one might not have been apparent.

---

14  Or nothing at all according to Cowart (personal communication 1980-2004).

More overtly, Theodore Roethke, bipolar, wrote in "In a Dark Time": "What's madness but nobility of soul/ At odds with circumstances? [...] The edge is what I have" (as cited in Hobbs and Roethke, 1971, p. 55). This poem is sometimes read as a transcendent mystical experience (Hobbs and Roethke, 1971), the purpose of which the author said was "...to find out what really happens when one attempts to go beyond 'reality'" (p. 57). Perhaps by dint of such evidence we could venture to say that poetry is an extant theory of Madness, because it is an enactment and embodiment of Madness itself (Cooper, 1978, p. 41):

> Destructuring/restructuring follows a dialectical rationality, a rationality of *depassement*. This is the logic of every form of creative activity; it is also the logic of madness and the language of madness. There is another logic, antagonistic to the logic of destructuring/restructuring, which in this age we may call capitalistic logic – a logic of destruction: a state of affairs exists or it is simply negated. In destructuring as in destruction there is negation (of alienated experience in the former case), but inherent in destructuring there is the negation of this negation, the actualization of the 'promise' that leads to restructuring.

> In the destructuring moment of madness there is a paradoxical union of ecstatic joy and total despair and it is on the basis of this experiential union that the words and acts of mad discourse arise.

Mad people have been writing Mad poetry for a long time, but non-Mad poets have been doing the work of unreason, too—sometimes working against, in fact, the very concept that rationality and unreason cannot, do not, somehow co-exist. Rumi, and Banani (1994), may posit Love as a competing force with reason, but classical Western and Cartesian binaries often draw firmer, broader dichotomies—namely that rationality and unreason are inherently opposite forces, and many have written on this tie between artists and madness, placing them firmly on the opposite side of reason. David Pilgrim (2016), seeking "...Holism in the Medical Humanities," writes that, post-Enlightenment, an "emphasis on the power of reason...chafed against the temperamental tendency of artists to celebrate, creatively represent and live by forms of unreason: the domain of intuition, the emotions, and the imagination" (The research agenda set by antiquity section). This is only a taste of the history more thoroughly mapped by Shayda Kafai (2013), in how madness is constructed in such binaries and "either/or positionality: one is either sane or mad, normal or abnormal" (para. 3); Kafai (2013) proffers another positionality that resists this rigid binary structure, building on Gloria Anzaldúa's work on border theory and Jacquelyn N. Zita's queer theory. As an embodied experience, Kafai (2013) experiences the world "in-between": "A mad border body exists in-between the fixed definitions of sanity and madness; this body is a duel inhabitant" (sic para. 12). Our experience of madness parallels this, and poetry, we think, does a similar, necessary work in reorienting our relationship to reason; our understanding of how unreason functions in the world; and what kind of knowledge we value.

## Circle Two: How Poetry Challenges Rationality

In *Crises of the Sentence*, Jan Mieszkowski (2019), citing Pahl citing Hegel, writes "then poetry, and perhaps literature in general, is the discourse in which the stability of the sentence form and the harmonious cooperation of grammar, logic, and representation cease to be givens" (p. 44). Poetry, as Pahl and Mieszkowski (2019) note, works both within these strictures and against them in myriad ways (as numerous as the individuals writing poems) and might posit entirely other ways of conceptualizing reality, being, and certainly the depths, nuances, and meanings of language.

English-language poetry after the printing press takes our understanding of the concrete word and cleaves it, showing where it cleaves, against its own music. Aram Saroyan did such work, exploring the dislocation of language from concrete meaning (Madness!). From the 1960's, he used the visual medium to complicate a reader's ability to verbally read what is indicated on the page. His most famous poem, "lighght" (Saroyan, 2013, p.31), dislodges a reader's understanding of how a poem, and further, the written word, works:

> "Lighght" is something you *see* rather than *read*. Look at "lighght" as a poem and you might not get it. Look at it as a kind of photograph, and you'll be closer. "The difference between "lighght" and another type of

poem with more words is that it doesn't have a reading process," says Saroyan (Daly, 2007, para. 7).

Daly (2007) further quotes Saroyan as saying that rather than a "beginning, middle, and end," the perception of "lighght" is *"instant"* (para. 8). A rhetor would indeed call this a reading process—and, the point still stands that there is a differentiation in Saroyan's work between visual perception of sign and cognition of what it signifies. While Saroyan and Daly (2007) focus more on its visual perception ("Look at it as a kind of photograph, and you'll be closer."), a reader perceiving this poem is confronted by something dislocating their understanding of spelling as a firm and concrete representation of sound. And, further of the written word's concrete association as signal to its intended sign.

It also may deepen it. By infiltrating that dislocation, that space, and offering a new perception, reflection on—a new *feeling* of *light,* and of language. "lighght" is merely the most famous of Saroyan's work in this approach. Among his always brief, sometimes single-word poems, you can also find "lighght"'s partner, "eyeye" (Saroyan, 2013, p. 30), and others that conflate the descriptive and the imperative, that conflate unrelated action with other meaning ("eatc," p. 157), or no clear meaning ("REMEIMBER," p. 215; "priit," p. 90). Consequently, the fight over whether such "misspelled words" *are* poetry, and deserve public arts funding, became a touchstone in the conservative/liberal binary of U.S. politics (Daly, 2007). This fight has shifted in the public eye, but I can tell you that, in my college composition classes, the central argument over what the conventions of language and art are and should be is alive and kicking.

There are Saroyan's (2013) koan-like aphorisms: "Be sure/ before you/ forget" (p. 130). There are his explorations of tautology and paradox: "My cup is yellow/ Or not, thought not's//Impossible/ It's yellow" (Saroyan, 2013, p. 116). There are pages that explore and defy traditional concepts of poetry and its approach to meaning without such "misspelling," such as the eight pages in his Collected Works that consist of four words in total: each pair of facing pages consisting of the same word, and nothing else: "chariot// chariot", "cowboy// cowboy", "polite// polite", "oxygen// oxygen" (Saroyan, 2013, pp. 250-257). There are poems that upend the traditional understanding of how language progresses on the page, in word and prose:

pagne

cham

(Saroyan, 2013, p. 156)

"I crazy," he writes (Saroyan, 2013, p. 91).

Whether Saroyan himself should be considered actually Mad, or considers himself actually Mad, is not established. Poetry written by the Mad has the chance to be completely rational and frankly status quo. It also has the potential for being radically transformative and creative. But a more holistic answer lies in an equal question, what qualifies as Madness? If anything opposed to reason, to classically Western concepts of sanity, is Mad, then much of human existence itself is deeply Mad. If reason is equated with good, and order, and normative behavior, then Madness becomes disorder(s), disease, and freakish—it becomes deeply undesirable. Such oppositions can arguably be tied into Western classical, anthropocentric, teleological concepts of human evolution, since reason is seen as a uniquely human capability, and "base" instincts and behavior as animalistic15. And yet such oppositions are also deeply anthropophobic, if you will—deeply self-hating. Humanity will never be purely divided, reason from emotion, and to denigrate such an integral part of self so consistently is surely harmful. And if Madness is inherently a challenge to the social order, then Madness is certainly to be pursued, since the Western colonial social order uses reason to justify unreasonable positions, and just such self-hatred.

And maybe Madness just is. It can have potential and not be realized.

So as for poets like Saroyan being Mad or not—the challenges his poetry posed, and continues to pose, to social conventions, and his influence on the contemporary poetic world, seem indeed a bit Mad. Poetry of the page allows for reinscription through visual staticness, the physicality of the visual field, reading and re-reading as forms of interrogation. Poetry, even when not written by the Mad, may be a realm of Madness, the court jester flying in the face of the king. Back to Kafai (2013):

---

15  This despite what we've seen problem-solving animals like crows do (Taylor et al., 2009; Jelbert et al., 2015).

The stigmas of madness, the falsity of the sane/mad binary and the assumption that one cannot exist simultaneously in the border spaces of sanity and madness are all perpetuated by silence, by the act of refusing to tell one's story. By claiming madness, by stating that I am a mad border body, I am acknowledging the ways history is rewritten through language. I am taking apart what I have been taught of madness in order to create my own story (para. 26).

## Erasure and Chat Transcript (2021)

"The definition of insanity is doing the same thing over and over again expecting different results."
(slp citing Aubry citing slp citing Narcotics Anonymous)

## excerpts from chat transcript (second erasure)

**Aubry:** Some of the erasure of our chat was to erase who spoke when, conflating the selves; enough to question who said what...I was feeling a desire to create with you...because sometimes it does feel like we are left among the rubble. I don't have enough spoons to take on craft videos where someone's like "I found a spoon and here's some resin and I created four chairs" and my response is "I have some gchats, I'll make some poems, bc I don't have the energy to create the content." It's like the poem I hate by whatshisname about the lanyard.

**slp:** I actually like that poem.

**Aubry:** I think about that bc I think about poetry, I wanted to give you something at your MFA graduation because you were giving me something so beautiful, support, reading poetry (of varying levels of quality). you'd been so generous with your thoughts, your time [...] I didn't have enough money to buy buffalo turquoise but I did have enough time to print a makeshift book. Also if I could erase anything. I want to erase the contraindications for Wellbutrin.

**slp:** I didn't realize you were on that

**Aubry:** Not anymore—it was glorious while it lasted, I was sad to see it go. [...] They talk about drugs getting into the water supply and I was like *this is the one, this is the one that needs to get into the water supply* bc it made me feel so good but I also knew inside that I was just really sad, but you know that feeling.

**slp:** I was just thinking actually that when my Wellbutrin was increased in response to my recent suicidality that it [...]

**Aubry:** I don't know what they had me on before Wellbutrin bc that was a time I was severely disassociating; it's like how ppl make for the common era; I can't remember before Wellbutrin, there was a period of 8 months where I have vague recollections, doing various things, I know they happened because I'm still here. I don't have a lot of details to offer people. I remember them offering a couple different drugs to me, the first one [...] the second one had me contemplating exactly how I wanted to kill myself [...] I've never wanted to kill myself but she took my jokes about falling off a cliff and turned it into a Road Runner-themed reality show..." the third one made me hazy, I wasn't sure if it was doing anything, and then I went on Wellbutrin and it's like the clouds parted and it came with a rainbow and a boner. I wanted more, like I wanted them to up my dosage [...]

**slp:** this is brilliant. I love you.

**adt:** I love you too, dear. . . .

## poem (first erasure)

conflating the selves; enough to question
feeling / desire / among the rubble.

"I found a spoon and here's some resin and I created four chairs"

buffalo turquoise / a makeshift book. Also
the contraindications for / it was glorious

in the water supply / *the water supply* / so good but / also
inside was just sad / just fucking

for the common era / 8 months / a rainbow and a boner.
out / at the gym / this is brilliant. I love you. / I love /

## Madder and madder / (matter and matter)

Nonetheless, we find it particularly important to form Mad communities, and have found the work of Mad poets to be central to our use of poetry as an adaptive tool and expression of interdependence. So we focus on the work of Mad writers. Other work bears up this idea that poetry is an extant Mad theory and process. Wallace Stevens, posthumously considered a depressed poet (Mariani, 2016), worked a great deal in his Modernist landscapes to engage the sound of language against concrete sense, of both signal and sign; in anything from "Bantam in the Pine-woods" to "The Emperor of Ice-Cream," clear allegories and commentaries can be drawn, but only from the depths of rupture from concrete rationalism—drawn from sonic and imagistic surrealism. Peter Middleton (2009) notes the poet's approach to metaphysics to be his own poetry, that is to say that a poem should "make the visible a little hard / To see" (as cited in Middleton, p. 71). He suggests that "by pursuing 'the less legible meaning of sounds,' [Stevens] is deliberately putting legibility under pressure" (Middleton, 2009, p. 75). Middleton (2009) also writes that Adorno and Dworkin have complicated the notion of interpretation:

> Many commentators on modernist aesthetics, notably Theodor Adorno, have drawn attention to modernist

strategies of resistance to interpretation, and especially to their fragility in the face of dogmas of reason and ideology. Writing about primarily visual modes of poetic illegibility, Craig Dworkin concludes his study by summarizing the paradoxes for interpretation in stark terms: "Reading the illegible," he writes, "nullifies its own account in the precise moment of its construction and obliterates the very object it would claim to have identified, creating a new space of erasure which cannot itself be read (155) (p. 75).

Namely, poetry often navigates what's legible and illegible—in vision, in sound, in semiotics—using shared signs to call out against language's strictures of rationality. Against limiting factors of the socially-agreed-upon, revealing the irrational within a seemingly shared, concrete, and rational mode.

Various contemporary poets continue this work. Jos Charles, noted for her volume *feeld* (2018), works within visual, sonic, and etymological spheres. In this work, an archival, aged language infiltrates the contemporary, and the contemporary, colloquial youth laughs back. On the jacket, Fady Joudah calls it "Chaucerian English [translated] into the digital twenty-first century":

> lorde i am I / lorde i am 2/ lorde i am infinite / imma tween off this feeld / inn mye laybor / mye breasthes borrowed / from the big guye / the werevs / the tired manners / hel yah / nowone owens ther serotonin anye more / eviktion is an aestetick act / & affect bye definition a cruele economics / lorde let this 1 be not

enuff / lorde let this 2 be 2 much / but lorde a hole / how
it buckles 2 the agonie off the hiv / mylkie & multypal / it
buckels 2 the writerlie & piggish fiste / if u don't havv 35
enemies yett / lorde / ur a dicke16 (Charles, 2018, p. 34)

In this work, the visual and the sonic are never fixed fields.
Frequently, they run aground one another—"i am I" as opposed to "i am 2," conflating the assertion of identity (pro-
noun "I") with assertion of uniqueness, that uniqueness expressed in Roman numeral I or as a kind of eye rhyme to the
Arabic 1. But this echo is mostly effected in retrospect, when
we reach "2" and then "i am infinite". This transformation
is at times playful, at times (M/m)addening, at times easy
to trace in its etymology ... and at times makes an entirely
new word, complicated by the layers of semiotic meaning
that overlay it: "bye definition", this poem says. In this "borrowed" time, "nowone owens ther serotonin anye more /
eviktion...bye definition a cruel economics."

The work also exists at the intersections of what it is to be
trans: a particular delight when Charles (2018) says to "mye
breasthes borrowed / from the big guye," "lorde / ur a dicke."

We read this and meander through theory. We are drawn
to equate this trans process—of language, of identity—with
a Mad one but not in a pejorative sense17. Rather, we see it

16  The spacing of the original text may appear different from repro-
    duced here.

17  Especially holding the historical ties of gender variance to mental
    health diagnoses and disability, distancing people from their "human-
    ness based on their proximity to normativity" (Smilges, 2023, p. 9),
    and the damage that has wrought *using* normativity as justification
    for a variety of inhumane treatment(s).

connecting to a desire to expand our notions of the borders of identity, perhaps drawing from Kafai's (2013) notions of Zita and Anzaldua, a border body as one inhabiting multiple spaces at once. In a similar way, Charles' language inhabits multiple spaces, while discussing a trans identity, alongside the glorious exultation of "lorde i am infinite." But we are weary and wary of conflicting epistemological stances. Perhaps the madness is in those who cannot see outside of their narrowly constructed definitions of gender and selfhood? We write them into this because we share complicated feelings. Can binaristic thinking clarify the space outside of it, and how does that manifest through transness re: madness re: queerness re: feminism re: crip identity (re: more?)? Madness, like the wandering madman referenced by Foucault in *Madness and Civilization* (1988), is both outside of the city and critical to defining its boundaries. He is abject and yet central to the other's very existence.

In a related vein, La Mar Jurelle Bruce (2021) argued through examinations of Black radical creativity that madness is a method/process for understanding abjection, which has potential for critical approaches to understanding transness and artistic production. Madness in Mad studies often refuses definition and exists in relationship with, and opposition to rationality (Foucault, 1988) especially in art and poetry (Smith, 2018). Madness' in-betweenness rejects monism, rejects in-betweenness as marked negatively through weakness or difference, and opens possibilities for further understanding a fuller experience of transness (e.g. Malatino, 2022).

Notably, however, Charles (2018) also self-identified writing as a kind of Mad process:

Writing was, for me, like a gate, or slab beneath a charred, dripping piece of a thing, collecting remains...

I was "depressed" and "suicidal," in a kind of pathological way I still can't grant myself. I was in the thicket of a kind of time that is very proximate to death. A time that, like a gate or rack, keeps one just before a visible opening (para. 3).

Herself wrestling with mental illness, Cathy Park Hong's *Dance Dance Revolution* (2007) works similarly in borderlands and linguistic states of in-betweenness and multivalence. This book and its narrative are deeply interested in such crossings and rewritings of borders, the resisting of systems (Madness!). Beginning with the prose in the Foreword, it conflates the fictional narrative with the non-fiction documentation of "the historian" (Park Hong, 2007); this conflation is particularly noteworthy as it appears in a book of poetry, so often conceived of as verse and not prose, and certainly not historical documentation. A kind of speculative narrative saga then unfolds in a fictional/future world where a "historian" (not yet born, recording events that have not yet taken place) records the words of a "Desert guide" on a journey of some length, through a somewhat dystopian landscape with a history of war and an entirely remapped, rewritten set of national borders (Park Hong, 2007). The historian's "father, who later moved on to become a phy-sician for *Doctors Without Borders*" (Park Hong, 2007, p. 21, emphasis added) lived in South Korea; there, he witnessed the protest of a speculative coup, in which many rose up "only to be massacred by a U.S.-backed government" (Park Hong, 2007, p. 21). In one of several "Excerpt[s] from the Historian's Memoir," the historian reveals they "went to mil-itary school in a tiny city that dissolved in its own quagmire," talking of "the city's *torn carapace*" (emphasis added) (Park Hong, 2007, p. 100). In the opening of the book, Park Hong's (2007) historian exits the airport to start on the journey and "could not make out any form, only refracted lobes of sun-light and the shadow flittings of tourists who just arrived" (p. 21). In each case—form, carapace, borders, light, and genre—nothing is as delineated as convention or expectation would have it.

At the same time, the Desert guide shares stories from her un/bounded life in this/these un/bounded dialect(s): "Mine gor-belly fadde a mout-rattla but soma-time/ he plant poily bromide in me crania: pep gems dat echo/me mind cham-ber time y time—*ahar, ahar,*/ Him saith" (Park Hong, 2007, p. 45); "En spitty noon Satriday, we trudged dreaded/ Nam-san mountain, gamboling past fen y fields whim farmers/ en straw chapos picked grinpepas, y past perma/ haired ajama who sole fizzy sodas/ imported de U.S. o A...." (Park Hong, 2007, p. 56). This multivalence is one not just of Madness and invention, but of the mad border-body. Park Hong and the Desert guide each inhabiting multiple linguistic and cul-tural borderlands, defying binary clarity in part through the sheer number of languages and cultures intersecting. The language of the book seems entered into with (perhaps) compulsion, difficulty, need, and joy by the actual poet. The phonetic representation of Korean-inflected accents and speculative slang is at turns recognizable and challenging; Spanish, French, archaic English, and more pepper the vocabulary; the grammatical construction of the phrases is not formal English, and resembles that of a multi-language learner; and the pure fire in how Park Hong (2007) approaches the page as a site of representation and reinvention is dazzling. Simultaneously, it seems *not* entered into as a poetic exploration. From the part of the narrator archiving it, it is offered as documentation of how the invented language of the book might become so (M/m)addening to a reader.

This book writes in a speculative creole, of sorts, a future imagining of how language not normally considered creole might become one (Park Hong, 2007). It is a language constructed of speculatively shared signs, an invented interpretive community (or, as above, a world of them). It then confronts the reader, who is not likely to share all the contributing languages, necessarily removing their fixed center of conventions. The book assumes, as part of its base, a challenge to the reader's own interpretive communities, and it does so with an insistent, frantic, deliberately Mad joy (and sorrow). Indeed, such dislocation and relocation might recreate a kind of Madness in the reader. A kind of "Waste Land," if the Waste Land's accrued symbology wasn't coded in allusion but in language itself (Eliot, 1922). It is not impossible that a reader might come to Park Hong's (2007) text with the necessary dialectical familiarity, or that a reader could decode all of those dialects—but it would be uncommon. Park Hong (2007) writes this into the poems themselves, the Desert Guide conveying a lesson learned from her father: *"You can be the best talker but no point if you can't speak the other man's tongue. You can't chisel, con, plead, seduce, beg for your life, you can't do anything, because you know not their language. So learn them all"* (p. 46). It is a book that requires a reader to simultaneously work for understanding, to augment knowledge for clarity, and suspend prior systems of knowledge to enter meaning.

## Madness! and reinscription

The language of madness is nothing more nor less than the realization of language. Our words begin to touch the other and that's where the danger of madness lies: when it tells its truth. One danger, the only danger of madness, is violent denormalization of trivial words and worlds of security.

If this rather linear literary analysis insists, repeatedly, that Madness is the resisting of systems, is this then a simple definition of Madness? Or in understanding this simplistic definition as inherent, then is Madness an ever-moving mark, undefinable? Is it like its near cousin disability and does it possess "a plasticizing ontology, infusing individuals and populations with varying degrees and qualities of humanness based on their proximity to normativity" (Smilges, 2023, p. 9)? Does Madness have to serve white, able-bodied goals? Smilges shows how disability as a term often does, and we are both white people hoping that Madness like its cousins queer and crip can have a capacity for cultural change. That promise remains to be seen and we do not want to obscure how Madness operates differently in racialized contexts. Rather we want to acknowledge the reality of our colonial context and challenge it, and for us, claiming our Madness is central to this path. Shayda Kafai (2013) wrote: "There is a fear in the telling and in the owning of madness. It lies in the constructed threat of the word, in the stigma of the disability. I am choosing to claim madness now in this space as a political act" (para. 1). We're given sanist words even as we seek mad and anti-sanist/desanist ways to describe ourselves. As we don't yet have the words to describe ourselves outside of these terms, we rely on the claim that Madness is political and that poetry can describe the ineffable. It is a tool, but more than a tool; it is a process but deeper than process. Erasure poetry is a form of reinscription. Reinscription, in part, the colloquial definition of madness—*doing the same thing over and over again expecting different results.*

Except reinscription of poetry *yields* different results—a way of understanding madness, a way of understanding the world. That process can create meaning, coping, easing, etc., through repetition with varied outcomes, and is benefitted by sharing process/outcome with other Mad folks. We as Mad people do not assume an answer, we assume a process, and maybe a painful and lasting process—in our case, the writing and rewriting of poetry over and out of previous dialogue—as a deeply productive technology in living with and exploring madness.

Origins are complex. Borders are constantly rewritten. Madness is a condition affected by the cure drive (Claire, 2017) and rationality is not, we think, an actual thing of the world, but an invention. It may be more important, then, to ask: how do we accept such an onto-epistemology? How do we embrace our own irrationality through Madness?

## Aubry: Platform

I found some peace in the uncertainty and futility presented in Zen kōans (Jp. 公案) especially in their blended forms as parables, dialogues, poems, and ruminations. As a queer person seeking a way outside of Biblical and Cartesian thinking, I enjoyed studying religious texts like the Mumankan (The Gateless Gate, Jp. 無門關 ). I constantly shared them with slp while we were in college. In the Mumankan there were kōans and responses to kōans which to some extent could serve *as* hermeneutics: there can be both a religious text and a plethora of historical religious responses, which become additional texts. This process reinscribes meaning over time, functioning itself as spiritual transmission and meaning over time. This structure (anti-) parallels some of the poetics of madness we are describing. A digression in Case 14, Nansen Cuts the Cat in Two (Jp. 十四　南泉斬猫) (Sacred Texts.com):

南泉和尚因東西堂爭猫兒。
Nansen Oshõ saw monks of the Eastern and Western halls quarreling over a cat.

泉乃提起云、大衆道得即救、道不得即斬却也。

He held up the cat and said, "If you can give an answer, you will save the cat. If not, I will kill it."

衆無對。泉遂斬之。

No one could answer, and Nansen cut the cat in two.

晚趙州外歸。 泉擧似州。

That evening Jōshû returned, and Nansen told him of the incident.

州乃脱履安頭上而出。

Jōshû took off his sandal, placed it on his head, and walked out.

泉云、子若在即救得猫兒。

"If you had been there, you would have saved the cat," Nansen remarked.

## Mumon's Comment

無門曰、且道、趙州頂草鞋意作麼生。

Tell me, what did Jōshû mean when he put the sandal on his head?

若向者裏下得一轉語、便見南泉令不虚行。

If you can give a turning word on this, you will see that Nansen's decree was carried out with good reason.

其或未然險。

If not, "Danger!"

Many kōans reconfigure thinking by telling a surprising story and that, in earnest, is what Madness does productively: it can take a treasured truth and reinterpret it many times. My experiences with disassociation and hallucination brought me to understand that every event has multiple stories. While feeling trapped by trauma, rape, or neglect — or more mildly triggered — I had the ability to fly above myself while driving. Or to sink into a mattress so low that my goose-bump-laden skin can become a foam topper for the next human. That I had a superpower in my own mind that was completely useless, necessary, unproductive, and dreamlike — not *super* at all: that in and through it, I could embrace dissonance, not always seeking answers. Understand my *way* of coming into being and out of it. I can see the cat being cut in half and I can wear the shoe on my head. I can tell and retell these stories to slp over many years and each time have a different response and understand their multiplicity.

## There can be no poetry // Poetry can be here, no? (slp)

Teador Adorno is often misquoted, or at least quoted out of context, for saying that *After Auschwitz, there can be no poetry*. Some critics interpret this not as a declaration that poetry is useless in the world imprinted with the Holocaust, but that what poetry is must be different, must reflect the world, must be of the world, "as fissured and fractured as the world itself" (Gordon, 2020, para. 34).

> "No poem after Auschwitz (Adorno)," [Paul Celan] notes. "What concept of the 'poem' is being presented here? The arrogance of the one who dares

hypothetically-speculatively to contemplate or poetically describe Auschwitz from the nightingale- or lark-perspective."

Like Adorno, then, Celan took to heart the idea that modern catastrophe would require a form of art commensurate with its horrors. Poetry could still be written, but it had to be as fissured and fractured as the world itself. Celan...insist[s] that poetic language must pass through "terrifying silence" and through "the thousand darknesses of murderous speech." [...] The Modern poem has "an awakened sense of ellipsis," he observed, and a "faster flow of syntax." It turns away from the lyricism of nightingales and descends into a darkened silence where it is 'freighted with world.' (Gordon, 2020, paras. 33-34)

## Genre-ish Discourse

We've said that poetry may be the most whole, extant theory of Madness; defining Madness is central to such theory, perhaps as part of the reinscription process.

Or perhaps no theory is best. Perhaps what is more central is illustrating how readers in a community approach poetry. What makes these poems, after all? Is it the rigidity of a process, is it formal bounds, its density of syllabic stress and one-syllable adjectives (Cooper, 1998)? Carolyn Miller (1984) defines genre as social action, which "encompasses both substance and form... [which] represents action, [and] must involve situation and motive, because human action, whether symbolic or otherwise, is interpretable only against a context of situation and through the attributing of motives" (p. 152). Is a poem defined by its intent as much as its formal life, by how it is perceived and received?

Stanley Fish "coined" the term "'interpretive communities,' [to address] such an issue by conceiving of reading not as an autonomous, free, and individual experience but as collectively framed by shared conventions, proper to a time or to a community" (as cited in Chartier, 2006, p. 130). Fish identified these "shared conventions" not merely as formal strictures, but as actual strategies employed by the readers in a community (Chartier, 2006). The community which reads the text is actually writing the text, both through interpreting the text according to shared interpretive strategies and through creating the climate and opportunity for the form to exist as such (Fish, 1976). Aubry and I approach the genre of poetry, the genre of erasure poetry, the genre of self-erasure, within the context of our lives and love as Mad people. We create texts through reading strategies born of shared experiences, as friends and Mad people, and further recreate texts.

17

// I thought — about applying
to both

Do you have an equal
Chance — ?

Look for — *Cripple Liberation*
*Front Marching Band Blues* —
border crossings —
Intersections

Do both — Don't overload
yourself

To some degree, then, poetry is an extant theory of Madness
and vice versa. It is valid for us because we say it is. In a
broader view, it is so by dint of Miller's (1984) definitions
of genre, who defined it within the context of the ways in
which "actual rhetors and audiences have of comprehending
the discourse they use" (p. 152).

Here, again, we return to deep motions of rationality
to explain Madness, which either has no words or simply
cannot function within the bounds of Western linguistic
conventions. The intentions of such conventions, after all,
are to enforce clarity and logic, to elevate individualized
concretized meanings of words over complexity. In this
way, the technology of poetry allows for this same medium
to express what is otherwise ineffable within its own conventions. The methodology of shared erasure poems allow
for Madness to be shared, normalized, held, and cared for.
The injurious madness of the world recedes and the joy of
shared Madness creates a new reality. Mad studies, we posit, must not only look into Madness, but reconsider stamp-
ing out methodologies for doing so; must reconsider that

Western academics, and Western language conventions, may fail, inherently, at providing a holistic or productive Mad studies.

## Into "Immanence" metaphorically

4

// thank god — for emotionally
distancing sarcasm

love —

thank god — no cancer

I just want no part in it
compassionate — like a
bodhisattva
all the time —

never stop looking at me

The study of ontology is the seeking of answers for how something comes into being (Simons, 1987). Often an example is given to explain ontology: most famously, a thought experiment involving a mountain. When does a mountain become a mountain? Is it a mountain when no one has seen it? Has it always been a mountain? Despite some obvious geological answers to these questions across time (see Smith and Mark, 1998) including when tectonic plates collide, what does a Mad onto-epistemology offer a mountain? Is a mountain the weight of not being able to leave the bed? Is it an antediluvian Deluezian (also Deleuze may have helped Gide molest children)? Is it a place where your friend died on a midday hike? Is a mountain the compound pain of complicated grief that hurts your knees and back? Is a mountain the hallucination of a mountain?

What does it mean to be mentally ill, and to suffer when the suffering is rooted in some intersection of simply living in the grief-stunned, loss-infused, bone-breaking world? And the difficulties of processing that world, itself complicated by the body, culture, and past wounds? To answer these questions, we often seek origins, a Mad onto-epistemology: when did I start to feel this way? What caused it? Origin points are not useless to seek. They can provide some solace in understanding, some path for coping. And yet, these questions betray us. Pain is a part of living, and there is rarely a specific point in time from which Madness arises. Madness is not inherently synonymous with suffering, and this conflation itself is part of the ontology of madness (pejorative): because I am not *supposed* to feel this way, then my perception of the state(s) of my being becomes itself punishment, self-inflicted, as I take up the mantle of ableism (just as I am supposed to).

And yet there is Madness. It is hard to know where to start.

Individual origin points may be temporally-fixed, time-bound—my father died when I was six; my brother raped me for years when I was a child. They may be chronic—long-term conditions of neurochemical imbalances or upregulated nervous systems; watching members of your community sustain blows from state-sanctioned violence; living in a heteronormative white supremacist failing capitalist state while resisting gendered expectations. Medicalized diagnoses rarely consider social conditions, but also, sometimes do—diagnoses get complicated: a dead parent is common enough in bipolar cases that it is an option for diagnostic criteria. This, as how ACEs can be traced to poor health later in life, as how epigenetics can express the poverty of your grandmother, suggests stress effects on the body of a child are one origin point for Madness in the bodymind.

So as we dive into the body for answers we dissect it. We scan our brains. We look for the wrong in a kind of maelstrom through neural (in)action. Foucault (1973) writes in *The Birth of the Clinic*:

> "In the Nineteenth century, doctors described what for centuries had remained below the threshold of the visible and expressible, but this did not mean that over indulging in speculation, they had begun to perceive once again, or that they had listened to reason rather than imagination; it meant that the relation between the visible and the invisible – which is necessary to all concrete knowledge – changed its structure, revealing through gaze and language what had previously been below and beyond their domain" (xii).

To what end is the medicalization of madness still "below and beyond" and trapped within the sanist and ableist construct of "visibility?" Is the process of treatment itself a concerted effort at invisibility? Or another way for us to push ourselves deep below and beyond the domain of medicalization: allowing ourselves to rot in a more palatable way?

And Foucault (1973), the philosopher king of postmodernism and likely molester of Tunisian children and youth, continues:

> In the rational space of disease, doctors and patients do not occupy a place as of right; they are tolerated as disturbances that can hardly be avoided: the paradoxical role of medicine consists, above all in neutralizing them, in maintaining the maximum difference between them, so that, in the void that appears between them, the ideal configuration of the disease becomes a concrete, free form, totalized at last in a motionless, simultaneous picture, lacking both density and secrecy, where recognition opens of itself onto the order of essences (p. 9).

We don't want to be neutral(ized). Complicated grief is a term in itself, a term *turned upon* itself—when all grief is the grief of origin, when grief *is* the ontology, then every grief that follows is a swirling maelstrom, an electrical storm feeding off its own generation, down to the neurons, to the neuroplastic pathways of the heart and the brain. Rationality soon loses effectiveness from the inside of such a storm, unless it is to express its own limits, unless it is to acknowledge the emotional difficulty of living this life. Then everyone who lives this life might be subject. But how do you live this life?

## Reinscribing Irrationality in Grief for the World (slp)

After every *Night*, every *Bury My Heart at Wounded Knee*, every *Roots*, every *xxx* or *xxx*, comes another *xxx*. There will always be a threnody after Penderecki's, and there will always be poetry after Auschwitz, because life, as Louise Erdrich (2005) says, "will break you" (p. 200). This is not an individual occurrence, but a perpetual spiral of events. So long as life continues, so will madness and in particular grief—grief, a lingering process of not being able to erase longing and pain, a reinscription of not being able to reinscribe. The process of reinscription broadly construed, multi-valent, of the horrors we enact upon each other, of the processing of trauma (individually, generationally, artistically). And in the artistic reinscription that is so critical in helping us move forward.

Didn't Lauren Olamina, that crip, say:

*All successful life is*
*Adaptable,*
*Opportunistic,*
*Tenacious,*
*Interconnected, and*
*Fecund.*

*Understand this.*

*Use it.*

*Shape God*18.

Leah Piezna-Samasarinha (2019, Crip fairy godmother)

I grieve at times that I am no Paul Celan of the word. But to grieve such is to overlook that Celan lost his parents to Kristallnacht, and may have, by different accounts, blamed himself ever after for it; that he survived work camps, living with loss I can barely imagine; that after going on to write poetry for several more years, he drowned himself at age 49. What a terrible aperture through which to view the self, then...particularly considering what I too have lost in my own life, to myself and to my grief. That I have almost lost *my* life to myself and my grief. I can really only go to Celan and talk not of those horrors but of how the poem might respond to them. Because if we are to remember, we will be fractured by it but must also carry that fracture forward, must find some kind of whole. Accepting such Madness eases the pains of my internalized ableism and/or sanism—if it is the nature of the world, then I am not built in contradiction to the fabric of the world but am perceiving it wholly. It might be difficult, painful, certainly *irrational,* something I cannot reconcile no matter the repetition of it all—but the torture of trying to reconcile the madness inherent in the world and in Madness is relieved. It might be better, then, for me to consider that I

---

18  Butler, O. (1993). Earthseed: Book of the Living, verse 19. *Parable of the Sower.* New York: Four Walls Eight Windows.

share the practice with him. Not separate him as icon from me as adept, but think of him as human, perhaps Mad, sharing this excavation of the world, of self, of grief, of meaning-making, of value-weighing. Of madness and Madness.

BLACK,

like the memory-wound,
the eyes dig toward you,
in the heartteeth light-
bitten crownland,
that remains our bed:

through this shaft you have to come—
you come.

In seed-
sense
the sea stars you out, innermost, forever.

The namegiving has an end,
over you I cast my lot.

|Paul Celan (transl. Pierre Joris) (157)

The '90s movie *The Abyss,* along with my old vocal teacher, offer this treacly, simplistic answer to humans: something along the lines of *you are capable of so much harm, but of so much beauty.* As though beauty can cancel out harm. As though, in the great equation of human harm on the glorious, tempestuous globe, enough art will outweigh the worst of it. I do not feel that human art—transcendent as it can be, truly mystic in nature—makes up for the (pejorative) madness of behavior in the world. There is no accounting for it. As Mary Oliver (2017) says, "We are not wise and not very often/ kind. And much can never be redeemed" (p. 62). As she also says, "Still, there is some possibility left" (Oliver, 2017, p. 62).

So if I am to survive, especially with some kind of bipolar/ treatment-resistant-

depression constantly stealing my (anti)methods from under me—I must find some other underlying approach. I have to stock up on them. Consider that in our different circumstances there is a sharing of Madness, and this sharing might be one. That Aubry is my (anti)method, his love for me is my (anti)method, our love for each other and how we understand one another. Interdependence is part of our method, and shared poetry a vehicle of our interdependence.

## ketamine log Wednesday January 20 2021)

I missed inauguration for this.

Lol it's okay.

[...] Oh yeah. I wrote and read poetry last night. For real. I read Cass and I read Paul Celan—and although I knew, o my god, how did I not know. I texted Cass late to say "something about [their chapbook] recalls to me Paul Celan...or vice versa" They responded "Oh" and "What an unexpected compliment" and I responded "maybe it's the ketamine"

Paul Celan. I broke through a barrier to find all the grief in the world. And all the regret at how I myself was unable to love better.

Your golden hair, Margarete
Your ashen hair, Shulamith

## 2

// I had a good day — not
great
but good — I didn't worry

## 3

// an image of you — shirt off —
outside
the house — screaming —
hence — desperate

yep — I want to beg

Let's not talk — about sex

Don't get started — I know

There are signs — there are
signs
We choose

## Getting to Reinscription through Mad Interdependence in Poetic Process

We are crip Earthseed
but we are not going anywhere
You are not an individual health defect
You are a systemic war battalion
You come from somewhere
You are a we
We know shit they'll need to know
We know shit they have no idea of
We have survived a million things they said would kill us
We prove them all wrong
Even death is different here
not a failure
but a glittery cosmos
(Piepzna-Samasarinha, 2019, Crip fairy godmother)

As Mad people, friends, and authors, we partly understand mad subjectivity as being shaped by cultural traumas (Alexander, 2012)—not only biomedical trauma as inflicted experience, but Mad subjectivities as arising within social processes, institutions, mores, values, etc., where "good mental health" and sanism is an oppressive norm. Sara Ahmed named for us the daily trauma done by "happiness duty" in

*The Promise of Happiness* (2010): through a Mad lens that be-ing/performing happiness becomes a moral duty to spread happiness like contagion. We propose ways to question, alter, explore, or add to Mad Studies through a particular process-based approach to writing—one productive technology to employ in a Mad way to explore Mad experience. Referring to Eli Claire, Jennifer Pool and Jennifer Ward (2013) argue that Mad people must "break open the bone" to upset the sanist nature of "good grief." When Mad people write about traumatic and sanist experiences—breaking open the bone—writing can also promote identity formation, easing and sometimes, though a cure is not always possible or desirable, healing. However, Pool and Ward's analysis of writing and their stories does not intend to analyze the process of writing. Often an iterative process itself, writing can be a location for processing experience, in and out of therapeutic confines—reinscription, in our experience, a conscious *re*-writing of and over previous text, is still further a method for understanding mad experience.

We're offering up a technology, a complicated tool, not "writing therapy," not a social scientific life story method, not autoethnography, writing with targeted goals of "improvement," or communicating particular messages. Instead, we've documented taking previous writings of personal experience and reinscribing them—in this case, our Gchat erasure poems. Repetition here is myriad, offering comfort and new outcomes, at the most literal level. Not only do we return, together, to discussions equally profound, playful, and banal—a literal retelling which is a reliving, reaffirming, and re-enlivening our relationship—we also create new texts, new experiences, sometimes transformative, through selective destruction of that beloved text. For us, creating art together benefits our lives, especially in relation to our shared experiences of madness and trauma. This process explores Mad peoples' daily lived experiences, which often don't get chronicled outside of a mad-specific anthology because the extraordinary or unusual defines you in a saneist society.

Mad people need radical interdependence. We should have learned as much from the disabled rights movements which keep moving, because the targets keep shifting. But bringing us together is also hard when so few people have the ability to take up the mantle of Madness. Before we thought to rely on each other we were trapped by individualism. slp has turned to therapists and psychiatrists; medications, nutrients and supplements; disordered eating and medically appropriate food plans; Internal Family Systems; emotional hyper-dependence on friends and lovers; and finally ketamine therapy. Aubry has turned to many years of therapy, disordered eating, spiritual practice including reclaiming tarot, depression, overwork, social seclusion, meditation, and various obsessions. But when we turned to each other we turned to poetry. We write separately and together.

Shared poetry, and erasure poetry—its own flavor, excavation, exploration, seeking of joy, absurdism, challenging of grief. It gives us an opportunity to rewrite, and write over, the origin points for trauma and mental illness. It allows us to write with them.

## 13

// You are at a wolf sanctuary

You are adept at
observation

I like both — the original

More pressure on — multiple
meanings

Stop making me write
poetry — about us

# References

Ahmed, S. (2010). *The promise of happiness.* Duke University Press.

Alexander, J. (2012). *Trauma: A social theory.* Polity Press.

Banani, A., Hovannissian, R., & Sabagh, G. (eds.) (1994). *Poetry and mysticism in Islam: the heritage of Rumi.* Cambridge University Press.

Bly, R. & Dutta, S. (1999). *The lightning should have fallen on Ghalib.* The Ecco Press.

Bruce, L.M.J. (2021). *How to go mad without losing your mind: Madness and Black radical creativity.* Duke University Press.

Celan, P. (2006). *Breathturn* (P. Joris Trans.). *Green Integer.*

Charles, J. (2018). *feeld.* Milkweed Editions.

Charles, J. (2018). How I wrote "Tonite I Wuld Luv to Rite." *The Adroit Journal.*

Chartier, R. (2006). Genre Between Literature and History. *Modern Language Quarterly, 67*(1): 129-139.

Claire, E. (1999). *Exile and pride: Disability, queerness, and liberation.* Duke University Press.

Cooper, D. (1978). *The language of madness.* Pelican Books.

Cooper, G. B. (1998). *Mysterious music: Rhythm and free verse.* Stanford University Press.

Cowart, E. (1980-2004). Personal communication.

Daly, I. (2007). You Call That Poetry?! How seven letters managed to freak out an entire nation. *Poetry Foundation.*

Eliot, T.S. (1922). *The waste land.* Boni & Liveright.

Erdrich, L. (2006). *The painted drum.* Harper Perennial.

Fish, S. (1976). Interpreting the 'Variorum.' *Critical inquiry,* 2(3): 465-485.

Foucault, M. (1973). *The birth of the clinic: An archeology of medical perception.* Vintage Press.

Foucault, M. (1988). *Madness and civilization: A history of insanity in the age of reason.* Polity.

Gabler, H. (2018). The draft manuscript as material foundation for genetic editing and genetic criticism. In *Text Genetics in Literary Modernism and other Essays* (pp. 209-220). Cambridge, UK: Open Book. http://www.jstor.org/stable/j.ctv8j3xd.13

Gordon, P. E. (2020). Poet of the Impossible: Paul Celan at 100. *Boston Review.* https://bostonreview.net/articles/peter-e-gordon-tks-paul-celan/.

Hoobs, J., & Roethke, B. (1971). The poet as his own interpreter: Theodor Roethke on "In a Dark Time." *College English,* 33(1).

Jelbert, S. A., Taylor, A. H., & Gray, R. D. (2015). Reasoning by exclusion in New Caledonian crows (Corvus moneduloides) cannot be explained by avoidance of empty containers. *Journal of Comparative Psychology,* 129(3), 283–290.

Kafai, S. (2013). The Mad border body: A political in-betweenness. *Disability Studies Quarterly,* 33(1).

Laing, R.D. (1970). *Knots.* Vintage Press.

Malatino, H. (2022). *Side affects: On being trans and feeling bad.* University of Minnesota Press.

Mariani, P, (2016). *The Whole Harmonium: The Life of Wallace Stevens.* Simon & Schuster.

Middleton, P. (2009). "The "Final Finding of the Ear": Wallace Stevens' Modernist Soundscapes." *The Wallace Stevens Journal Vol. 33*(1). 61-82.

Mieszkowski, J. (2019). *Crises of the Sentence.* University of Chicago Press.

Miller, C. R. (1984). Genre as social action. *Quarterly Journal of Speech, 70*(2), 151–167.

Oliver, M. (2017). *Devotions.* New York, Penguin Publishing Group.

Park Hong, C. (2007). *Dance dance revolution: Poems.* (1st ed.) W. W. Norton.

Pilgrim, D. (2016). The aspiration for holism in the medical humanities. *Health, 20*(4), 430-444.

Piepzna-Samasarinha, L. (2019). *Tonguebreaker.* Mawenzi House Publishers Ltd.

Pool, J. & Ward, J. (2013). "Breaking open the bone": Storytelling, sanism, and mad grief in LeFrançois, B., Menzies, R. & Reaume, G. (eds.) *Mad matters: A critical reader in Canadian mad studies.* Toronto, Canada: Canadian Scholars Press.

Sacred Texts.com (n.d.) The gateless gate. https://sacred-texts.com/bud/zen/mumonkan.htm

Saroyan, A. (2007). *Complete minimal poems.* Primary Information/Ugly Duckling Press.

Simons, P. M. (1987). *Parts. An essay in ontology.* Oxford, UK: Clarendon Press.

Smilges, J.L. (2023). *Crip negativity.* University of Minnesota Press.

Smith, P. (2018). *Writhing writing: Moving towards a mad poetics.* Fort Worth, TX: Autonomous Press.

Smith, B. and Mark, D.M. (1998). Ontology with human subjects testing: An empirical investigation of geographic categories. *American Journal of Economics and Sociology, 58*(2): 245-272.

St. Pierre, E. (2021). Why post qualitative inquiry? *Qualitative Inquiry. 27*(2): 163-166.

Taylor, A. H., Hunt, G. R., Medina, F. S., & Gray, R. D. (2009). Do new Caledonian crows solve physical problems through causal reasoning? *Proceedings of Biological Sciences, 276*(1655), 247–254.

# The Trans Depressive

*j. logan smilges*

I have a sad secret. It's a secret that is both sad to tell and literally about sadness.

The secret is this: I feel most trans when I'm depressed.

It sounds fucked up, right? That I feel most confident in my transness, most secure in my relation to the other trans people, and most at home in my trans identity when I am curled up in bed and crying about being undesirable or about being totally worthless or about nothing at all. To be clear, I'm not talking about gender dysphoria or the distress that some trans people experience as a result of the disjuncture between their felt gender and their bodies or the social recognition that their bodies receive. I enjoy my muscled femme faggotry and have spent a considerable amount of time pursuing body-modification techniques to construct myself as I appear today. What I'm talking about is the legibility of my gender *as trans* that comes through most clearly when I'm *going through it*. It's almost like gender dysphoria in reverse: not my transness making me feel depressed but my depression making me feel trans.

For a long time, I assumed that this relationship between feeling trans and feeling depressed meant that I was a bad trans person. I often found myself asking a series of questions like these:

> *If I can't articulate my depression as gender dysphoria but still feel as though it is imbricated with my gender, does that mean I have internalized transphobia? If hating myself makes me feel trans, does that mean I hate all trans people? If I hate all trans people, am I even still allowed to be trans, especially since I'm nonbinary, which leaves me feeling like a fake trans person most of the time. And like, as a transfeminine person whose body is hypermasculine, I already feel a lot of guilt claiming common ground with women and other femmes who experience cissexism differently than I do, so maybe it's misogyny? But honestly, I'm pretty confident in how much I hate men with penises—you know, outside of the bedroom, where they are occasionally useful—so if I hate most men and women, do I just have a people problem? I am also autistic, so I guess the people problem kind of checks out, even though it low-key feels super ableist to think that. And it's kind of hard to imagine a misogynistic transphobe who isn't ableist. Since I struggle to articulate why I'm depressed, maybe it's just my conscience hinting at all of these reasons for how terrible of a person I am.*

You get the picture. This sort of spiraling would continue on until I'd tucker out, break down into heaving sobs, or hurt myself. It's hard to stop being depressed when your mind keeps feeding you new reasons to be depressed.

Recently, however, I've found myself drawn to Cameron Awkward-Rich's (2017) rendering of the "depressed transsexual" as a way to read the fact that my depression makes me feel trans without turning it into a question of ethics (p. 823). For Awkward-Rich, the depressed transsexual offers both an alternative genealogy of trans affectivity that is opposed to "the affirmative project of trans studies" and a new methodology with which we might read trans affect as it unfolds (p. 823). Though he seems to be primarily interested in the depression occasioned by trans-antagonism, I am nevertheless taken by his proposal to accept "pain...as a given, not necessarily loaded with moral weight" (p. 836). The depressed transsexual allows me to investigate the relationship between my transness and depression without feeling guilty about it. Instead of asking whether I should feel the way that I do, I can approach it as a rhetorical issue, that is, as one concerned with how meaning is created and assigned. What is it about depression that makes me *feel* trans? What does trans feel like, and why for me is it depression?

Ruminating on these questions has led me to explore both the clinical histories of trans and depression as medical diagnoses and the growing interest among trans and disability scholars in affect as a social phenomenon. To my surprise, I discovered that my sad secret linking depression to feeling trans has a thoroughly documented medical history, even if it is a history that has largely been effaced from the modern medicalized narrative of trans experience. What I had assumed to be my own private, sad secret turns out to be one of the most pervasive and dominant models of gender nonconformance in the public sphere, one encapsulated by a figure whom I call the *trans depressive*. As the foil to a medical model of transness that posits depression as a symptom of Gender Dysphoria, the trans depressive operates under a gender-dimorphic model of depression that characterizes gender nonconformance as an expression of disabled affect. The trans depressive is someone whose depression not only accompanies their transness but helps to generate it, converting their disordered expressions of emotion into forms of gender variance hinged on inappropriate affectivity. Alcoholic women, tearful men, people who feel both too much and not enough. Feminine boys like me, fainting onto the chaise next to the window and wishing someone would bring them some smelling salts.

As defined by a model primarily organized around affect, the trans depressive does not rely on a clinical diagnosis of depression nor on a formal identification as transgender. The trans depressive is not always a depressed person who comes out trans, though they very well could be. Instead, the trans depressive is a figure whose affect is indexed outside of their assigned gender, thus suggesting that binary gender itself is an affective construct. Here and throughout this chapter, I understand "affect" as a broad category of feeling that includes not only nameable emotions but also the many other ways that our bodyminds respond to stimuli and orient themselves to the world. A bad mood can make someone a trans depressive. A second glance into the mirror. A breakdown. A muffled sob. A long shower. A dirty look at a stranger. A nap. A hug that lasts a moment too long or second too short. A trans depressive could be anyone who finds themself feeling not right and subsequently accused of occupying gender all wrong.

What I propose in this chapter is that the trans depressive might open alternative routes to thinking (and feeling) trans and depression together. By tracing the development of the trans depressive from its origins in mid-twentieth century psychiatric models of gender nonconformance through the diagnostic invention of Gender Dysphoria and Depressive Disorders, I reveal the medical precedent for a gender-dimorphic model of affect. This model shapes both the clinical symptomatology of affective disorders, such as depression, and the affective norms governing trans experience. The trans depressive pulls gender-dimorphic affect into focus, so we might name it, trace its string of clinical and cultural effects, and release ourselves from the project of gendering into happiness.

## A Sad Story of the *DSM*

Historicizing the trans depressive requires us to take a closer look at its constitutive parts—trans and depression—as social constructs and lived experiences that owe much of their cultural legibility to their mutual histories of medicalization. While these histories long precede the development of American psychiatry (Stryker, 2008; Sadowsky, 2021), the 1980 publication of the *Diagnostic and Statistical Manual of Mental Disorders, 3rd ed.* (*DSM-III*) was the first to include both "transsexualism" and "major depressive disorder" as official diagnoses (American Psychiatric Association [APA], 1980). Variations of these diagnoses existed in earlier editions of the *DSM*, but the third edition was the first to articulate models of depression and trans experience that closely resemble the ones in use today.

In contrast with previous editions, which had grouped mental illnesses according to their alleged causes, the *DSM-III* adopted a more empirical approach that sought to organize conditions based on their discrete symptoms (Metzl, 2003). In the *DSM-II*, for instance, depressive characteristics were littered across several disease categories, including psychoses, major affective disorders, neuroses, personality disorders, and transient situational disturbances. A patient presenting with depressive symptoms might be diagnosed with a condition in any one of these categories, depending on the whims of the clinician on staff. Among the primary intentions behind the *DSM-III* was to "make diagnosis uniform" by reclassifying conditions according to their distinctive characteristics (Sadowsky, 2021, p. 149). The addition of "major depressive disorder" and "transsexualism" to the *DSM-III* was thus a testament to the field of psychiatry's growing confidence that being depressed and being transsexual were unique conditions in their own right, each with its own symptomatology that could be ascertained independently from the symptoms for other conditions.

As historians of medicine have been quick to point out, however, psychiatry's hope to prove its own objectivity with evidence-based science has had mixed results. On one hand, the *DSM-III*'s investment in uniformity reflected the APA's interest in eliminating clinician bias from the field. In the manual's introduction, the authors urge clinicians to take on an "atheoretical" stance that involves "the lowest order of inference necessary" (APA, 1980, p. 7). This "lowest order" is characterized as a "descriptive approach," implying that if clinicians merely describe their patients' visible symptoms, rather than speculate about their patients' unconsciouses, then they can avoid perpetuating the gendered, racialized, and sexed biases that plagued previous editions of the *DSM* (Metzl, 2003, p. 53). On the other hand, the fantasy of an "atheoretical" science is demonstrably impossible and typically results in disguising one "situated knowledge" with another (Haraway, 1988). Jonathan Metzl argues that the invention of psychotropic medications accomplished just this by making it possible for the APA to allege the infallibility of psychiatry as an evidence-based science without necessarily interrogating the premises by which diagnoses and medications are distributed. "Like psychoanalysis of years past," he writes, "medications both treat the symptoms and teleologically maintain the categories in which the symptoms operate" (p. 63). Even if explicit references to psychoanalysis were removed from its pages, the *DSM-III* continued to uphold "all the cultural and social baggage of the psychoanalytic paradigms" (p. 7). Psychiatry was not so much becoming less theoretical as it was simply burying its theory beneath the deceptive transparency of observation-based diagnosis.

Particularly relevant to our discussion here is the way such buried theory hid much of the connective tissue linking gender and depression. In *American Melancholy: Constructions of Depression in the Twentieth Century*, Laura D. Hirshbein (2009) shows how psychiatry's biomedicalization worked to confirm, rather than trouble, the idea that depression was a woman's disease. "Depression in women was becoming a circular concept" she writes. "[W]omen were believed to be depressed more than men and were selected for clinical trials more than men, and then their greater presence within trials appeared to affirm that they were depressed more than men" (p. 90). It was sexist confirmation bias paired with a poor research design. Worse yet, the gender bias of these early studies calcified particular symptoms as reliable criteria for the category of depression itself, despite that they were not equally represented across genders. Symptoms such as "poor appetite," "loss of interest," and "inappropriate guilt" may have been common for depressed women (APA, 1980, p. 214), but they were not particularly common among depressed men, whose symptoms tended to be either ignored or associated with substance abuse (Hirshbein, 2009, p. 101). Hirshbein explains, "patients were defined as depressed because they matched researchers' assumptions about what depression looked like..., and their symptoms were used to diagnose depression in general" (p. 99). Since there was no effort put forth to expand the list of depressive criteria or even interrogate the conditions under which a particular symptom qualified as a depressive criterion, the gendered assumptions of psychoanalysis were guaranteed to perseverate. No matter which way you cut it, women were going to appear more depressed, and depression was going to appear more feminine.

## A Sad Story of Trans Pathologization

While many scholars in addition to Hirshbein have addressed the feminization of depression (Cvetkovich, 2012; Davis, 2013; Metzl, 2003; Sadowsky, 2021; Schiesari, 1992), less discussed has been how the feminized symptoms for depression laid the groundwork for the evolving diagnoses applied to transgender people. Tobias B. D. Wiggins (2020) has noted that since the addition of "transsexualism" to the *DSM-III*, each successive revision of the diagnostic category has further emphasized that *distress* with one's gender, often exhibited by depressive symptoms, is "the requisite and differentiating characteristic of mental illness" (p. 61). In the *DSM-III*, for instance, transsexualism is defined by a two-year period of "a persistent *sense of discomfort and inappropriateness* about one's anatomic sex and a persistent wish to be rid of one's genitals and to live as member of the other sex" (APA, 1980, p. 262) (emphasis mine). The *DSM-IV*, which reclassifies transsexualism as "Gender Identity Disorder" (APA, 1994, p. 532), splits the diagnosis into two separate criteria, including "evidence of *clinically significant distress or impairment* in social, occupational, or other important areas of functioning" (p. 533). And the most recent edition, the *DSM-5*, maintains this second criterion for the updated category "Gender Dysphoria," offering the explanation that "Although not all individuals will experience distress as a result of [gender] incongruence, many are distressed if the desired physical interventions by means of hormones and/or surgery are not available" (APA, 2013). Thus, the medicalization of trans experience has less to do with whether a person identifies themselves as trans than with whether they are experiencing distress as a result of their identification. The biomedical technologies made available through diagnosis, such as hormone replacement therapy and various gender affirmation surgeries, are framed similar to Prozac for depression: their primary purpose is not to help a person actualize their desired bodymind but to "prescript an affective movement from discontent toward a happy future" (Wiggins, 2020, p. 62). Any bodymind modification is merely a biomedical means to an affective end.

The parallel with depression specifically, as opposed to affective disorders more generally, shifts into focus when we consider how psychiatrists expect Gender Dysphoria to manifest symptomatically. The *DSM-5* (APA, 2013) explicitly mentions the "development of depression, anxiety, and substance abuse" as examples of the "impairment" caused by Gender Dysphoria, and it lists a series of "Functional Consequences," such as "[r]elationship difficulties, sexual relationship problems," "negative self-concept, increased rates of mental disorder comorbidity, school dropout, and economic marginalization" that are all resonant with the effects of depression. Indeed, the *DSM-5*'s "Diagnostic Features" for "Major Depressive Disorder" include "social withdrawal," "reduction from previous levels of sexual interest or desire," "feelings of worthlessness," and "a precipitous drop in grades." The overlapping criteria between Gender Dysphoria and depression demonstrate how Gender Dysphoria itself is catalogued as a variant of a depressive disorder.

Additionally, that "substance abuse" is listed as an expression of gender dysphoric impairment brings to mind depression's gendered dynamics. A common assumption among psychiatrists is that whereas women "exhibit more internalizing problems," such as the conventional symptoms for depression (e.g., fatigue, sadness, guilt, etc.), men "exhibit more externalizing problems," including addiction and violence (Elliott, 2013, p. 97). Alcohol Use Disorder, especially, is one of the few mental disorders in the *DSM-5* that is attributed primarily to men (APA, 2013). Hirshbein identifies the apparent masculinity of alcohol abuse as an issue of bias analogous to the overrepresentation of depression in women. Historically, when subjects were selected for clinical trials for psychotropic medications, such as Prozac, researchers intentionally "excluded those who had complicating factors such as alcoholism," thereby preventing the study of many men who were likely depressed, as well as women who failed to present feminine depressive symptoms (Hirshbein, 2009, p. 98).

The effects of this clinical exclusion have been significant not only for the classification of depressive disorders but also for the treatment of men's mental health. The gendered bifurcation of depression and addiction has led to what Dena T. Smith et al. (2018) explain as "a reliance on gender comparisons (men vs. women) rather than examination of within-gender differences in mental health outcomes" (p. 79). This tendency toward comparisons overlooks the frequency with which many men experience depression and makes it more difficult for clinicians to diagnose men who present tradition-al (read: feminine) depressive symptoms. While it would be a mistake to suggest that all instances of addiction are reducible to depression, it is worth acknowledging that for some peo-ple addiction may be a *"correlate of misery"* that functions as an alternative depressive symptom to those already classified within the rubric of depressive disorders (p. 79).

Such a correlation between addiction and depression ex-pands and retrenches Gender Dysphoria's rhetorical depen-dence on negative affect as its defining characteristic. Gen-der Dysphoria can be diagnosed not only through feminine distress as expressed through depression but also through masculine distress as it is performed by addiction. Gender Dysphoria's flexible capacity to manifest as two entirely sep-arate mental disorders reflects a shared feature of all psy-chiatric disabilities that Jenell Johnson (2011) has called "af-fective impairment" (p. 187). For Johnson, the entanglement of Gender Dysphoria, depression, and addiction is not coin-cidental but representative of psychiatry's ongoing assump-tion that "emotion [is] the primary impairment of mental illness" (p. 192). For Gender Dysphoria, distress becomes a catch-all term for disordered affect, regardless of how that affect is expressed (e.g., crying or drinking) or what caused it.

While the *DSM-5* (APA, 2013) attempts to clarify that a diagnosis of Gender Dysphoria "focuses on dysphoria as the clinical problem, not [gender] identity per se," the inclusion of the distress criterion both individualizes gender dysphor-ic distress as a personal pathology and demands that such a pathology exist in order for a person to be given access to transition-related healthcare (Davy, 2015, p. 1166). As Wiggins (2020) puts it, "The manual tangentially names societal issues that dramatically impact trans people's lives, while simultaneously essentializing trans subjectivity as an inherently biologically based suffering" (p. 67). This suffering indexes an affective impairment, one that Johnson (2011) explains as "not one of kind [but] one of degree," wherein "mental illness emerge[s] not as abnormal ideation or emotion, but as a disordered economy in which the supply of emotion exceed[s] the demand" (p. 191). Trans people feel too much, do too much, are too much. This is Gender Dysphoria as gender excess as affective intensity: "a surfeit of abnormally strong emotions...and especially negative emotions like sadness, fear, and shame" (p. 191). To be trans, medically speaking, is to feel the wrong amount of the wrong feelings.

## A Sad Story of Affective Gendering

Gender Dysphoria succeeds in medicalizing trans existence by way of pathologizing trans affectivity. Trans people have to feel bad in order to be diagnosed with Gender Dysphoria, and the biomedical technologies made available through diagnosis are meant to cure these bad feelings by making trans people feel good. Put differently, negative affect authenticates a person as trans. Negative affect is what makes a trans person visible within a medical model, transforming depressive symptoms into unmistakable characteristics of a dysphoric trans person. Andrea Long Chu (2018) has lamented this affective economy of biomedical transition because it shores up the authority of psychiatrists and other medical providers to decide whether a person is allowed to access care based on how happy they would be following medical intervention. As she and Emmet Harsin Drager (2019) admit elsewhere, sometimes "dysphoria maybe never goes away" (p. 104), but this possibility is unthinkable according to trans medicine, wherein the singular purpose of transitioning is to cure dysphoria. Regardless of how any given trans person feels, they must articulate themselves within a framework of disabled affect or risk being denied access to biomedical intervention. Chu (2018) explains, "As long as transgender medicine retains the alleviation of pain as its benchmark of success, it will reserve for itself, with a dictator's benevolence, the right to withhold care from those who want it." This "dictator's benevolence," sustained by a medical model of transness, presumes not only that distress must be alleviated through transition but also that there must be distress to alleviate.

By arguing that Gender Dysphoria pathologizes trans affectivity, I am referring to the dual processes by which trans people's existing negative affects are collated as symptomatic of their need for biomedical intervention *and* the way negative affect itself is retroactively read into trans people's clinical histories. Sara Ahmed (2010) puts it thus: "Certain subjects might appear as sad or wretched...because they are perceived as lacking what causes happiness, and as causing unhappiness in their lack" (p. 98). In order to want to transition, the *DSM-5* implies, a person must feel bad. Must be miserable. Must be depressed. Must be acting out. Trans affect must be pathological because gender transition would otherwise be undesirable. The tethering of gender transition to pathological affect makes apparent that affect itself is gendered terrain. What people feel, what they are supposed to feel, and how they are expected to express those feelings are all structured in part by a binary gender system. The clinical separation of depression from addiction is one example of the gender norms regulating people's emotions, but the distress criterion for Gender Dysphoria further exposes the way that any indulgence of negative affect can be taken as a sign of gender nonconformance if expressed at the wrong intensity or in the wrong form.

Echoing Chu's complaint that the idealization of happiness in trans medicine prevents some trans people from accessing care, Ahmed (2010) argues that "[t]he demand for happiness is increasingly articulated as a demand to return to social ideals, as if what explains the crisis of happiness is not the failure of these ideals but our failure to follow them" (p. 7). To not be happy is to fail not only at happiness but also at "social ideals," such as gender normativity, that are meant to produce happiness. Trans medicine positions biomedical transition as the sole mechanism by which gender-related distress can be relieved, thereby implying that a realignment with gender normativity will bring trans people happiness (Malatino, 2019). Even for people who are not trans, unhappiness can still be read as symptomatic of gender nonconformance if they fail to adhere to binary gender norms, as in the case of men with undiagnosed depression. People who are not happy are failing to live up to the ideals that would make them happy. If people would do gender correctly, perhaps they would be happier. This is, of course, the fundamental assumption underpinning a diagnosis of Gender Dysphoria: if we fix the gender, we can fix the affect.

But what this medical model appears to overdetermine, in addition to the other critiques I've already described, is the order of causality surrounding trans distress. The *DSM-5* alleges that trans distress is "about" a person's gender incongruence (APA, 2013), insinuating that the incongruence *causes* the distress. Curing the incongruence through transition is thus meant to eliminate the source of the distress. I am left wondering, though, about how to differentiate gender dysphoric distress from variations of gender nonconformance precipitated by distress itself—those forms of gender nonconformance indexed by failed affects and emotions, those that do not neatly align with existing diagnostic classifications or clinical expectations. I am here referring to my sad secret, to the binary gendering of depressive characteristics and of the norms that regulate how our behaviors are affectively coded or made legible as emblematic of particular emotions.

What happens when a person's expression of negative affect does not align with the norms of their assigned gender? What happens to the man whose depressive symptoms go unrecognized because clinicians expect to see them only in women? To the woman with an addiction? Or to the nonbinary person like me who has a penchant for melodrama? Answers to all these questions lie within the realm of the trans depressive, who opens up the relationship between negative affect and gender nonconformance to additional configurations than the one prescribed by trans medicine. While a medical model presumes that a trans person's depressive characteristics are always already an effect of their gender incongruence, the trans depressive makes possible alternative arrangements, such as by regarding depression and transness as mutually constitutive or even by locating depression as a trans origin.

## A Sad Story of Trans Depressiveness

The value of these alternative arrangements is held in their capacity to honor trans people's negative affects without pathologizing them and to simultaneously contest the terms of gendered affect and affective disability. By taking seriously the generative potentialities of depression, its ways of producing both new orientations to the world and new variations of the gendered self, perhaps it will be easier to build on the coalitional opportunities made apparent at the nexus of trans and depression as modes of affective impairment. The clinical histories of trans and depression reveal the dual contingencies of Gender Dysphoria on depression and of negative affect on binary gender. Additionally, these histories show how each category finds its method of articulation through the other. Trans appears as a manifestation of pathological affect, and depression produces iterations of gender nonconformance. The trans depressive is how we might name the crossroads of these categories' distributed emergence.

In a way, I find the figure of the trans depressive comforting, not because it is necessarily liberating on its own but because it offers me a genealogy for my feelings and the possibility of community—that there may be other trans depressives living through and against the pull of bad feelings making us into bad genders. There is a slim chance that my depressive tendencies will ever go away. I'll likely always be a sad boy, and a part of me will probably always be sad about this sadness. But another part of me knows that being sad for so long has helped to shape other parts of me, parts that I love and treasure and perhaps parts that others might love and treasure about themselves, too. Many of these parts are the ones that I take to be indicative of my transness—my tearfulness, my moodiness, the way I pout when my man doesn't touch me enough. These pieces of me vibrate strongest when I'm sad.

In those moments when I am depressed, I feel furthest from the man others expect me to be, not because I hate being perceived as a man but because my feelings simply do not fit neatly within the category of a man. Being perceived as a man just feels incorrect. For now, these feelings are not equivalent to dysphoria or wanting to occupy my body differently. Maybe in time that will change; maybe it won't. Similarly, these feelings are not purely depression or reducible to an affective disorder, though that's certainly part of it. These feelings are a more complicated kind of trouble. A trouble that renders this muscled femme faggot—sniffling under a blanket, wringing their hands, and clenching their toes—gendered by their madness: a trans depressive.

# References

Ahmed, S. (2010). *The promise of happiness*. Duke University Press.

American Psychiatric Association. (1980). *Diagnostic and statistical manual of mental disorders* (3rd ed.). American Psychiatric Association.

American Psychiatric Association. (1994). *Diagnostic and statistical manual of mental disorders* (4th ed.). American Psychiatric Association.

American Psychiatric Association. (2013). *Diagnostic and statistical manual of mental disorders* (5th ed.). https://doi.org/10.1176/appi.books.9780890425596.

Awkward-Rich, C. (2017). Trans, feminism: *Or*, reading like a depressed transsexual. *Signs, 42*(4), 819-841.

Chu, A. L. & Drager, E. M. (2019). After Trans studies. *Transgender Studies Quarterly, 6*(1), 103-116.

Chu, A. L. (2019, November 24). My new vagina won't make me happy: And it shouldn't have to. *The New York Times*. https://www.nytimes.com/2018/11/24/opinion/sunday/vaginoplasty-transgender-medicine.html.

Cvetkovich, A. (2012). *Depression: A public feeling*. Duke University Press.

Davis, L. (2014). *The end of normal: Identity in a biocultural era*. University of Michigan Press.

Davy, Z. (2015). The DSM-5 and the politics of diagnosing transpeople. *Archives of Sex Behavior, 44.* 1165-1176.

Elliott, M. (2013). Gender differences in the determinants of distress, alcohol misuse, and related psychiatric disorders. *Society and Mental Health*, 3(2), 96-113.

Haraway, D. (1988). Situated knowledges: The science question in feminism and the privilege of partial perspective. *Feminist Studies*, 14(3), 575-599.

Hirshbein, L. D. (2009). *American melancholy: Constructions of depression in the twentieth century*. Rutgers University Press.

Johnson, J. (2011). Thinking with the thalamus: Lobotomy and the rhetoric of emotional impairment. *Journal of Literary & Cultural Disability Studies*, 5(2), 185-200.

Malatino, H. (2019). Future fatigue: Trans intimacies and Trans presents (or how to survive the interregnum). *Transgender Studies Quarterly*, 6(4), 635-658.

Metzl, J. M. (2003). *Prozac on the Ccouch: Prescribing gender in the era of wonder drugs*. Duke University Press.

Sadowsky, J. (2021). *The empire of depression: A new history*. Polity.

Schiesari, J. (1992). *The gendering of melancholia: Feminism, psychoanalysis, and the symbolics of loss in renaissance literature*. Cornell University Press.

Smith, D. T., Mouzon D. M., & Elliott, M. (2018). Reviewing the assumptions about men's mental health: An exploration of the gender binary. *American Journal of Men's Health*, 12(1), 78-89.

Stryker, S. (2008). *Transgender history*. Basic Books.

Wiggins, T. B. D. (2020). A perverse solution to misplaced distress: Trans subjects and clinical disavowal. *Transgender Studies Quarterly*, 7(1), 56-76.

# The Blackbird's Sonnet

*Jacquie Pruder St. Antoine*

There is nothing familiar or comfortable about where we are going.

How do you imagine that which you cannot conceive?

We don't know what these new ways of being/knowing/doing will look like, we don't have a clue. We don't have any idea what it looks, feels, smells, sounds, or tastes like or how it will even happen, we know "only that it needs to. And that it needs to be created by and for and with neurodivergent/mad/disabled/neuroanarchoqueer/rock/plant/water/animal/human peep(hole) coa lishons" (Smith, 2018, p. 165).

Yeah, I'm one of those tree/soil/flesh/animal/star/people. One of the Mad ones.

Madness is an individual experience, but one that illuminates the saneist/ableist/sexist/racist/classist forces that build the -ism forces. These -isms do not exist in singularity, but rather in intersecting oppressions and ordered pairs, building to a logic of domination (Warren, 2015). These forces (plenty of which grant me privilege as a cis-het white human) are entangled with my experiences as a Madwoman and can be only examined through my own cloudy lens. To examine Madness ethnographically would be to continue the Othering that has plagued not only my life, but the lives of my fellow Mad wanderers. It would be a continuation of the powers that have sought to eliminate me, or at least the parts of me that are viewed as undesirable. We've done enough of that.

Autoethnography is my shield and sword.

But it can't just be my story,

ya know?

It has to be color and scent, paint and yarn and buttons, shrieking laughter in the night and deep grieving wails, lines and slashes, new words (or worlds) that are real, imagined, or something wholly out of this stratum. Nah, words aren't right for describing what it is like to be Other. It is needles in kitchens and glowing green digits on your stove clock. Other is the *whomp, whomp, whomp* in your ears and swimming in the pond among frogs. Other is broken and whole, spilled paint and stained glass. These are the moments, sea glass, strips of birch bark, and shimmering glitter of the Others and how we *do* and *be* the Mad turn.

At least, maybe.

## May We Never Be Useful Trees

Sitting on the swing in the backyard,
my eyes cast on the fallen tree and tangled brambles.
Their berries are not yet a lush purple-black,
but a mixture of soft white petals and knobbly green.
The forceful drum of a woodpecker echoes on the trees.
Branches sway side to side in a hypnotic rolling tide waltz.

At dusk from this spot wander tentative white-tailed deer,
sometimes with their joyful young.
With the new velvety antlers sprouting,
they clash against one another
as the rabbits scurry about nearby
(while I sometimes from indoors fuss at them to not eat the
Brussels sprouts...
but truth be told I don't mind much if they do,
this place was theirs before I was born).

On the ground beneath the apple tree where the swing is
roped
are blue jay feathers,
what remains from a friend who gave his life
to a Cooper's Hawk who has a nest high up in one of the
pines.
We find feathers among the browning needles and pine cones.
I mourn this bird-person.
I hold a vibrant feather between my thumb and index finger,
twisting it back and forth to catch the light.
My heart pulls in my chest, it aches.

Some human folks would tell you that these people,
the tree and woodpecker and blackberry people,
can't and don't know.
They would say they can't and don't feel.
Juniper-people and rock-people, are
"aware of nothing and, therefore, experience neither suffering

nor fear of death. They can and should be treated as resources for conscious beings" (Phelps, 2012, p. 216).

But...
Wildflowers grow less competitively next to their kin,
    develop different stem heights when growing next to
        siblings,
    protect themselves from inbreeding (Owen, 2007),
    but since humans do not have roots weaving beneath the
        soil
    and our language cannot capture this vibrant matter
    we are unable to understand
        (and thus reduce)
    this divergent consciousness.

Some human folks would tell you the same about me,
that I can't and don't know.
Women, and those traits traditionally viewed as "feminine",
can't and don't know things.
"Humble in character and submissive" (Griffin, 1978, p. 22)
women-human-people
are less objective.
This justifies and naturalizes
the domination of men over women.
It positions me as lacking in relation.
The centering of men
and Othering of women (Griffin, 1978; Plumwood, 2002)
is just one hierarchical relationship

that can be examined to understand the ways
historically created assumptions,
    (cause every month is white-man-person history
    month)
formed,
internalized,
exchanged,
built,
perpetuated,
protected,
defended
"as 'regimes of truth,'
  come together to
    create,
    rationalize,
    maintain,
    guard,
    multiply
    these patterns of belief and behavior" (Martusewicz,
      2019, p. 3).

These oppressive systems
are quiet
(not like a forest, because have you ever been in one?
If you have ever met a blue jay you know what I'm saying.)
but like an empty shopping mall,
or the top of a parking garage.
Quiet and seemingly benign,
working hard to make it appear

that hierarchies
    (and the disparity
        in power,
        resources,
        rights,
        freedoms,
        and advantages
        that flow from hierarchies)
        are natural,
        good,
        normal,
        and beyond modification (Jensen, 2015).

Centrism centers and Others to invent superiority;
    man/woman,
    white/black,
    reason/emotion,
    mind/body,
    culture/nature,
    human/nature
    with each of these intersecting and building to a logic of
        domination
    (Martusewicz, Edmundson, & Lupinacci, 2015; Foster &
        Martusewicz, 2019; Martusewicz, 2019).
We are taught
    "to idealize the human mind or soul over a bodily, earthly
    existence, and the spiritual over the material, assuming a
    natural hierarchized division" (Martusewicz, 2019, p. 47).
Centrism separates the haves

from the have-nots.

Men have,

women have-not.

It is about separating queer people,

disabled people,

mad people,

and "neurodivergent people

(the neurohaves from the neuronots)...

it's about separating colored people

(because white is not a color, heh),

it's about separating colonized people (we're all colo-

nized)" (Smith, 2017, p. 86).

And it is about Mad people, too.

Experts know/ feel/ create/ do,

Mad folks do not.

These experts have growing lists,

about all the things broken in brains.


The Diagnostic and Statistical Manual of Mental Disorders,

Fifth Edition,

affectionately called DSM-5 (American Psychiatric Associa-

tion, 2013)

by close and personal friends,

outlines two-hundred and ninety-seven

(297!)

mental disorders,

each with specific diagnostic criteria,

an outline of potential causes,

and recommended interventions.

That's an awful lot of mental disorders,
so each has a number code.
For convenience.

Irrational, confused, distressed.
Intense, prolonged, avoidant.
The terms are psycho-medical and psycho-legal,
known to the masses as depression, psychosis,
and the like (LeFrancois, Menzies, & Reaume, 2013).

"What do you suppose it's like to be a knower,"
I ask the giant apple tree from which my swing hangs.
I look up at the soft white flowers that cover the branches.
When the wind catches the exquisite blooms,
petals cascade down from the crooked, twiggy offshoots
like snow falling on a warm day.

The tree creaks and yawns quietly,
the stretching and rolling of decades.
"I suppose they might tell you
knowledge is objective and sure.
That criteria is neutral and observable.
That knowing and knowledge
are culturally removed
and certain (Martusewicz, 2019),"
I go on as my eyes trace the lines in the tree's bark,
going down the thick base
to where the roots curl into the dirt.

These knowers say trees growing in the forest
should be useful
and women who work in offices
should be emotionally stable (Griffin, 1978).
Knowers ask if each tree is worth the space it grows in
and if the work provided by women is necessary (Griffin,
    1978).
Do we grow straight to reach the light
    and produce
    and produce
    and produce?
I look up at the knobby branches of the tree,
    a tree which I have never known to produce apples
    any larger than my palm,
    but which feed the deer-people, bird-people, and
    ant-people,
    fertilize the soil-people,
    provide for the bee-people,
    bring joy to the human-people.
"They'd say you aren't worth the land you inhabit,"
 I utter to the tree,
"That you are overripe
 and past your best growing years..."

And so like...
    So what?
    What does this have to do with
        candy-colored pills in brown bottles near your

kitchen sink,
 white-walled doctor's offices and stiff leather
 couches.
So what does it tell us about
 an opened paperclip scraping across an inner wrist,
 maintaining spreadsheets of every gram of food,
 throwing away dishes you cannot bear to wash.
What and how we do/be/create/survive/exist
the Mad turn is rooted in this huge,
 fancy, fantastic word
 (one that I didn't know about until years into my graduate coursework).
Epistemology is one of those jargoned words
that keeps feelers from participating
in conversations about what it is like to do/be Mad.
What is knowing and knowledge,
who gets to know and create knowledge,
what counts as truth and fact?
Some thinkers might tell you
knowledge is only created by those white guys,
the knowers who are objective and unemotional.
Some thinkers might tell you
KNOWledge
(with a capital KNOW)
is always culturally removed (Martusewicz, 2019)
 but other folks say our understandings are
 (and will always be)
 incomplete (Martusewicz, 2019).
 That "Truth and Knowledge are dead and turning moldy"

(Smith, 2018, p. 59).
The human-people who are considered knowers
and the thinking that is considering knowing
isn't Mad.
We inherited an institutional, ideological, and psychological
    system
    (that isn't broken, it's operating)
which "naturalizes a whole series of hierarchized relation-
    ships that essentialize the power of the human mind to
    control and possess the world" (Martusewicz, 2019, p. 47).
    White coats,
    prescription pads,
    academic journals,
    textbooks,
    diagnostic checklists,
    bell curves –
        medical, psychiatric, and academic knowing,
        and the people who create and perpetuate that know-
            ing,
        are the ways we are told we may come to know.

## We are Blackbirds in the Bulrush

Meandering steps take me down the slope
to where the grass turns to marsh.
Cattails shoot from the wet ground,
swaying side to side in the breeze.
I was told decades ago this was a pond
where water flowed in from the creek.

You can still see the creek on maps,
 though anymore the water is mostly still.
I have traced it back across the miles to where it begins,
now I know it to be Tarabusi Creek.
Follow it farther and it leads to the River Rouge.
Though it is smaller than it once was,
as I understand anyway,
you can hear it trickle quietly after heavy rains.
Deer still gather to drink from it,
it gives life to the cattails that reach above my head.

I recall my partner and oldest daughter
scooping water from the marsh
in a clear jar,
letting it settle in our kitchen window.
Over days you could see
an entire universe that existed inside.
I could not even begin to tell you
the names of the small,
   swimming,
   shelled,
   and worm-like beings
   that inhabited just those twelve ounces of marsh water
      and mud.

Some human - people,
(especially those who exist in
corporate - commodified - capitalist - modernist - western -
      eurocentric - white - neoliberal - dominant

- industrial culture)
"assume that art, philosophy, and spirituality are impractical,
that they're just impractical luxury activities" (Akulukjuk &
Rasmussen, 2019, p. 67).
But other folks,
the human and non-human beings that
live - breathe - exist - disrupt - be - question - take up space,
"believe that art is all around us.
Inuit definitely know this.
They didn't have to differentiate
art from the rest of the world -
art is something that is in everything" (Akulukjuk &
Rasmussen, 2019, p. 69-70).
Art is in everything.
Maybe it is not *in* everything,
rather art *is* everything.
Or, everything is art.
I see deer tracks in the snow,
microscopic crustaceans in the mud,
the sensual red and winding vines of wild strawberries,
joyfully fuzzy dandelions reaching through sidewalk cracks
as being as wonderfully made as a concert composition or museum-hung portrait.

And stories, no matter how painful,
are not luxuries but spiritual, personal, political necessity.
Not just pretty stories,
no fairytales here,
but hard and painful stories.

Vulnerable stories.

Stories that make you shriek with laughter

or gnaw your inner cheek until it is raw and pulpy.

Stories that hurt and evoke and writhe.

Poem stories, dance stories, song stories, film stories, paint
stories –

I am convinced that these stories cannot be told in ways
that aren't wired, weird, wild.

Stories you forgot about,

that ache as they pour out from your pores,

not because they happened to you,

but because the story isn't just yours.

It is the story of those you care deeply for, too.

That's what aches.

If it was just my story I could bear it,

I could hold it quietly and tenderly.

We build ourselves up to speak these stories into the universe,

the multiverse, the perceived reality in which we find ourselves.

[Full disclosure, questioning what we deem reality
is one of my so-called symptoms that can send me
quickly down a thought spiral. Every horrible news
story, potential hazard, experience of suffering or
pain, reaffirms the terrors that intrude (Jago, 2002). If
I think these things – though often it feels as though
they are not my thoughts – surely it means that I am

capable of doing something terrible. Perhaps one day, against my will, I will jerk the steering wheel and send myself into the barrier. This thought is the spark that begins a large, winding spiral. Inward and inward it winds, the spiraling becoming smaller and smaller for days and weeks until it has so long spiraled that I forget I am in a spiral at all. It is often in the spiral that I begin to feel like an imposter walking around inside a suit of flesh. I wonder if I can possibly be a real person; surely a real person would not think this way. There is a terrible sense of watching myself "disappear, unable to act in self-defense" (Jago, 2002, p. 743). Worse yet, the spiral often extends so long I go beyond disappearing and begin to wonder if I ever existed. "It's as though I've never been" (Derby, 2013, fig. 3), or that, perhaps, what I view as my life is all some type of projection. I become consumed by the thought that perhaps none of it is real. Once I heard an interview with Neil deGrasse Tyson in which he said it was very likely that our existence is a program on someone's hard drive (Moskowitz, 2016). Hearing him say that made me feel less alone. It also made me feel absolutely terrified.]


"One story always begets another" (Poole & Ward, 2013, p. 100).
Stories not for navel-gazing individualism,
but for connecting.
In the reception of my story it becomes your story,

and reverberates.
Stories rolling into stories,
bending and twisting.
We call these communal stories
by an academified (L. Johnk, personal communication, May
    21, 2016) name.
We call these stories autoethnography,
because they are greater than the singularity
of the teller's experiences.
Each is "more than one person's story" (Lockford, 2017, p. 31).
It is in our collective Disabled-Ecojustice-Mad-EcoFemi-
    nist-Crip-entangled-multi&antidisciplinary-Neuroqueer-
Poetic-ArtstBased-Divergent-relational-qualitative-onto-
    logical-epistemiolgical telling/yelling/keening/dancing/
    crying/painting/writing/singing/performing
that allows for reflexivity (Marti, 2017)
and resistance (Denizen, 2017).

Here I stand at this marsh-place,
sturdy reeds reaching to the billowy clouds.
The woodpecker still drums somewhere
beyond the clearing
and red-winged blackbirds
(if you've met these birds,
you know they are mean as can be)
dive in and out of the cattails.
*Conk-ra-leeeeeeee -*
They demand to be noticed,
their swooping and shrieking

cut only by the tedious, monotonous,

industrious efforts of the adept woodpecker.

*Conk-ra-leeeeeeee -*

The cry screams in angry horror.

I suppose they are likely Mad-bird-people.

How could they *not* be?

Looking down at the water,

seeping between the bulrush

and impossibly long grasses,

making out a reflection is nearly impossible.

The murk distorts the blue sky above,

the lines of my face,

the wind-dancing reeds.

Some waters are too murky

for clear reflexivity,

mine certainly are,

so each that looks on brings their own context.

The truth

(with a little t)

comes with what we see reflected,

(I suppose what the Mad-blackbird-person sees

is not what this Mad-human-person sees).

What we see comes to light only in being seen and spoken,

in the telling and reception (Peterson, 2016).


Just as I suppose the industrious woodpeckers

look at the Mad-blackbird-people

and wonder....

Huh...

Some human-people
look at the Mad-human-people
And wonder...
Huh...
But they don't just wonder.


They excluded us
on the Ship of Fools sailing down the Flemish canals (Fou-
    cault, 1988).
They lobotomized us
and wrapped us in wet sheets
in attempts to end our Madness (Whitaker, 2002).
Madness has been used
to account for a representational danger,
one that deems the Mad not quite human (Goffman, 1986).
They locked us,
and anyone else who did not abide by the social norms,
away in asylums used as instruments of control (St-Amand
    & LeBlanc, 2013).
Men turned difference
into an opportunity for dominance (Jensen, 2017);
They set out to master nature,
decided earth should be called land;
trees, timber;
animals called domesticated or hunted (Griffin, 1978).
They "reified **genera** and **species**
of *saturated* difference
by naming and codifying them:

**anencephaly**
**Prader- Willi syndrome**
**cerebral palsy**
**cri-du-chat syndrome**
**microcephaly**
**Down syndrome**
**moderate cognitive disability**

and all the numbered Others of them (Smith, 2018, p. 54).

They defined emotions into hysteria,

a Madness situated in the womb and of women (Griffin,
1978).

Responses to the limitations placed on women in the 19th
century,

reactions to real injustices,

were used as proof of irrationality

and cause for intervention (St-Amand & LeBlanc, 2013).


They didn't just pathologize us -

label, objectify, medicalize, arrest, psychiatric hold, institu-
tionalize, regulate, bell curve, norm, lobotomize, segre-
gate, sterilize, quantify, measure, test, and dissect us.

After they did all that,

then...


They stole our stories.

Professionals co-opted survivor knowledge

into a buzz-word to benefit public health systems

while demanding disclosure (Penney & Prescott, 2016).

They stole our stories.
While I share my truths with a hope of radical change,
a psychiatric system uses them
to further its own interests (Voronka, Landry, Reid, McFar-
    lane, Reville, & Church, 2012).

They stole our stories.
Madness does not fit with cultural values of rationality and
    credibility.
They told us we were too close,
too unreliable, too sick, too confused,
too clouded to tell/speak/know/feel
what any, all, or some of it meant.
So they asked for our stories,
then erased us "in/from the 'record'" (Harris, 2017),
and called it ethnography.

They stole our stories.
Then they molded them,
made them marketable,
produced stage shows, films,
music, works of art, academic papers,
books, novels, short stories, and poems,
directed by Ron Howard, starring Dustin Hoffman
and Joaquin Phoenix,
that won awards
about us,
but without us.

They stole our stories.

They used them as proof;

proof of derangement and deterioration.

Proof of difference, deviance, difficulty, deficit (Smith,
    2008).

They used them to provide scientific-sounding arguments,

 to "serve as rationalizations for doing harm

to the most vulnerable elements of society," (Groce &
    Marks, 2000, p. 821).

They used them as entertainment and

acting exercises, characters, and plotlines.

They perpetuated stories that painted us

as violent and unpredictable,

unable to hold jobs and care for families,

scary and dangerous and pitiful,

without acknowledging the

"emotional, relational, biological, cultural, and historical
    forces" (Jago, 2002, p. 733)

that shape our experiences.

## A Bird-Person of a Different Color

Onetwothreefourfivesix

onetwothree, onetwo

1-2-3, onetwo, One

onetwo, One Two

ONEtwo

   *Deep breath*

123

onetwothree
One-two-three
One, two, three, 456
One, two, three, four, five, six
One, two, three, four, five, six
Regaining breath, I count.
But only ever to six.
I bring myself back to the air in my lungs,
back to the tight throat and grinding teeth.
Return myself to the bottoms of my feet,
wet through my stained (previously) white canvas shoes.
Attention drifts from the soppy shoe-bottoms,
to the stinging skin picked away from my thumbnail.
*Conk-ra-leeeeeeee,*
screeches the red-winged blackbird.
Smiling, I recall how the red-winged blackbirds
dove at me and my sister and our dogs,
a glossy Golden Retriever and pale Yellow Lab,
as we swam in the murky pond,
caught frogs with our muddy hands,
and learned how to be stewards of a place
from our father as children.
I put my thumb in my mouth,
the scarlet blood that seeps out disappearing.

The counting helps.
It brings me back to the marsh,
to the creaking frogs and
the wind as it catches tree branches.

The counting helps.
It grounds me to the marsh,
tethers me to the blackbirds' shrieking
by an invisible string.
Six has always been my number,
the one I resort to when things become overwhelming.

> The faster I can say the numbers the better. Sometimes
> I only make it to two because counting to six takes too
> long. There was the one time things all fell apart. That
> time I lay in bed for days and pressed my spine against
> the cold cement cinder blocks of my apartment and
> counted. And counted. And counted. I organized my
> closet, and lay on the bathroom floor to feel the cool
> tile against my cheekbone, and tried not to breathe so
> fast that I became light-headed.

That was one time. Every time is different.
There were pills in red bottles near the kitchen sink.
Then I assumed there was a pill
to fix the fast thoughts and the worry
and the pacing and panic.
I told them my stories
and they told me something was wrong with me,
that everybody didn't think about

> Reality not being real.
> Sleep being a portal to a carbon copy of your life.
> Staying awake because when you sleep maybe you're
>     dead.
> Your mind leaving your body and not being able to leave
>     your car at Target.

I told them my stories in quiet rooms,
sitting on uncomfortable chairs.
They nodded and they wrote them down,
they laced their fingers together and asked me
about my childhood, my parents' divorce, my ex-boyfriend,
     my job, my students, my family, my marriage, my labor
     and delivery, my assault, my habits, my fears, my com-
     pulsions, my routines.
And I told them.
I told them because I didn't know what else to do.

Telling them didn't make me feel better.
Taking the pills didn't really either.
So I learned to live with it, through it,
I came to accept myself as part of it.

So instead I waded through,
I painted and I lifted weights,
planted pole beans and
ran until my lungs heaved.
Threw a frisbee for a dog-friend,
got a North American guide of birds
and bought all the black oil sunflower I could carry.
Observed the Sabbath
as I filled the feeders.
Took blonde girls for stroller rides,
read books (so many books) and
listened to Nirvana, Lady Gaga, and Bruce Springsteen.

Climbed a mountain in Colorado and
read about Australia, Kenya, India,
and Japan with middle schoolers.
Wrote hard about things that hurt.


I learned what I could about
arts-based research and autoethnography,
finding connection,
an opportunity to listen,
hope to heal,
disruption of the comfortable (Lockford, 2017),
and vision as means to engage imagination.

Autoethnography, poetry, fiction, dance, music, and narratives offer alternatives to traditional academic scholarship that is "inclusive and disruptive to the status quo, particularly when it comes to disability perspectives" (Nocella, George, & Lupinacci, 2019, p. 3). Rejecting ethnography that Others and dissects, engaging in "inquiry situated in experience" that integrates both theory and practice "by embodying frameworks for understanding and using those frameworks as tools for thinking and living" (Adams & Jones, 2018, pp. 152-153). In short, refuse the notion that you can ever be outside this thing we call research. Refuse the notion that there is some singular truth. We are always inside and part of it, whether we call it fieldwork or not. This understanding requires embracing emotions and connections, accepting a perspective in which there are multiple truths, and

adopting (maybe even seizing) a notion that written
representations can never be the same as actual lived
experiences (Smith, 2018).

So I committed to these methods,
for myself and for others.
I made a commitment to being truthful
over Truth as a place to start,
but it can't be where we end.
It isn't enough.

Rather than being defined
by the diagnostic power of professionals,
I claim the title of Mad.
I reclaim Mad as a way
to "radically and creatively invest it
with disability history, politics, and pride
while simultaneously questioning paradigms
of independence, normalcy, and medicalization" (Taylor,
     2017, p. 12).
I reject a "fetishization of sameness and individualism"
     (Nocella, 2017, p. 143)
and instead, with the neurodivergence movement,
accept the "infinite variations of neurocognitive function-
     ing" (Walker, 2014) within humans.

My madness isn't past tense (Smith, 2018).
Recognizing that I have been pathologized
by a culture that Others me

doesn't make it easier to breathe.

"I'm not broken.

I don't need to be fixed.

I don't need a pill" (St. Antoine, 2017, p. 100).

Knowing that my disability is constructed

doesn't make living less difficult.

I reject the inferiorizing and marginalization,

but I can't escape it.

Rejecting a medical model, capitalist, human-centric narrative

of my bodymind doesn't make it any easier to exist in this
culture.


Simply existing as a Madwoman

is an act of powerful influence and resistance.

Existing as an openly Madwoman

in academic spaces is political and ethical necessity.

Because I have the privilege to make it so,

I have to.

Challenging the dominant context of institutionalization

requires "millions of small acts and restraints" (Berry, 2002,
p. 202).


It isn't just about including Mad people and Mad stories.

The Mad Turn has to be anti-racist.

It must denounce loudly supremacy in all forms

   Human supremacy, white supremacy, male supremacy,

   ablebodyminded supremacy.

Our work must challenge hierarchies

in all their intersecting and building forms.

We have to talk/write/sing/perform/create

about hard and ugly things –

like eugenics, the Galton guy, racism, sexism, classism, ableism, colonialism, sanism [Because disabled, Deaf, black and brown, racial and ethnic minority, indigenous, Mad, women, impoverished human-people were sterilized, institutionalized, segregated, murdered in the name of pseudo-science that invented tests to prove some folks had superior, valuable genes (Farber, 2008; Cohen, 2016; Smith, 2018). And wouldn't you guess the folks with superior genes, which include "health, energy, ability, manliness, and courteous disposition" (Galton, 1904, pp. 2), were white, upper-class men. Everyone else, they were to blame for insanity, criminality, pauperism, sexually transmitted infections, epilepsy, the decaying moral fiber of 'Merica, promiscuity – so even after sterilizing, they kept them institutionalized (Comer, 1936) because if the state can demand such a sacrifice as sterilization for the supposed benefit of society, the state is able to demand every lesser sacrifice (Berns, 1957)].

We have to talk/write/sing/perform/create

multiple, cascading (little t) truth, fiction, and art –

[Because, like stories, fiction has truths to share about the world (Smith, 2019) and through it deep wounds can be revealed (Stanley, 2019). In doing the talking-writing-singing-dancing-performing-creating-imagining, we are the inquired and the inquirer. As Mäkelä (2019) describes, it is "questionable to call it "making" art. Oftentimes it feels more like *the art is happening through me*" (p. 115). The art itself has a soul and we can make and use it to impact an audience, we attempt to convey something which ripples out into our world (Akulukjuk & Rasmussen, 2019). This work is never finished, it remains always a question, always a work in progress (Smith, 2019), always a draft because with each reading/listening/experiencing/viewing new meanings, understandings, emotions, and receptions will evolve.]

We have to talk/write/sing/perform/create
about hope and wonder –
[Because as Wendell Berry (2010) writes, it is hard to have hope. It often feels harder every day. For "hope must not depend on feeling good" (Berry, 2010, p. 91). Often, it doesn't feel good – it is hard and uncomfortable and requires a great deal of courage. In order to work toward a more just and equitable world, to resist injustice, to demand you "be with us or get out of the way" (Smith, 2018, p. 182), we must choose hope – decide on it, prioritize it. Day after day after day.
"hope is a choice.
it's a decision.
like love, lots of times it takes real, hard work.
sweat. labor.
dreaming of and working for what is right and good is always worth doing" (Smith, 2021). Interdependence, meaningful work (Martusewicz, 2019), challenging

damaging systems, cultivating a graceful path (Jensen, 2015), perhaps these are places in which we may begin to find our hope. "Find your hope, then, on the ground under your feet" (Berry, 2010, p. 93).]

We have to talk/write/sing/perform/create

about love –

[Because creation in all forms is "holy, whole, and demanding of our care... We are constantly being compelled toward love without recognizing it. And we don't recognize it because we have been taught that love is inferior to reason as a way of being and that the world is other, there for us to use as needs and wants be" (Martusewicz, 2019, p. 46). As hope is a choice, is work, so too is love. We are not able to make sense of it and words cannot possibly capture it. But we are called to do this work above all others and, many times, it begins by loving our crazy/bonkers/unbalanced/ kooky/disturbed/deranged/quirky/fruit loop selves despite it all (and you know the *it all* cannot possibly be contained to the words on this page).]

Doing this work,

doing disability studies, Mad studies, ecojustice education, eco-feminism

"requires us to be ANTIdisciplinary.

to embrace complexity.

Instead of working to simplify, we need to work to complexify" (Smith, 2018, p. 158)

There is no doubt
we will continue to be "confronted by a general acceptance"
by those that surround us
that there is "no reason to question any of it" (Martusewicz,
    2014, p. 35).
There is and will continue to be pressure to
assimilate, sit down, be quiet, be rational, be palatable, stop
    questioning, pass.
To this apathy and rationalizing,
I choose love "in the form of active collective responsibility
and meaningful work as an antidote for despair
and exhaustion" (Martusewicz, 2019, p. 19).


So this *thing* we call the Mad Turn,
it isn't a *thing* at all.
The Mad Turn is us.
    We are/be/breath/do/live/walk/roll/crawl/dance/scream/
    sing/write/paint/perform/run/
    lift/sleep/wear/where/laugh/keen/mourn/rejoice/exist/
    love/lose/speak/utter/worship/cry
    the Mad Turn because it is us,
    all of us (probably you, too).
    Just surviving, living (un)well
    living Mad,
    is our most academic, political, and radical act.


This is how we do/be/are the Mad Turn.
We live. We talk about it and how

painful and haunting,

wonderful and miraculous

it is to exist Mad.

Mad people dancing, Mad people writing, Mad people singing, Mad people talking,

Mad people creating, Mad people imagining, Mad people
doing, Mad people teaching –

This is the Mad Turn.

We are the Mad Turn.

It isn't going to be pretty. It isn't going to always make
sense or be linear.

It'll hurt, sometimes it'll hurt a lot.

It can't be quantified, it can't be measured, it can't be
contained in books or journals.

The Mad Turn spills off the margins (heck, what are margins?)

because the Mad Turn is living unapologetically Mad lives.


The woodpecker has stopped drumming,

his work done (for the moment at least).

But, the red-winged blackbird still

screams, still dives.

To make sense of the enclosure

we have experienced,

to make un-sense of it,

to un-learn it,

unpack it as a construction of "what is what,"

to feel it more deeply,

to become and survive it.

The red-winged blackbird still screams, still dives,

because she doesn't know what else to do.

Whatever it is that makes it so painful,
whatever it is that makes my despair so deep,
"It is always here, always becoming, always present.
It never goes away.
It doesn't know how.
And I wouldn't know what to do without it.
I don't know what to do without it" (Smith, 2018, p. 133).

## Afterword

Once upon a time,
I met someone who changed my life.
At the time,
I couldn't know how they would,
or even that they would.
But they did.
Not sure who I would be without this person,
sometimes I wonder if I would even still be around.
In 2015, I could not have written these words.
While I would love to say this is all of the story,
this is but one small piece of it.
There are so many things that remain unwritten and unsaid.
Some of them need saying,
some of them do not.

I have talked about my Madness
at lots of professional places.
Every time I speak,

I am met with silence when it comes time for questions.
After the session has ended, someone always approaches,
almost always a woman,
who says, "Me too."

This is the power of autoethnography,
arts-based research, poems, and stories.
Hearts change.
Stories matter.
Statistics have a place.
Statistics stun,
but I haven't yet seen them move people to action (Lock-
    ford, 2017).
Stories matter
"because power is enacted and felt upon the body,
and it is there that the true cost is measurable" (Lockford,
    2017, p. 30).

In writing and telling,
there are words
that I have never shared publicly.
There are moments of fear.
It must begin somewhere.
It isn't just me,
I think we all feel deep pain.
I think we all feel torment.
Sharing stories is integral for my work as a Mad person,
it is integral for my survival, too.
It is only by telling hard, terrifying truths

that I think we can change the world
(by breakfast tomorrow).

## Pinky-Promise I am Not Making this Stuff Up

Adams, T. E., & Jones, S. H. (2018). The art of autoethnography. In P. Leavy (Ed.), *Handbook of Arts-Based Research* (pp. 141-164). Guilford Press.

Akulukjuk, T., & Rasmussen, D. (2019). Art is that which takes something real and makes it more real than it was before. In R. Foster, J. Mäkelä, & R. A. Martusewicz (Eds.), *Art, Ecojustice, and Education: Intersecting Theories and Practices* (pp. 59 - 70). Routledge.

American Psychiatric Association. (2013). *Diagnostic and statistical manual of mental disorders* (5th ed.). Author.

Berns, W. (1953). Buck v. Bell: Due process of law?. *The Western Political Quarterly, 6*(4), 762-775.

Berry, W. (2002). Conservation and local economy. In N. Wirzba (Ed.), *The art of the commonplace: The agrarian essays of Wendell Berry* (pp. 194-204). Counterpoint.

Berry, W. (2010). Sabbaths 2007, VI. In *Leavings: Poems* (pp. 91-93). Counterpoint.

Cohen, A. (2016). *Imbeciles: The Supreme Court, American eugenics, and the sterilization of Carrie Buck.* Penguin Press.

Comer, S. D. (1936). The growing need for a national eugenic program. *Bios, 7*(3), 176-187.

Denizen, N. K. (2017) A manifesto for performance autoethnography. *International Review of Qualitative Research, 10*(1), 44-45.

Derby, J. (2013). Accidents happen: An art autopathography on mental disability. *Disability Studies Quarterly, 33*(1).

Farber, S. A. (2008). U.S. Scientists' role in the eugenics movement (1907-1939): A contemporary biologist's perspective. *Zebrafish, 5*(4), 243-245.

Foster, R., & Martusewicz, R. A. (2019). Introduction. In R. Foster, J. Mäkelä, & R. A. Martusewicz (Eds.), *Art, Eco-Justice, and education: Intersecting theories and practices* (1-10). Routledge.

Foucault, M. (1988). *Madness and civilization: A history of insanity in the age of reason.* Vintage Books.

Galton, F. (1904). Eugenics: Its definition, scope, and aims. *American Journal of Sociology, 10*(1), 1-25.

Goffman, E. (1986). *Stigma: Notes on the management of spoiled identity.* Simon & Schuster, Inc.

Griffin, S. (1978). *Woman and nature: The roaring inside her.* Counterpoint.

Groce, N., & Marks, J. (2000). The Great Ape Project and disability rights: Ominousundercurrents of eugenics in action. *American Anthropologist, 102*, 919-822.

Harris, A. (2017). An adoptee autoethnographic femifesta. *International Review of Qualitative Research, 10*(1), 24-28.

Jago, B. J. (2002). Chronicling an academic depression. *Journal of Contemporary Ethnography, 31*(6). 729-757.

Jensen, R. (2015). *Plain radical: Living, loving, and learning to leave the planet gracefully.* Soft Skull Press.

LeFrançois, B. A., Menzies, R. & Reaume, G. (2013). Introducing mad studies. In B. A.

LeFrancois, R. Menzies, & G. Reaume (Eds.), *Mad matters:*

*A critical reader in Canadian mad studies* (1-22). Canadian Scholars Press, Inc.

Lockford, L. (2017). Now is the time for autoethnography. *International Review of Qualitative Research, 10*(1), 29-32.

Marti, J. E. (2017). *Starting fieldwork: Methods and experiences.* Waveland Press, Inc.

Martusewicz, R. (2014). Letting our hearts break: On facing the "hidden wound" of human supremacy. *Canadian Journal of Environmental Education, 19,* 31-46.

Martusewicz, R. A. (2019). Love in the commons: Eros, eco-ethical education, and a poetics of place. In R. Foster, J. Mäkelä, & R. A. Martusewicz (Eds.) *Art, EcoJustice, and Education: Intersecting Theories and Practices* (pp. 166-177). Routledge.

Martusewicz, R. (2019). *A pedagogy of responsibility: Wendell Berry for EcoJustice Education.*Routledge.

Martusewicz, R. A., Edmundson, J., & Lupinacci, J. (2015). *EcoJustice education: Towarddiverse, democratic, and sustainable communities.* Routledge.

Moskowitz, C. (2016, April 7). Are we living in a computer simulation? *Scientific American.* Retrieved from https://www.scientificamerican.com/article/are-we-living-in-a-computer-simulation/

Nocella II, A. J. (2017). Defining eco-ability: Social justice and the intersectionality of disability,nonhuman animals, and ecology. In S. J. Ray & J. Sibara (eds.), *Disability studies and the environmental humanities: Toward an eco-crip theory* (pp. 141-167). University of Nebraska Press.

Nocella, A. J., George, A. E., & Lupinacci, J. (2019).

Introduction: Defending and sharing space and place for Eco-ability voices for total liberation. In A. J. Nocella II, A. E. George, & J. Lupinacci (Eds.) *Animals, Disability, and the End of Capitalism: Voices from the Eco-Ability Movement* (pp. 1-8). Peter Lang.

Owen, J. (2007, June 14). *Plants can recognize, communicate with relatives, study finds.* Retrieved from http://news.nationalgeographic.com/news/2007/06/070614-plants.html

Penney, D., & Prescott, L. (2016). The co-optation of survivor knowledge: the danger of substituted values and voice. In J. Russo & A. Sweeney (Eds.) *Searching for a rose garden: Challenging psychiatry, fostering mad studies* (35-45). PCCS Books Ltd.

Phelps, N. (2012). Infinite ethics: An inclusive vision for a diverse world. In A. J. Nocella, J. K. C. Bentley, & J. M. Duncan (Eds.), *Earth, animal, and disability liberation: The rise of the eco-ability movement* (pp. 205-222). Peter Lang Publishing.

Plumwood, V. (2002). *Environmental culture: The ecological crisis of reason.* Routledge.

Poole, J. M., & Ward, J. (2013). "Breaking open the bone": Storying, sanism, and mad grief. In B. A. LeFrancois, R. Menzies, & G. Reaume (Eds.) *Mad Matters: A Critical Reader in Canadian Mad Studies* (pp. 94 - 104). Canadian Scholars Press Inc.

Smith, P. (2021, January 21). Hope is a choice. it is a decision. like love, lots of times it takes real, hard work. sweat. labor. dreaming of and working for what is right and good is always worth doing. there are no benefits for cynicism [Facebook status update]

Smith, P. (2018). *Writhing writing: Moving towards: Moving towards a mad poetics.* Autonomous Press.

St. Antoine, J. P. (2017). Madness in the time of grunge. In D. A. Ryskamp & S. Harvey (Eds.), *Spoon Knife 2: Test Chamber* (pp. 92-101). Autonomous Press.

St-Amand, N., & LeBlac, E. (2013) Women in 19th – Century asylums: Three exemplary women; A New Brunswick Hero. In B. A. LeFrancois, R. Menzies, & G. Reaume (Eds.), *Mad matters: A critical reader in Canadian mad studies* (38-48). Canadian Scholars Press, Inc.

Taylor, S. (2017). *Beasts of burden: Animal and disability liberation.* The New Press.

Voronka, J., Landry, D., Reid, J. McFarlane, B., Reville, D., & Church, K. (2012). Recovering our stories: A small act of resistance. *Studies in Social Justice, 6*(1), 85-101.

Walker, N. (2014, September 27). Neurodiversity: Some basic terms & definitions. Retrieved from http://neurocosmopolitanism.com/neurodiversity-some-basic-terms-definitions/

Warren, Karen J. (2015) Feminist Environmental Philosophy. In E. N. Zalta (Ed.), *The Stanford Encyclopedia of Philosophy (Summer 2015 Edition)*. Retrieved from https://plato.stanford.edu/archives/sum2015/entries/feminism-environmental

Whitaker, R. *Mad in America: Bad science, bad medicine, and the enduring mistreatment of the mentally ill.* Basic Books.

# the possibilities of a post-psy Mad studies

## another damn man[maid]ifesto

*phil smith*

Richard Ingram,
who created the ideer
of Mad Studies,
said that id
needs tuh be    a way
       away way
of doing and being that
"unsettles *all* academic disciplines...
it needs to have
as part of its end goal
the shaking up,
the disturbing,
of all forms of academic knowledge."   (Ingram, 2016, p. 14).

Ingram said that, in creating idself,
Mad Studies would need to practice
"sly normality," "...by showing

that there is method in our madness;
and on the other side,
preserving madness in our method...
It has to retain components of madness..."

(Ingram, 2016, p.<br>13).

how might we create
a Mad Studies that is
Mad    in       method
a Mad  un       method
a Mad anti      method
a       method
in Mad-Studies-that-might-be
that unsettles and is unsettling?
we have known for      some time

        sum thyme

        sub lime

        mean time      [greenwich colonialist
                        center of the    whirring
                                        word
                                        whirled]

despite the absolutely      incredible

                    bull-headed
                    ostrich-like

unwillingness of many
to pull their heads out of the sand
    among other plazas of ill repute
    i'll leave where those might      be
    on the human anato              my

to your sufficiently extraordinary collective
imaginings
that the kind of knowledge  may      king

            see          king

            explo(d)    ring

            manifeste    ring      destiny

done by        the psy-complex

            the sci-complex

            the spy-complex

            the cyclop[s]lex          (exlax?)

as well as social science schoolar      ship

                                     boat

                                     dinghy

                                     thingy

gimme dat gimme dat gimme gimme dat thing(y).

is not

has never been

cannot ever be

objective                               (Berg & Seeber,
2016; Gallagher,
1998; 2001; 2006;
Gallagher, Connor,
& Ferri, 2014;
Smith, 1999a;
1999b; St. Pierre,
2006; 2016).

the        empirical approach

         empire

         colonial

to understanding the world
goaded on by neoliberalism                    (St. Pierre, 2006)
and founded on an approach to science
called logical positivism
(the idea that knowledge
"...is grounded in scientific facts,
scientific evidence gathered
in the 'real' world from observation..." (St. Pierre, 2016, p.
                                                          23),

"is only an idea,
not the truth as it claims"                    (St. Pierre, 2016, p.
                                                          24),

the project to build
brick by brick
block by block
a solely empiricist foundation
for scientific understanding
is an entirely failed project.
a failure that we have known
for literally decades
we are   wholly                                (St. Pierre, 2006)
        holy
        holely
done wid dat.
it's over.
finished.
done.
kaput.
fini.

the failed project of empiricism
is based on scientism -
the ideology that empiricist work
is the    only
          best
way to understand and explore the world.
it's done undt over with,
but I want to     ack ack ack knowledge
that scientISM, positivISM, and empiricISM
remain at present entirely transcendent          al

                                                  Big Al

in research and policy,
and those who continue to work in it
don't even know it collapsed.
The ideology of scientism
asserts that all other views are,
by definition,
suspect
(in da crime uv da century).
it is a perspective
that claims itself to be neutral
(a claim that is itself, of course,
ideological, and not neutral):
"...those advocating neutrality
have worked themselves into a position...
of being able to accuse others
of being ideological
without having to acknowledge or account

for their own ideologies..." (Gallagher, 2001,
Gallagher pointed out two decades p. 242).
   ago that
"...a major goal of empiricist science
has been to develop law-like generalizations
which are essential for  explaining,
                predicting
                and controlling
the objects of study..." (Gallagher, 1998,
                                  p. 495).

this kind of goal
in science, about people,
is prepost      erous
   test        osterone
     "...seriously predicting [the] actions
     [of others] in a scientific sense...
     is an unrealizable goal
     offered by many..." (Gallagher, 1998,
                                  p. 498).

this kind of    empiricism
creating an    empire
of knowledge
in/uv/oven    Western
            White
            Enlightened
            Abled
hegemony
relies on     analytical
            anal tickle statistics

in order to make claims of     generalization,

    objectivity,

    and neutrality

        (St. Pierre, 2016).

analytical statistics

are not theyownselves

neutral or objective:

they are morally suspect

(uv crimes against all da udders).

the field of analytical statistics

was built and designed with one purpose:

to meet the needs

of Victorian era racism and ableism;

    "...the development of... statistical procedures

    were subjected to various manipulations

    necessary to accommodate eugenic ideology"

        (Gallagher, 2006,

        p. 99).

the     classist

    racist

    sexist

    saneist

    ableist

    all the other ists

        underpinnings of eugenicism

(now masquerading as empirical research)

continues to haunt and permeate research today

        (Smith, 2008).

Francis Galton,

cousin of Charles Darwin,

coined the term eugenics,

and fashioned the pseudo-science

in order to        disenfranchise,

                sterilize,

                and euthanize

those that the dominating        White,

                          male,

                          able bodyminded

                          middle-to-upper class

deemed less than human            (Smith, 2008).

to do this,

"Galton designed the normal curve,

and many of the currently used statistical procedures,

for the very purpose

of creating and enforcing social hierarchies"

                        (Gallagher, 2006,

                        p. 99).

even if the false claims to      objectivity

                        and neutrality

made by the version of empiricism

relied on in Western, Eurocentric science

was not riddled with ideological      holes,

                        holy holy holy

                        lord grid almighty

the eugenicist foundation of analytic statistics

makes it a project

that is morally re        prehensi        ble
                        prehensile (tail tall tale).

and besides,

"not everything that counts can be counted"
                        (Collini, 1999, p. 120).

the use of analytical statistics

in the psy-complex

in the spy-complex

is a moral choice that cannot be def        ended,
                and must        end.

perhaps worster,

all of this knowledge was created,

and continues to be so,

in institutions of higher education

in which knowledge itself

has become commodified,

and the work of researchers

increasingly        corporatized

      commodified

      reified,

"...privileging certain forms of knowledge

above others..."        (Berg & Seeber, 2016, p. 54).

this kind of commodification

creates a "knowledge economy"

that "emphasizes instrumentalism and marketability"
                (Berg & Seeber, 2016, p. 53).

Denzin and Giardina put it all togedder:

    ...those in higher education –

    especially those scholars

    in the humanities and social sciences

    doing        critical,

                    feminist,

                    poststructural,

                    postmodern,

                    and posthuman research –

face a cross-roads, one in which

(a) the act of research is inherently political;

(b) that act is governed by a particular free-market politics
of research in the corporate university;

(c) (post-)positivism still dominates this conversation; and

(d) anti-foundational approaches to research are often
marginalized or forced to sit alongside foundationalist
perspectives...        (Berg & Seeber,
2016, p. 5).

and yet.

change away from empiricism

(an exorcism of empiricism)

in the psy-complex

has been and is fought

with a tremendous amount of zeal

by those whose careers have been,

and continue to be,

founded on it

funded by it.

This dominating paradigm
(rooted, ultimately, in   racist,

                 patriarchal,

                 eugenicist

                 ableist

                 saneist ideology)

continues to hold enormous sway.
as a result,
"whole knowledge systems
and the ways of life they make possible
are being threatened
at the beginning of the 21st century..."   (St. Pierre, 2006).
many in the fields that make up the     psy

                                    spy

                                    pry

                                    die

                                    lie

                                    sly complex

continue to hold it up as       the only way

                              the best way

to do research and scholarship
(with others, I have to say,
"We wondered
what kind of social theory
those social scientists
had been reading for fifty years"     (St. Pierre, 2014, p.

                                                              8).

their protestations
are similar to those
made after                Copernicus
                          Kepler
                          and others
showed unequivocally
that the earth went around the sun,
rather than the reverse.
the geocentric model,
one that had remained
firmly in place
for thousands of years,
and which was based
on simple observation and common sense,
was so taken for granted
that those who claimed otherwise
were seen as being      here    tical
                        hear    tickle.
and so it is now in the
Mad-Studies-that-might-be.
the power and dominance
of those asserting the superiority
of the empiricist model
in the psy-complex
(even though we know
it's all just a lie              (Whitaker, 2001;
                                 2010; Whitaker and
                                 Cosgrove, 2015))

has been, and remains, over     whelming.

[under]

it reflects a

"...willful ignoring

of an extensive and readily available critique..."

(St. Pierre, 2006).

this critique

has been ongoing for some time,

and many have understood it

to be a critique of so-called quantitative research

which it certainly is.

increasingly, though,

this critique is also being made

about qualitative research as well:

"the conventional humanist qualitative methodology

described in     textbooks

and handbooks

and university research courses

is, indeed, an invention, a fiction – we made it up"

(St. Pierre, 2017, p.

38).

St. Pierre goes on:

"other formations,

other methodologies,

or *no methodology at all,*

are possible

when other images of thought

are in play,

such as the      Liebnizian,

                  Nietzchean,

                  Deleuzian,

                  postmodern,

                  nonrepresentational,

                  immanentist

trajectory that post qualitative inquiry makes room for."

                               (St. Pierre, 2017, p. 38).

further,

"...we are in a     post-epistemological/

                 post-ontological

age

where there can be no extra-linguistic grounding

for our claims to knowledge"      (Gallagher, Connor, & Ferri, 2014, p. 1135).

as a consequence,

post-qualitative researchers

are beginning to assert that

"language has been given too much privilege

in the dominant paradigms of 20th century thought"

                             (McLure, 2017, p. 52),

no matter from which theoretical base

that thought arises.

instead, new ways of    knowing-being-doing

                     do-be-do-be-do

arising from within

a post-psy Mad Studies

will be   outside of
　　　　opposed to
language.
the unwillingness to move on
from empiricism into gnu scholarly terrain,
by so many,
might seem otherwise   laughable
　　　　　　　　　　a divinely comic psy-opera.


but move on     we must
　　　　and will
　　　　and can
　　　　and do
from     within and
　　without a post-psy Mad Studies
understandervating that
"the Real,
after all,
is only desire and simulation;
it never existed at all"                    (St. Pierre, 2013, p.
　　　　　　　　　　　　　　　　　650).

what is this next new Mad Studies
　　geography?
It is a place
　　　　(literal and metafloric)
"...in which we are beginning to realize
that foundations
for our knowledge are no longer possible –

a post-epistemological/post-ontological world..."

(Gallagher,

Connor, & Ferri,

2014, p. 1134),

which

"...calls for        post-methodological,

                     post-humanist,

                     post-empirical, and

                     post-qualitative frameworks..."

(Denzin &

Giardina, 2016, p. 7),

which I and others call the posts      (St. Pierre, 2016a).

it is a kind of knowing-being in which

"meaning always escapes the capture, the

closure of language. This understanding

also refuses the logic of representation

which posits a hierarchy of

knower-language – the real in favor of

a flattened ontology with representations

on the same plane as humans and the real."

(St. Pierre, 2017, p.

39)

this      wild

           weird

           whored

           whirred

           word

           whirled

is extraordin     are

air:
it is a place      where
"...there are no nouns in the typical sense,
because things are      their relations,
                        their doings, and
                        their movements—
with every noun actually describing
something that is going on"            (Vannini &
                                       Taggart, 2015, p.
                                       48).

in this   doing
          being
that      things are,
is the place that
researchers-without-foundations-or-methods live,
"...inventing inquiry in the doing"      (St. Pierre, 2015, p.
                                         81).

the point of this work? it is
"...to engage in a rebellious practice...
to rebel and smash windows, as necessary"
                                       (Krejsler, 2016, p.
                                       1).

what does this inquiry want to look
    like?
St. Pierre,
and her mentor Lather,
point out that

"this inquiry cannot be tidily described
in textbooks or handbooks. There is no
methodological instrumentality to be
unproblematically learned. In this
methodology-to-come, we begin to
do it differently wherever we are in
our projects."                                    (Lather & St.
                                                   Pierre, 2013, p.
                                                   635).

it is a kind of
"thinking without method"                         (St. Pierre, 2017, p.
                                                   37).

when i talk about this world,
this place,
i don't mean to speak of it
as something that is separate from this self –
we are the same.
i create the world,
and it creates me.
i, with others, choose to
"...be-do-live something different"               (St. Pierre, 2014, p.
                                                   5).

that being-doing-living includes,
necessarily,
deconstruction of text,
following          on        Derrida,
                   on        Deleuze and Guattari,
                   on        Foucault,

and understanding that

> "the text is always already of,
> with the world;
> it is never 'just text.'
> everything (including language, the text)
> exists at the surface,
> at the level of human activity..."

(St. Pierre, 2014, p. 12).

this deconstructive analysis
also necessarily involves creation of text.
instead,

> "the "posts"... use... ontologies that
> describe the world as unstable and
> becoming... epistemologies that describe
> meaning, too, as unstable and unable to be
> contained in language...; and... onto-
> epistemologies that do not separate
> "knowing" and "being" but describe the
> world as intra-actions—or entanglements—
> of subject and object, human and non-
> human..."              (St. Pierre & Jackson, 2014, pp. 716-717)

it does so without
"...producing alternative or successor regimes
with accompanying metanarratives"        (St. Pierre, 2000, p. 26).

it should be

"...increasingly unintelligible to itself..." (St. Pierre, 2000, p. 27).

it embraces    "queer,

feminist,

race,

postcolonial,

critical, and

poststructural theories"

(St. Pierre, 2002, p. 25),

among a host of others that must include    Mad theory

Mad knowing

Mad being.

in the    field

pasture

meadow

paddock    of Mad studies,

it is most decidedly nod about

advancing the cause of the psy-complex(es).

this work is not    rooted in quantitative research methodology.

this work is not    rooted in qualitative research meth-odology.

this work is not    rooted in mixed methods research methodology.

this work is not,    one must assert, method at all,

but rather a critical ontology of ourselves, to paraphrase

St. Pierre

(2014).

this kind of work –
this after-method, non-method work –
is embodied in  Mad Studies
emboweled in  Mad Studies
alongside        Mad Studies
inside              Mad Studies –
is in a place of coming-into-existence,
just on the cusp
of being                              created or
                                          imagined or
                                          done.

it may be that the only way
for it to be truly enacted will be,
as St. Pierre                              (2017).
and Kuhn and Max Planck have indicated,
when previous generations
of researcher-scholars have finally died off,
allowing next generations
of new think-being actors to do new things.


whut might this mad stud tease
look like?
"mad studies would do well
to adopt a deft meta-methodology
capable of        stretching,
                        darting,
          and       navigating
diasporic spirals and crisscrosses.
It would do well

to persist in incorporating
intersectional insights from
    disability theory,
    critical race theory,
    feminist theory,
    queer theory,
    deconstruction,
and    phenomenology,
among other established fields...
mad studies is most potent
when it critically and ethically
animates madness itself as methodology...
mad methodology resists rote positivism
and defies the cult of objectivity;
it listens for    ghosts,
            madpeople,
            outcasts,
    and    disembodied voices
that trespass,
like stowaways,
in modernity;
it perceives the expressive potential
in the so-called rants and raves of madpeople;
it is poised to find message within messiness
and philosophy within "pathology";
and it respects the peculiar vantage points
of those who are askew.
Whereas rationalists
tend to discredit and depoliticize the madperson,

a mad methodology

centers that madperson

within projects of critique and liberation."

                                        (Bruce, 2017, p.

                                        306)

St. Pierre                              (2017)

suggests that this kind of work

will be undertaken by

"those who might be lost

from the beginning

and prefer to stay lost as they 'inquire,'

whatever that involves"              (2017, p. 42).

i'm        completely

and        totally

and        irrevocably    lost

                          loused

                          last

                          list.

in that spirit, then:

    i have no idea what i'm doing.

    i have no idea what i'm doing.

    i have no idea what i'm doing.

# acknowledgement of the giant shoulders we stand on

Berg, M. & Seeber, B. (2016). *The slow professor: Challenging the culture of speed in the academy.* Toronto, Canada: University of Toronto Press.

Bruce, L.M. (2017). "Mad is a place; or, the slave ship tows the ship of fools." *American Quarterly* 69(2), 303-308. doi: 10.1353/aq.2017.0024

Collini, S. (1999). *English pasts: Essays in culture and history.* Oxford University Press.

Denzin, N. & Giardina (2016). Qualitative research through a critical lens. In N. Denzin & M. Giardina (Eds.) *Qualitative research through a critical lens* (pp. 1-16). Routledge.

Ferri, B., Gallagher, D., & Connor, D. (2011). Pluralizing methodologies in the field of LD: From "what works" to what matters. *Learning Disability Quarterly* 34(3), 222-231. doi: 10.1177/0731948711419276

Gallagher, D. (1998). The scientific knowledge base of special education: Do we know what we think we know? *Exceptional Children, 64*(4), 493-502.

Gallagher, D. (2001). Neutrality as a moral standpoint, conceptual confusion and the full inclusion Debate. *Disability & Society, 16*(5), 637-654. doi: 10.1080/09687590120070042

Gallagher, D. (2006). If not absolute objectivity, then what? A reply to Kauffman and Sasso. *Exceptionality, 14*(2), 91–107.

Gallagher, D., Connor, D. & Ferri, B. (2014). Beyond the far too incessant schism: Special education and the social model of disability. *International Journal of Inclusive Education, 18*(11), 1120-1142. doi:10.1080/13603116.2013.875599

Ingram, R. (2016). Doing Mad Studies: Making (non)sense together. *Intersectionalities: A Global Journal of 2016 Social Work Analysis, Research, Polity, and Practice, 5*(3), 11-17.

Krejsler, J. (2016). Seize the opportunity to think differently! A Deleuzian approach to unleashing becomings in education. *Educational Philosophy and Theory*, p. 1-11. doi: 10.1080/00131857.2016.1163247

Lather, P. & St. Pierre, E. (2013). Post-qualitative research. *International Journal of Qualitative Studies in Education, 26*(6), 629-633.

Smith, J. & Gallagher, D. (2008). An essay on the politics of schooling and educational research. *Cultural Studies ↔ Critical Methodologies, 8*(3), 284-301. doi: 10.1177/1532708607310793

Smith, P. (1999a). Ideology, politics, and science in understanding developmental disabilities. *Mental Retardation, 37*, 71-72.

Smith, P. (1999b). Drawing new maps: A radical cartography of developmental disabilities. *Review of Educational Research, 69* (2), 117-144.

Smith, P. (2008). Cartographies of eugenics and special education: A history of the (ab)normal. In S. Gabel & S. Danforth (Eds.), *Disability and the politics of education: An international reader.* Peter Lang.

St. Pierre, E. (2000). The call for intelligibility in postmodern educational research. *Educational Researcher, 29*(5), 25-28. doi: 10.3102/0013189X029005025

St. Pierre, E. (2002). "Science" rejects postmodernism. *Educational Researcher, 31*(8), 25-27).

St. Pierre, E. (2006). Scientifically based research in education: Epistemology and ethics. *Adult Education Quarterly, 56*(4), 239-266.

St. Pierre, E. (2013). The posts continue: Becoming. *International Journal of Qualitative Studies in Education, 26*(6), 646–657. doi: 10.1080/09518398.2013.788754

St. Pierre, E. (2014). A brief and personal history of post qualitative research: Toward "post inquiry." *Journal of Curriculum Theorizing, 30*(2), 2-19.

St. Pierre, E. (2015). Practices for the 'new' in the new empiricisms, the new materialisms, and post-qualitative inquiry. In N. Denzin & M. Giardina (Eds.) *Qualitative inquiry and the politics of research* (pp. 75-96). Left Coast Press.

St. Pierre, E. (2016). The long reach of logical positivism/logical empiricism. In N. Denzin & M. Giardina (Eds.) *Qualitative Inquiry through a critical lens* (pp. 19-29). Left Coast Press.

St. Pierre, E. & Jackson, A. (2014). Qualitative data analysis after coding. *Qualitative Inquiry, 20*(6), 715–719. doi: 10.1177/1077800414532435

Vannini, P. & Taggart, J. (2015). *Off the grid: Re-assembling domestic life.* NY: Routledge.

Whitaker, R. (2001). *Mad in America: Bad science, bad medicine, and the enduring mistreatment of the mentally ill.* Perseus Publishing.

Whitaker, R. (2010). *Anatomy of an epidemic: Magic bullets, psychiatric drugs, and the astonishing rise of mental illness in America.* Crown.

Whitaker, R. and Cosgrove, L. (2015). *Psychiatry under the influence: Institutional corruption, social injury, and prescriptions for reform.* Palgrave Macmillan.

# about the editor

phil smith is completely post-everything—he is SO after that. formerly a big deal perfesser guy, with teaching gigs in vermont, michigan, and illinois, he slipped disability and mad studies cranky rants into courses he taught. at eastern michigan university, as a full professor, somewhat implausibly, he was director of the brehm center for special education scholarship and research, and head of the department of special education. phil received the 2002 vermont crime victim service award, the emerging scholar award in disability studies in education in 2009, and the eastern michigan university college of education innovative scholarship award in 2015.

his writing—academic and creative—has been published widely, since 1977. phil has had dozens of papers published in a buncha different journals, *including Disability Studies Quarterly, Taboo, Rural Special Education Quarterly, Qualitative Inquiry, Intellectual Disabilities, Review of Educational Research,* and *Health and Place. he*'s published a whole lotta book chapters, and made over 120 presentations and keynote addresses in local, state, national, and international venues.

he studied creative writing at a couple of universities, as well as photography, filmmaking, and education. a poet, playwright, novelist, and visual and performance artist, his creative books include *pomes; plaze; hagiography, or the electron; hats; keweenaw bay songs; landscapes; machines; doors and walls and windows; still life; the reach; this place is north; poems come;* and *cutting wood.*

phil describes himself as a Mad and Critical Disability Studies scholar, as well as a whatever-comes-after-qualitative researcher. his academic work includes two books exploring disability studies, *Whatever Happened to Inclusion? The Place of Students with Intellectual Disabilities in Education* and *Both Sides of the Table: Autoethnographies of Educators Learning and Teaching With/In [Dis]ability;* as well as a textbook entitled, *Disability and Diversity: An Introduction.* his book, *writhing writing: moving towards a mad poetics,* published by Autonomous Press, won the 2020 American Educational Studies Association Critics Choice Award. he's edited another book for Autonomous Press, *Tinfoil Hats: Stories by Mad People in an Insane World.*

for more than 25 years, in a variety of contexts and roles, he worked as a Disability and Mad justice activist, and served on the boards of directors of a number of regional, state and local organizations, including the Society for Disability Studies, where he was President.

he's Mad (but not, mostly, angry) as hell, a walkie, and identifies as disabled. a life-long Yankee, he lived for a coupla decades in Michigan, spending as much time as he could beside Lake Superior, where loons, wolves, moose, and bald eagles peeked in the windows of his cabin. now he lives on the side of a mountain at 1800 feet, in an even smaller cabin without a toilet or running water, fussing and ranting with his tree and animal neighbors. you can find his work at https://www.amazon.com/stores/Phil-Smith/author/B012XFCOBW

# about the authors

**Jersey Cosantino** (they/them), a former K-12 educator, is a doctoral candidate in Cultural Foundations of Education at Syracuse University, holding certificates of advanced study in women's and gender studies and disability studies. A Mad studies and trans studies scholar, Jersey employs Mad trans oral history methodologies that center the experiences and subjectivities of Mad, neurodivergent, trans, and gender non-conforming narrators. Challenging sanism, ableism, and transmisia, their research confronts medical model discourses and the pathologizing gaze of the psychiatric industrial complex. Jersey identifies as Mad, neurodivergent, Autistic, queer, trans, and non-binary and is white with education and citizenship privilege. A co-facilitator for SU's Intergroup Dialogue Program, Jersey holds a master's in education and graduate certificate in mindfulness studies. They are also the co-editor of the *International Mad Studies Journal*, a consulting editor for the *Journal of Queer and Trans Studies in Education*, and a former Trans Lifeline call operator.

**Adam Davies** (they/them), PhD, Ontario Certified Teacher, Registered Early Childhood Educator is a Mad, neurodivergent, queer, nonbinary white settler Assistant Professor of Sexualities, Genders, and Social Change in the College of Arts at the University of Guelph in Guelph, Canada. Adam's research interests are in anti-oppressive practices in education, mad studies and mad poetics in education, critical disability studies, queer theory, femme theory, and trans studies in Education. Adam has a PhD in Curriculum Studies and Teacher Development with specializations in Women and Gender Studies and Sexual Diversity Studies from the Ontario Institute for Studies in Education, University of Toronto, Toronto, Canada.

**Rebecca-Eli M. Long** (they/them) is a disabled scholar, activist, and artist whose work disrupts ableist structural violence. An avid knitter, Rebecca-Eli uses creative forms of knowledge-making to advance social change. They are a PhD candidate in Anthropology and Gerontology at Purdue University where they strive to make autistic futures—individual and collective—more possible. Learn more about their work at www.rebecca-eli.com.

**Samuel Z. Shelton** is a doctoral student of Women, Gender, and Sexuality Studies at Oregon State University. Their dissertation project aims to advance an intersectional feminist theorization of trauma that can inform and transform critical, social justice education. Their other research interests include: access(ibility); gender and technology; politics of care; and consent as liberatory practice. You can learn more about Sam by visiting their website: samsheltonswebsite.com

**Monica K. Shields** identifies as white, non-binary, neurodivergent, disabled, and Mad. She has femme and cishet passing privileges and an invisible disability. She spent decades in public education in a variety of roles. After completing a doctoral degree she moved to Puerto Rico to do nonprofit work. Monica feels all emotions in a deep and profound way and has strong empathy for all life. She struggles with change, even changes that are good, and believes everything is political. Monica gets overstimulated at the library and laughs at her own jokes.

**j. logan smilges** is an Assistant Professor of English at Texas Woman's University. They identify as (neuro)queer, trans, and disabled, and their scholarship, teaching, and activism are led by commitments to transfeminism and disability justice. Their writing, which can be found in *Disability Studies Quarterly*, the *Canadian Journal of Disability Studies*, *Rhetoric Review*, and elsewhere, lies at the nexus of disability studies, trans studies, queer studies, and rhetoric. Currently, Smilges serves as the co-chair for the Disability Studies Standing Group at the Conference on College Composition and Communication.

**Jacqueline Pruder St. Antoine** is a mother, a mad person, a partner, a reader and writer, a sister and daughter, a mad studies and disability studies scholar, an artist and performer, a student and teacher, a lover of Brussels sprouts and dinosaurs, a compulsive exerciser, a feeder of birds, a wannabe gardener, a halfway decent chocolate cake baker. She works to bring a mad studies perspective to new spaces and investigate new ways of being, doing, understanding, and representing. Jacquie aims to make her work arts-based performative in nature, accessible, and emotive, exploring the nuances of madness, disability, and what it means to exist in an ableist, saneist, multi-verse.

**slp** is a poet, musician, writer, and educator, with an MFA in poetry, an under-promoted album, a typewriter, and too many instruments to play, whose work has been published in *Denver Quarterly, HIVES, Jacket2, Bear Review,* and *burntdistrict*; it has also been finalist for the Ahsahta Sawtooth Prize (2016, 2012), Ahsahta Press Chapbook Competition (2012), and Slope Book Prize (2012, 2012). slp has published in mad studies with colleague and best friend Dr. Aubry Threlkeld and is a Senior Instructor at Colorado State University. slp is happily queer, less happily mad but trying to work with it, and grateful to live near the river and mountains with a half-sighted dog named Monk. The love of (t)he(i)r life was a schnauzer named Fred.

**Aubry Threlkeld** (they/them) is currently an Associate Director at the Harvard Summer School and an independent educational consultant. Dr. Threlkeld has served in a range of academic capacities at various institutions and given more than 200 invited talks internationally in pedagogy, disability studies, 2SLGBTQIA+ studies, Mad studies and cultural studies. They have more than twenty-five publications focused primarily on the practical work of curriculum development for children and youth with disabilities, trauma-informed pedagogy, and more recently Mad studies and poetry. They have a Doctorate in Education from Harvard University, a Masters in Science from Mercy College, a Masters in Business Administration from Endicott College, and a Bachelors of Arts from Middlebury College. They are Mad-Queer, Genderqueer, Disabled, and a white person of Romani descent.

www.ingramcontent.com/pod-product-compliance
Lightning Source LLC
Chambersburg PA
CBHW022044020426
42335CB00012B/533